AF324915

Psychopathology
and
World Politics

Psychopathology and World Politics

Ralph Pettman

University of Melbourne, Australia

World Scientific

NEW JERSEY · LONDON · SINGAPORE · BEIJING · SHANGHAI · HONG KONG · TAIPEI · CHENNAI

Published by

World Scientific Publishing Co. Pte. Ltd.

5 Toh Tuck Link, Singapore 596224

USA office: 27 Warren Street, Suite 401-402, Hackensack, NJ 07601

UK office: 57 Shelton Street, Covent Garden, London WC2H 9HE

British Library Cataloguing-in-Publication Data
A catalogue record for this book is available from the British Library.

PSYCHOPATHOLOGY AND WORLD POLITICS

ISBN-13 978-981-4338-69-1
ISBN-10 981-4338-69-9

In-house Editor: Yvonne Tan

Typeset by Stallion Press
Email: enquiries@stallionpress.com

Printed in Singapore.

Preface

It is a question worth looking into whether modern psychology and
psychiatry have provided us with the conceptual tools which would
enable us to construct ... a ... pathology of international politics.
(Morgenthau, 1973 [1948], p. 6)

Most of those who analyze or practice contemporary world politics do
so as proponents of Enlightenment modernism, that is, as
Enlightenment rationalists. Even when they are not party to this particular way of thinking, they cannot avoid its global effects and the
success it has had in terms of globalizing particular ways in which
world affairs should work.

This meta-discourse arose in 17th-century Europe in the form of
a concerted effort to prioritize the human capacity for reason. The
result was a scientific revolution and a growing body of reliable
knowledge about the natural universe. The result was an industrial
revolution that placed advanced military power at the disposal of a
handful of regimes that subsequently used it to build global
empires. After two huge wars, these empires fell apart. They did
leave behind, however, European ways not only of ordering world
affairs but also of creating material wealth and crafting societies
and selves.

The pursuit of pure reason is not possible. Only someone endowed with divine luminous wisdom could sustain the objectivity and detachment such a way of knowing requires.

Analysts and practitioners may aspire to such a pursuit, but in practice they make assumptions about human nature and human nurturing practices. Each aspirant subsequently sees his or her part-view of the world as the only true view, though the difference between them betrays their specificity.

The pursuit of human reason as an end in itself has also by now come to result in a range of auto-critiques. There are post-modernists, for example, who turn the priority placed upon reason back upon itself in order to ask what the reasons are for prioritizing reason. There are post-structuralists who question the neutrality of language as a way of communicating what modernists learn as well as the integrity of the modernist identity in this regard. There are romantics who back off from reasoning to seek the truths that emotion makes possible. There are phenomenologists who bracket-off reasoning in the attempt to describe things-in-themselves while intuiting the primary categories of the mind and how they intend the world that the mind thinks it is attending to. And there are sacralists who endorse the spiritual perspective that rationalists eschew as metaphysics at best or as superstition at worst.

Amongst these auto-critiques is one not listed above, namely, the psychopathological one. What is distinctive about this auto-critique is the way rationalists turn their ability to reason back upon the brain as the organ where reasoning occurs as well as upon the mind as an emergent property of a properly functioning brain.

This work highlights this auto-critique. It explores those occasions when the brain/mind ceases to function properly and the effects this has on world affairs.

What is to be done, for example, when a leader ceases to act in a seemingly sane fashion and yet still commands the loyalty of those who maintain him or her in office? What is to be done when a leader's advisers seem rational but are clearly not, for example, when they accept the prospect of large-scale nuclear war, or industrially induced global warming, without actively decrying the enormity of the human costs involved? Indeed, what is to be done when whole societies seemingly go insane?

This is to raise more questions than a single study can adequately answer. Indeed, the full extent of this approach has yet to be ascertained. The study of psychopathology is a very large one and only a start can be made here, not only on describing psychopathology itself but also on ascertaining its relevance to world affairs.

This does not preclude articulating this perspective, but it cannot be more than a beginning. It is hoped that what follows will prompt others to consider more closely what deserves to be a burgeoning field.

Nor does this preclude others arguing that the study of psychopathology and world politics presents important problems. How, for example, do particular levels of analysis relate to each other? How do individuals relate to communities or collectivities?

Like the question of the range of issues this auto-critique raises, this does not mean that no attempt should be made to address these problems. It is hoped that what follows prompts others to consider these concerns, too.

What follows delineates two strategically-chosen case studies. It describes in general terms what psychopathology might be and its relationship to world affairs. It looks at denial and at "speaking the truth" as a potentially therapeutic antidote, highlighting the contemporary discourse about nuclear weapons. It then looks at delusion, at what being "in touch" with reality might entail, and how this sense might be deployed with regard to a so-called "failed state" like the Solomon Islands. These two case studies demonstrate that a discussion of psychopathology and world politics can go beyond generalities. They suggest that it is possible to have hypotheses to do with conflict, for example, that include conscious as well as unconscious dimensions. So: what follows begins by discussing psychopathology in general and how it applies to world affairs in particular, that is, it looks at how an understanding of the unconscious dimension to the brain/mind helps foster an understanding of how world politics works. It then looks at denial, what it means to talk of truth in this context, and how truth-telling affects disavowal. It ends by looking at delusion, what it means to talk about reality in this context, and how reality affects the limits delusion sets to an individual or social sense of what knowing involves.

About the Author

Ralph Pettman is professor of international relations at the University of Melbourne, Australia. He has a PhD in international relations from the London School of Economics and Political Science. His previous appointments include teaching and research posts at the Australian National University, the University of Tokyo, Princeton University, the University of Sydney, Cambridge University, the New School for Social Research, the Frankfurt Peace Research Institute and Sciences Po, Paris. He has held a number of administrative positions, most notably with Australia's foreign aid bureau, its human rights commission and its broadcasting commission. His most recent books include *World Affairs: An Analytical Overview* (World Scientific, 2010); *Intending the World: A Phenomenology of International Affairs* (Melbourne University Press, 2008); *Reason, Culture, Religion: The Metaphysics of World Politics* (St. Martin's, 2004); and *Commonsense Constructivism, or the Making of World Affairs* (M. E. Sharpe, 2000).

Contents

Acknowledgements

An abbreviated version of the first two chapters was published in the *Cambridge Review of International Affairs*. They appear here in their original form with the kind permission of the above journal.

An early attempt to discuss the psychopathology of nuclear deterrence appeared as a chapter in a work by Gordon Rodley (ed.), *Beyond Deterrence* (Centre for Peace and Conflict Studies, University of Sydney, 1989). Those parts of the third chapter that draw upon this attempt appear here with the kind permission of that Centre.

An initial draft of the analysis in the fourth chapter of the Japanese approach to conflict resolution was written as a keynote address to the Fifth Afrasian International Symposium, Kyoto. A revised version of that address appears here with the kind permission of the Afrasian Centre for Peace and Development Studies, Ryukoku University.

With regard to research facilities I would like to thank the London Institute of Psychoanalysis, the London School of Economics and Political Science, the University of London's Senate House, and the Institute of Political Science in Paris, for the use of their libraries. I am also most grateful to the last for providing me with support services for a month and for making the writing of the second chapter such a memorable experience.

On a more personal note I would like to thank Rosy and David Walker, who not only put a roof over my head in London but whose hospitality extended to Paris as well. Their extraordinary generosity was a constant source of sustenance and delight.

Dr. Andrew Firestone, Consultant Psychiatrist, DPM (Conjoint), MRCPshcyh, FRANZCP reviewed the technical chapters of this work and I deeply appreciate his willingness to do so. He is in no way responsible for any shortcomings with regard to the above, but he did save me from making some serious mistakes and point me in the direction of some key resources.

This is my last scholarly monograph. As I look back on a lengthy academic career, I do wonder what all the scribbling was about. Admittedly it had its rewards. This was particularly the case when tough mental puzzles responded to sustained intellectual scrutiny. It is now time to go for a walk in the world, however, not so much to get anywhere in particular but for its own sake.

Introduction

When Harold Lasswell first published *Psychopathology and Politics*, he wanted to find a way of compensating for the idea that politics is about institutions. He wanted to investigate the mental profiles of all the sorts of people that politics involves. What stands, he asked, "behind [the] agitators, [the] administrators, [the] theorists, and [the] other types who play on the public stage ...[?]" (Lasswell, 1960 [1930], p. 8).

Nor did he intend to stop there. Once these individual stories had been told, he wanted to find out if it was possible to understand the "whole social and political order" in this way (Lasswell, 1960 [1930], pp. 8–9).

What follows takes Lasswell's lead. It construes world politics in terms of people rather than in terms of objectified entities like nation-states, multinational corporations or global social movements. It sees individual life-histories as making it possible to understand whole social and political orders. It does not, in other words, accept the attempt — still very prevalent — to describe and explain world affairs in terms of reified institutions. Rather, it seeks to understand the people who inhabit world affairs and the patterns made by their various practices. It seeks to understand how they act and why, that is, the shape and cause of the thinking they promote and protect.

In following Lasswell's lead, the present work also takes as its jumping-off point the concept of psychopathology. It starts with the idea that there are abnormal or dysfunctional ways of thinking and feeling and ways of behaving that characterize these abnormal or dysfunctional mind-states.

There are obvious problems involved in determining how to describe and explain world politics in psychopathological terms and when it is appropriate to do so. This is a relatively uncommon approach and its fruitfulness is not self-evident to those unfamiliar with its analytic potential.

For example, there are problems in defining what psychopathological abnormality and dysfunctionality mean. These problems are not insurmountable. Normality and functionality can be defined as having to do with average or ideal qualities, and abnormality and dysfunctionality can be defined likewise. These problems still make it difficult to determine when it is most appropriate to turn to psychopathology for descriptive and explanatory (and prescriptive) help, however.

And while it is consistent with Lasswell's approach to look at the psychopathological profile of important state leaders like Adolf Hitler and Josef Stalin, or Woodrow Wilson and Richard Nixon, this can result in a "great man" approach that critics decry as reductionist because it highlights the influence of important leaders instead of that of a strategic environment, an economy, a society, a historical heritage or a culture.

Psychopathological profiling need not be reductionist, however. Quite to the contrary, it can be an attempt to add a missing dimension to how world affairs is understood. It can compensate, for example, for the way political thinking "shies away" from the "hidden, the unknowable, the unseen" in the society and the self. And while the attempt to include insane discourse as a meaningful part of political theorizing has little contemporary support, if only because of the way it reminds analysts that political life has "internal considerations", there are those who do see insane discourse as containing "symbolic truths" that "focus attention not only on the conscious orientations of power, but also on the unconscious ... processes that precede our fundamental … attitude toward [political] power and authority". Thus, the language of delusion, as discussed in Chapter 5, can be considered an "implicit commentary on the inner origins of power and authority". Likewise the language of schizophrenia, which, in reflecting the "extremes" of human society, is less a "perversion" of society as an "integral part of it" (Glass, 1985, pp. 11–13).

Psychopathologists tend to believe that abnormality and dysfunctionality of this kind pertains exclusively to individuals. As such, they argue that it cannot be used to analyze whole cultures, countries or societies.

Despite what psychopathologists tend to say, however, there are times when key political communities and even whole cultures, countries or societies can be called neurotic or psychotic. This can happen in two main ways.

Where the political community or the culture, country or society is a modernist one, it is possible to summarize the mental state of the individuals in it and to arrive at a conclusion about the neurotic or psychotic condition of the entity as a whole. Because of the modernist character of the group concerned, this will be a collectivist conclusion.

By contrast, where the political community or the culture, country or society is a pre-modernist or traditionalist one, it is even more apparent what the summary mental state of those involved might be. Because of the pre-modernist or traditionalist character of the group concerned, any conclusion about its neurotic or psychotic condition will be manifest in communalist terms.

Having accepted the relevance of psychopathology to world politics, it remains necessary to demonstrate how the relationship between the two disciplines might be described and explained. These are large bodies of knowledge that have very diverse dimensions.

Demonstrating all of the ways in which they impinge upon each other would be a daunting task indeed. That is why what follows is illustrative only.

It begins by highlighting how in very general terms a connection can be made between psychopathology and world affairs. It outlines briefly what psychopathology is and how it impinges upon how world politics is usually understood.

It then explores denial and delusion. More particularly, it explores those kinds of denial and delusion that are sufficiently serious to be deemed pathological. Denial and delusion manifest on both an individual level and on a collective or communal one. The denial and delusion experienced by the socially embedded individuals who constitute a pre-modernist or traditionalist people manifest as a communal sentiment that only someone familiar with politico-cultural solidarism can appreciate. The denial and delusion experienced by the socially dis-embedded individuals who constitute a modernist people manifest as a collectivist sentiment that only someone familiar with politico-cultural individualism can appreciate.

The following work begins, in other words, by describing how the modernist mind-gaze can be turned back upon itself to objectify the unconscious motives that underpin this mind-gaze and how, as a consequence, contemporary world politics is notably less rational than appears to be the case. Lasswell considered Freud the great innovator in this regard. Lasswell believed that Freud had documented every aspect of how we think including the unconscious one. He saw him as having determined scientifically the "laws of mental life" (Lasswell, 1960 [1930], p. 12). Whether Freud deserves such acclaim continues to be debated (Gomez, 2005; Gay, 1988). In the light of Freud's findings, Lasswell saw the healthy mind as being a flexible mind, that is, as being one with the ability to vary its responses depending upon its immediate environment. By contrast, he saw the pathological mind as a fixed mind, "like an automobile with its control lever stuck in one gear …" (Lasswell, 1960 [1930], p. 16). Profound traumas inflicted by the members of one culture upon the members of another, for example, can be passed on from generation to generation, causing such mental suffering that it is difficult for the afflicted to adapt well to a world they neither initiated nor condone. The plight of indigenous peoples worldwide is a case in point. Likewise, those who deny the significance of global warming as an environmental issue may end up causing large-scale conflicts and loss of life despite their belief that this will not happen.

After looking at the modernist mind-gaze, the present work then argues, as does Lasswell, that the radical reliance upon reason and logic blinds as well as enlightens. It not only emancipates, it also incarcerates. In a cultural context where it is generally considered sufficient to describe, explain (and prescribe for) the subject matter in rationalistic terms, it seems that this might not be the case. It seems that unalloyed rationalism might not do justice to the unconscious motives of those involved and that it might be necessary to ask how the world is construed in unconscious as well as conscious terms. As Lasswell argues, unconscious motives and meanings continuously compromise the ability to make conscious judgments about what is real. They distort how the mind sees reality despite the best of efforts to achieve an objectified and rationalistic account of that reality (Lasswell, 1960 [1930], p. 36). In short, it is not enough to improve world politics by telling the rational faculties to do better. "Until this fundamental proposition is adequately comprehended …", said Lasswell, the discipline will continue to promote "self-deception" rather than "self-analysis" (Lasswell, 1960 [1930], p. 37).

This being the case, it is necessary to think not only of prioritizing reason but of other ways of using the mind. Lasswell saw the "distorting results of unseen compulsions" as inhibiting reliance on rational faculties. The present work concurs. Like Lasswell, it argues that assuming "heroic doses" of "logical thinking" can overcome "emotional aberrations" is only likely to reinforce these aberrations. It is not likely to mitigate them (Lasswell, 1960 [1930], p. 31).

In detailing other ways of using the mind, Lasswell highlighted the psychoanalytic technique of free association. He highlighted the way such a technique provided release from the shackles of linear analysis. He also highlighted how knowledge of the self might emerge that the more "socialized" versions of the self would rather not confront (Lasswell, 1960 [1930], pp. 32–33).

Does free association have a place in understanding world politics? Could individual leaders be put on the psychoanalytic couch? Could whole cultures be treated like this?

What role free association has is limited by the reluctance of most leaders to take part. It is also limited by the inappropriate nature of such a therapeutic regime for entire populations.

This does not prevent the attempt to answer this question in another way, however. It does not prevent, for example, exploring the importance of denial and delusion as part of the unconscious construction of world politics and what happens when the attempt is made to confront denial with "truth" and delusion with "reality". Truth-telling and reality-assessment can be used to access and articulate deeply felt, indeed, psychopathological politico-cultural instances of denial and delusion. They can be used to deal with denial and delusion in a politically emancipatory way. Someone in denial who is confronted with the limits of their understanding may feel insulted by the assertion that they suffer from such limits. They may actively resist the idea that there is a truth that can give them access to a depth of understanding that their conscious mind does not. However, there is arguably no other way to deal with this particular form of mental dysfunction despite the fact that part of being in denial is manifesting the unconscious certainties that underpin the psychopathology of denial itself. Someone suffering from a delusion who is likewise confronted with the limits of their understanding may also feel insulted by the assertion that they suffer from such limits. They may actively resist the idea that there is a reality that can give them access to a depth of understanding that their conscious mind does not. However, there is arguably no other way to deal with their particular form of mental dysfunction either, despite the fact that part of suffering from a delusion is resisting the need to deal with the unconscious certainties that underpin the psychopathology of delusion itself.

The key point is that in both cases it is not enough to tell the afflicted to behave differently or to change their strategic, economic or social environment. Because of the subconscious nature of the motives involved, a more radical intervention is required than the rationalistic requirement that people recognize the need to do something different.

What is Psychopathology?

Psychopathology refers to forms of behavior that seem so dysfunctional that they denote ill-health. It refers to those "morbid" mental phenomena that some people must deal with some of the time and other people must endure all of the time. It is, in short, the "systematic study of abnormal experience, cognition and behavior — the study of the products of the disordered mind" (Oyebode, 2008, p. 3).

As such, it is one of those concepts that is easier to recognize than it is to define (Davis, 1984, p. 1; Page, 1975, pp. 3, 49). The problem is that psychopathology is concerned with "every psychic reality which we can render intelligible ...". It is concerned, that is, with the way the self endlessly attempts to comprehend the world. This makes it necessary to know what people experience in general before it is possible to say what might be wrong with them in particular. It makes it necessary to know the full nature of their psychic reality. This reality can only be known by objectifying the human psyche and then compensating for the limits and distortions of detachment by the use of empathy and understanding (Oyebode, 2008, p. 3). Only after such a comprehensive appraisal is it possible to determine what the conscious as opposed to the unconscious means and what the inner as opposed to the outer world entails. Only then can it be said what might mentally be the matter (Jaspers, 1972 [1913]).

It should also be noted that psychopathology is used to refer to various techniques that are currently believed to provide people who behave in a mentally unwell way with some kind of help. It has a prescriptive as well as a descriptive and an explanatory dimension.

In other words, psychopathology is supposed to provide a rational basis for identifying those who suffer mentally as opposed to those who suffer physically. It is also supposed to allow for the identification of those who suffer psychosomatically, that is, those who suffer physically because of their state of mind (for instance, those who develop an ulcer because they worry too much), as well as those who suffer psychologically because of the state of their brain or some other part of their body (for instance, those who lose their memory because of Alzheimer's disease). Psychopathology is supposed in all such cases to provide a rational basis for restorative or at very least palliative care.

This approach to psychopathology was directly contested, a generation ago, by those who believed that changing the definition of disease from one highlighting the "physicochemical derangement of the body" to one highlighting the "disability and suffering of the person" would be potentially disastrous (Szasz, 1974, p. 40). Critics like Szasz argued that such a change could only result in many more people being considered ill than ought to be the case. Such a change, he said, could only end in "abuse" since it would do no more than provide "professional assent" to the "popular rationalization" that life-issues are like bodily diseases. This would rob individuals of their personal responsibility, he said. It would make them powerless patients who would require medical prescriptions. It would cease making them self-reflexive individuals capable of self-help (Szasz, 1974, p. 262). It would put them in an intolerable situation where they would have to accept rules that they did not make and play roles they did not construct for the benefit of those who had imposed a bargain they did not strike. From this perspective, people did not "go mad" so much as get "driven mad" because they could not escape the "social pressures" obliging them to act in this way (Cooper, 2001 [1961], pp. viii–ix). Goffman called the outcome "self-alienating moral servitude" since those who wanted to escape such servitude had first to submit to it. Those who wanted to fight such a regime had first to admit defeat. They had to accept the outlook of those whose job it was to enforce the way the world was defined (Goffman, 1962, p. 386). More generally, it relegated the "wildly charismatic or inspirational area of our experience" to the "desparate region of pseudo-medical categorization" from which critics saw clinical psychiatry as having sprung (Cooper, 2001 [1961], p. ix). Or to put the same point in less rhetorical terms, it meant having a profession intimately allied with the "alienated needs" of the societies it functioned within (Cooper, 1970, p. 10).

Regardless of what such critics said then and continue to say, however, abnormal and dysfunctional conditions are found in every human community and in every historical epoch. They are recognizable features of all eras and of all the societies found therein. In other words, in the major cultures of the world, psychopathological phenomena are similar or the same despite individual differences (Jaspers, 1972 [1913]).

Therefore, psychopathology is not just a contemporary phenomenon, nor is it confined to those societies that currently use the concept. Indeed, "every known language includes at least one word that specifically refers to seemingly irrational disturbances in psychosocial functioning", thereby distinguishing such disturbances from "crime, immoral conduct, and other types of deviance ..." (Page, 1975, p. 5).

To reiterate: there are particular psychopathological disorders that are identifiable as such regardless of when and where they occur (Mezzich and Berganza, 1984; Schumaker and Ward, 2001). They may not be as numerous as current classification systems suggest they may be, since close scrutiny of these systems results in few conditions that have unambiguous physiological and/or psychological causes (Poland, Von Eckardt and Spaulding, 1994). They are also described differently in different cultural contexts. Nonetheless, they are recognizable in every culture and in every era, and though this is not a conclusion beyond dispute, they result in similar concerns (Millon, 2004).

It is these concerns that are most reminiscent of Lasswell's image, cited previously in the Introduction, of a car stuck in one gear. When people or peoples exhibit a lack of "voluntary control" and manifest a "troubled and troublesome" state of mind; when there are notable "disturbances" in their thinking, their emotions, their ability to communicate or their ability to act purposefully regardless of the cultural context; when these disturbances are serious enough to impede "effective and satisfying" conduct; when they result in behavior that is "more persistent, less appropriate … less controlled, more severe, more incapacitating, and more disturbing" than should otherwise obtain (Page, 1975, pp. 5, 15); then a *prima facie* case exists for talking in terms of mental abnormality or dysfunctionality — whether individual, collective, or communal.

In other words, all societies in every era have found ways to identify and deal with mental disorders. They differ in what they think brings them about and how they should be treated. The members of a pre-modernist community, for example, might see madness as resulting from a curse or as possession by evil spirits or as the effects of the moon. The members of a modernist society, by contrast, might see madness as biologically or socially induced, that is, as a consequence of a personality disorder or of unconscious drives or the side-effect of some organic disease. What in the first instance might be treated by shamanistic exorcism or bloodletting is more likely to be treated in the second instance with drugs or a form of psychotherapy (Davis, 1984, pp. 142–164). The main point is that both pre-modernist and modernist societies label particular mind-states as abnormal or dysfunctional, regardless of how misguided their understanding might be, and that they actively intervene to deal with these mind-states in the light of their understanding (Draguns and Tanaka-Matsumi, 2003).

This suggests that it is far too radical to argue, as Szasz did, that "[t]here is no medical, moral, or legal justification for involuntary psychiatric interventions. They are crimes against humanity" (Szasz, 1974, p. 268). This might be so in most places most of the time. It is not, however, the case in all places all of the time. There are cases of chronic reactive depression, for example, where the person who is suffering is self-evidently ill. In these cases, only the most radical and decisive intervention is likely to help. Nor is it enough to suggest to those affected that they think about what they should do — they no longer can. Meanwhile, there is ample non-anecdotal evidence to suggest that psychotherapy of various kinds is more effective than no psychotherapy at all (Bloch and Harari, 2006, pp. 14–16).

Who is Normal and Who is Not?

This still begs the question of who is normal and who is not, that is, what is dysfunctional and what is not. Several contemporary disciplines address this issue, each one of which has its own perspective on what is involved. Psychiatrists, psychologists and psychoanalysts, for example, tend to articulate different ideas about cause and prescription. This makes normality and functionality into portmanteau concepts that allow for diverse definitions. This, in turn, makes them difficult to specify with any degree of precision. It leaves considerable scope for psychiatrists, psychologists and psychoanalysts to invent diseases in lieu of discovering them (Szasz, 1974, p. 13) and to seem to know more than is really the case. It is one thing, for example, to learn "formulae and technical terms" and to seem to have the "answer to everything"; it is quite another to adopt an approach that acknowledges the limits of what one is trying to do (Jaspers, 1972 [1913], p. 50).

As noted earlier, normality can be seen in terms of an average or an ideal. As an average, it is a mean that individuals may briefly correspond to, though not usually for long. As an ideal, it is a preferred state in terms of functioning, in accord with an inherent design that, again, individuals may briefly approximate but usually not for long. The former is a statistical concept while the latter is an optimal one (Robins, 1977, pp. 2–3).

Regardless of whether normality is an average or an ideal, the question then becomes: when does an eccentric pattern of behavior (with regard to culturally accepted means or preferred states) become pathological? When do people manifest an inability to cope that is so notable and deviates so far from the social mean or preferred ideal that they seem to need treatment of some kind?

When, for example, does repressing an unpleasant memory so that it no longer directly impinges become pathological rather than a means of seeking mental comfort? When does rationalizing what is being done so that it seems to be beneficial become evidence of unwellness rather than of a desire for self-justification?

And when should those who seem to have chosen delusions be deemed so ill that they should no longer be treated as self-indulgent?

When does projecting feelings of inadequacy onto seemingly malevolent others become persecution and paranoia rather than a desire to escape feelings of self-blame or a lack of self-confidence? When, that is, does compensating for inadequacy become a neurotic wish to succeed rather than vaulting ambition? When does the eschewal of personal or social traits that are deemed undesirable become a "reaction formation" rather than a need not to parade those traits in the public domain? When does retreating from adversity become "regression" rather than a process of renegotiating a radical change in the environment? When does imitating a significant role-model become "identification" rather than adopting the ideas and practices of someone who is admired? When does imitation of this kind become so intense that it becomes "introjection" rather than extreme identification with another self or culture (Page, 1975, pp. 14–15)? When should someone who is weak or oppressed, who speaks softy but is not heard, who then speaks more loudly and is deemed anti-social, be categorized as insane for deciding finally to shout out loud (Szasz, 1974, p. 119)?

It is clear from the above that determining where the line should be drawn between normality and abnormality, or functionality and dysfunctionality, is, in all but a few cases, far from self-evident. This is not to say that no such line exists. The fact that at the turn of the last millennium a major hospital in Jerusalem had several patients, each one of whom claimed to be Jesus Christ, and all of whom denounced the others as false prophets, suggests that there are delusions that are evidence of illness rather than self-indulgence (Morris and Hill, 2000; Rokeach, 1981 [1964]). Instances of this specific form of insanity are relatively rare, however. Most of what is called mental illness is a more or less moderate case of a syndrome deemed recognizable as such in the everyday world. It is usually within the range that is recognized as necessary to allow for effective functioning there.

The Political Implications of Defining Normality

It is also clear from the above that, except for those concerns that are recognizable as such in every place and time, conditions like these are closely related to the cultural context in which they are found and that this has important political implications. For example, normality and abnormality and functionality and dysfunctionality are labels that are used to create in-groups and out-groups. They are used against those out-groups that an in-group wants to label as undesirable. Diagnosis under these conditions is not neutral. It does not transcend the interests of the in-group as it would in the case of a physical disease. It promotes those interests in a culturally specific and politically self-aggrandizing way (Goffman, 1962, pp. 364–365).

The incarceration of political enemies in mental asylums is clear evidence of such an implication. This occurs particularly under conditions of authoritarian rule, though it is not unknown under democratic ones either. Again, these issues were thoroughly aired a generation ago by critical analysts concerned with the medicalization of mental illness. "There is no doubt", as one such critic said, "that psychiatrists [for example] may be called on to help 'adapt' individuals to a status quo that is itself brutalizing for those whose social role makes them an integral part of a pathological social system" (Devos, 1976, p. 279). Goffman called this process "mortification". He described it as placing a barrier between the person or persons who were labeled abnormal or dysfunctional and the wider world. He said this involved destroying the former's previous identity and imposing one more relevant to the role they were expected to play as someone abnormal or dysfunctional. This included depriving them not only of their property but also of their name, their dignity and even their personal or social integrity. At the same time, it included the provision of substitute possessions deemed more suitable to the cultural context they now found themselves in. It also included the imposition of "forced deference" so that those who were mortified had to live lives that were completely alien to them. More subtly, it included taking the defensive responses of those being mortified and making them part of the process. Goffman called this "looping". In society at large, for example, wherever people have to conform to an environment that radically insults their sense of self, they are usually given some leeway with regard to expressing their discontent. By the time they are grown-up they have usually learned what is necessary to function in the world, so that the matter of appropriate or inappropriate behavior only tends to arise when they are assessed as productive or not. In institutions like mental hospitals, however, "didactic feedback" can be erected into a "basic therapeutic doctrine" (Goffman, 1962, pp. 14–48).

Less obvious is the way every culture sets terms of reference that make some kinds of politics legitimate and other kinds illegitimate and the way concepts of normality and abnormality are germane to setting these terms. The modernist project, for example, emphasizes knowing as a matter of using reason as an end in itself. It places a related emphasis on the appropriate form of being, that is, socially-alienated individualism. This makes the active promotion of a politics of personal autonomy almost automatic. The success of modernist science has made it possible for modernists to globalize their culture to a historically unprecedented degree. It has made it possible for modernists to globalize their preferred ways of ordering the world's strategic, market and social affairs as well. This has had profound political consequences for the global order. Those who accept these consequences are deemed to be functional. Those who do not are deemed dysfunctional.

Least obvious of all is how, when modernists began objectifying what seemed to them to be the very seat of reason, they began to objectify the brain and the mind and to see abnormality and dysfunctionality as the consequence of two sets of causes, one brain-based and physical and the other mind-based and psychological. The physical causes they saw as the more metabolic and organic ones. This was to posit a "disease" model of psychopathology (Davis, 1984, pp. 1–8). The psychological causes they saw as the more mental and emergent ones. This was to posit an "adaptation" model of psychopathology (Davis, 1984, p. 8).

The Modernist Conception of Consciousness

In promoting this dichotomy, modernists were promoting a difference between the brain and its awareness. This was an idea that was first advanced in the early days of the modernist project. It was one that construed the mind and the brain as separate and discrete. It also construed a similar difference between what is acquired naturally and what is learned growing up (Descartes, 2006 [1637]; Taylor, 1966, p. 11). These distinctions became part of the history of psychopathology as a modern-day science (Jaspers, 1972 [1913]).

While objectifying reason resulted in a clearer conception of the brain and the mind, the process did not stop there. It was taken a step further and used to question this conception itself.

The dichotomies that the brain/mind and nature/nurture alternatives represent were redefined as a consequence — they were turned into continua. The clear-cut differences that brain/mind and nature/nurture highlight became complex, unitary, non-additive concerns that are not fully understood.

Further reflexivity undermined the assumptions of modernity itself. Modernity was set up in opposition to knowing-by-believing. Consequently, though many modernists still subscribed to a spiritualist perspective, modernity as a doctrine promoted secularity. Secularism in turn promoted secular coping strategies, secular counseling, or scientific treatments, like those that involve psychotropic drugs. Modernists themselves who suffered mentally chose to self-medicate using alcohol, narcotics and other such substances. Non-modernists, meanwhile, like those who belonged to communities still relatively untouched by modernist mores, were more likely to eschew the secularity of modernity and to see psychopathology in terms of spirituality. Thus, they tended to see healing in terms of rituals and ceremonies that emphasized the relationship between the people and the land. They tended to want to restore harmony, not just in organic and physical or mental and psychological terms, but in sacral ones as well. This was pre-scientific rather than scientific language, but in psychopathological terms it was not inappropriate. It was not necessary to return to demon possession and shamanistic exorcism or witchcraft and bloodletting to find a meaningful role for non-modernist knowing in this regard.

Despite all the reflexivity that modernity ultimately encouraged, the notion that there was a dichotomy between the organic or physical and the mental or psychological persisted. More particularly, modernists continued to see the causes and consequences of psychopathology in dichotomous terms. They admitted that the brain and the mind, for example, were not the dichotomous alternatives they were initially seen to be when the modernist perspective was brought to bear psychopathologically. They acknowledged that closer analysis revealed that the brain was the mind and the mind was the brain in mixed ways that the attempt to objectify both did little to describe and explain. This said, we still have those who want to alleviate the suffering that psychopathology causes by seeing it primarily in terms of organic or physical causes. Analysts like these tend to prescribe treatment regimes that deal with the brain. They cleave pre-eminently, though not exclusively, to a psychiatric approach. By contrast, we still have those who want to highlight environmental causes. Analysts like these tend to prescribe treatment regimes that deal with the mind. They cleave pre-eminently, but not exclusively, to mental and psychological or psychoanalytic approaches.

Organic or Physical Causes

Those who highlight the importance of an organic or physical approach tend to argue, as Jaspers did, that psychopathology finds in neurology, internal medicine and physiology its "most valuable auxiliary sciences". As our knowledge of such causes advances, he says, the need to posit psychological causes becomes less acute.

As knowledge of the limits of human awareness expands, however, psychopathologists find no organic cause capable of accounting for those limits. Jaspers himself posited a dichotomy between the brain/mind as a somatic/psychic entity, likening the current research situation to exploring a foreign land from opposing directions and one, moreover, where the explorers fail to meet because of the terrain that separates them (Jaspers, 1972 [1913]).

This said, the fact that psychopathology and the main psychopathological syndromes are found in every culture is evidence in itself for assuming the universality of organic causes. How these syndromes are manifest may depend on what is learned locally. What they are called may have highly specific linguistic referents. However, human beings do respond to "intolerable stress situations" in similar ways, for example. They also react to life's problems with the "rigidity" associated with "neurosis", the "conversion symptoms" of "hysterics", the "inner retreat" of "schizophrenics", the "hopeless despair" of the "depressed", and the "disorganized hyperactivity" of "manics" (Page, 1975, p. 165).

Of the causes of psychopathology that are self-evidently organic there are, firstly, the direct insults to the brain that result from such things as drug abuse or physical trauma. The psychopathological symptoms that arise from insults like these can only be dealt with by avoiding the cause itself or by attempting to address the damage they create. The paranoid delusions that can arise from drug use, for example, are likely to require a program of sustained detoxification before these delusions can be dispelled. Likewise, someone with Capgras syndrome, whose brain has been injured and who recognizes family members but not as such, may have to wait until their brain heals before they stop seeing their parents and siblings as masterful imposters.

Secondly, there are the more insidious insults to the brain like those that result from malfunctioning body parts. This includes the malfunctioning of the brain itself. These insults can have sustained effects on brain function. Down's Syndrome, for example, manifests in a characteristic pattern of physical symptoms, as does a malfunctioning central nervous system, blocked cerebral arteries, or an advanced case of dementia. All can be manifest in psychopathological terms.

Insults like those above can be manifest in terms of both psychoses and neuroses. The former is more serious than the latter.

Psychoses are thoughts, feelings or perceptions that are not real. As such, they can be distinctly upsetting. Fact can be confused with fiction, as in the case of hallucinations, and the capacity to fit in with society can be radically impaired. A person suffering from psychotic delusions, such as the paranoid belief that they are being discussed behind their backs, can result in a sense of persecution that is sufficiently serious to distort the ability to sustain social interaction. Such a person is less likely to realize that there is anything the matter, is less likely to respond to psychotherapy, and more likely to respond to psychiatric intervention in the form of a clinically attested course of psychotropic medication or shock therapy.

Neuroses are generally less severe. The sense of reality is typically not lost and neither is contact with society. Neurotics are more likely to remain aware of their symptoms, to seek assistance and to respond to psychotherapy. They are less likely to require medication except for secondary symptoms like depression or amnesia (Page, 1975, p. 34).

The attempt to classify different kinds of psychopathology in terms of organic or physical causes is an ancient one, though it comes into its own in modern times. Two and a half millennia ago, for example, medical practitioners in ancient Egypt, China and Greece were trying to understand psychopathology in natural rather than supernatural terms and providing categories in the process that highlighted brain dysfunction rather than, say, divine possession. For example, the school of Hippocrates is said to have identified hysterias and psychoses as such, as well as phobias, hypochondria and obsessive-compulsive disorders (Page, 1975, p. 23; Millon, 2004). It is modernism that invented the contemporary concept of insanity, however, and it is modernism that created "houses of confinement" for those so defined, just as it did for those deemed criminal (prisons) and those deemed physically unwell (hospitals) (Foucault, 2001 [1961], pp. 14, 35).

In the contemporary era, the attempt to establish an organic or physical conception of psychopathology was championed most notably by Emil Kraepelin, a medical clinician who saw mental diseases as exhibiting specific patterns indicative of specific biological and genetic causes. By understanding these patterns, he believed that it would be possible to intervene more effectively. As a consequence, he spent 40 years shaping and re-shaping his "general symptomatology" (in practice, a long list of the "disturbances" he saw in our perceptions, thoughts, feelings, purposes and actions). The list he devised summarized the "forms" of mental disease as he saw them. These diseases led to another list that included what he saw as the psychoses caused by infection, exhaustion, intoxication, involution or the thyroid, as well as those diseases he called dementia praecox, dementia paralytica, organic dementia, manic-depression, paranoia, epileptic insanity, psychogenic neurosis, and insanity caused by degeneracy. He also saw certain personalities as being psychopathic personalities and certain forms of mental development as defective (Kraepelin, 1981 [1907], pp. ix–xvi).

Though he is often seen as the quintessential European psychiatrist, it is only fair to say that Kraepelin also demonstrated an interest in comparative psychology, having visited Cuba, Mexico and the United States to find out how psychiatry was done there. Before his death he was researching Buddhism in preparation for a trip to India (Kraepelin, 1981 [1907], p. xi).

This interest did not extend to an attempt to locate his conclusions in the context of a more comprehensive approach, however. Indeed, his whole analysis remains notable for what it did not say. It did not, for example, talk about mental illness as socially or culturally caused. When he confronted the issue of what factors he should include in a provisional classification, he not only said that there was no "sure foundation" on which to build a "final" or "standard" summary, but the summary he did build was based entirely on a physical foundation (Kraepelin, 1981 [1907], p. 116). While he distinguished between modes of insanity caused by a "faulty metabolism and auto-intoxication", by diseases of the brain itself (such as a head injury or syphilitic lesions), by senility, by a "morbid" constitution, by epileptic attacks, by a psychopathy of some kind and by retarded development, he did not distinguish between physical and psychological forms of mental illness since he placed no credence on mental illness as having a psychological foundation.

Is it fair to highlight this failure? In his introduction to Kraepelin's text, Carlson says that critiquing Kraepelin for not adopting a more psychodynamic approach is like critiquing Newton for not discussing electronics (Kraepelin, 1981 [1907], p. xii).

The problem with Kraepelin's conclusions, as well as the problem with all those who followed uncritically in his footsteps, is that only some kinds of psychopathology (e.g., some kinds of psychosis) are sufficiently unambiguous to allow for a clear description and a reliable intervention. Most psychopathological conditions are psychopathology "in name only" (Page, 1975, p. 38). As abnormal or dysfunctional forms of behavior, they have more than one cause, while the same symptoms can characterize a variety of conditions. They are very poorly defined, in other words.

Harsher critics strike at the rationalist root of Kraepelin's enterprise. "What we call psychiatric practice", they say, "is a certain moral tactic ... preserved in the rites of asylum life, and overlaid by the myths of positivism" (Foucault, 2001 [1961], p. 262).

In the face of such imprecision, Karl Menninger posited a non-dichotomous, more dynamic approach that allowed for a continuum of mental states ranging from wellness to illness and allowing for the movement of peoples along this continuum. Menninger and his colleagues described five levels of dysfunction ranging from normal coping strategies (such as tears), through levels characterized by worry and breakdown, to paranoia and suicide (Menninger, Mayman and Pruyser, 1977 [1963], pp. 153–270). This helped modify some of the consequences of the classification approach; however, it still left a large number of the categories intact.

The key issue remains the fact of ambiguity. This continues to make it difficult to say with certainty what is going on and how best to respond to alleviate the suffering involved.

Describing people as psychopathologically abnormal or dysfunctional also results in their being seen as deviant and being socially stigmatized in ways they do not deserve, particularly when it is the social environment that is to blame. As a consequence, psychopathology can amount to a massively misdirected attempt to see in suffering people or peoples the cause of what is not their fault. Laing's notion of insanity as the only sane response to an insane environment, that is, as a "special strategy" devised in order to live in an "unlivable situation", attempted to capture one consequence of this massive misdirection. After all, Laing said, "[s]ociety highly values its normal man. It educates children to lose themselves and to become absurd, and thus be normal." In this light we would do well to wonder, he said, why it is "[n]ormal men" who have killed "perhaps 100,000,000 of their fellow[s] ... in the last fifty years" (Laing, 1967, pp. 95, 24).

The notion of a sick environment and not just sick people would suggest the need to consider political rather than personal change. As Szasz said in the preface to his critique of psychiatry: "Who defines what constitutes [mental] illness, diagnosis, treatment? Who controls the vocabulary of … psychiatry, and the powers of the physician-psychiatrist and citizen-patient?" (Szasz, 1974, p. viii).

More radically, to say that Euro-American medicine only treats "bodily" ills is to say, Szasz argued, that there is "no such thing as mental illness". From this perspective, mental illness is "[merely] a metaphor" (Szasz, 1974, p. ix). This, in turn, is to make of a psychiatric diagnosis no more than a "stigmatizing" label, since the difference in this view between physical and psychological illness is no more than the difference between "types of languages or modes of representation" (Szasz, 1974, pp. xii, 79).

Laing made a similar point when he argued that a category like schizophrenia is a "social fact" and therefore a "political event" (Laing, 1967, p. 101). As such, it allowed those with legal, medical and moral power to oblige those so labeled to pursue a "career" as a schizophrenic (Goffman, 1962, p. 127). This career deprived those said to have this condition of their existential and legal status as rational and autonomous individuals — at least until the label was changed or removed. More importantly, it deprived people of the chance to undertake the kind of "voyage" that did not call for a cure but, rather, called for the opportunity for the healing process to do its work and to overcome the state of alienation we call being normal. Psychiatrists concerned for our welfare might try and intervene. They might even, Laing said, succeed. However, there was "still hope", he said, "that they will fail" (Laing, 1967, pp. 136–137).

The position that critics like Szasz and Laing took is an extreme one. Despite what they said, mental illness is a demonstrable event. There are enough instances in every culture of people who suffer psychologically, and their suffering is sufficiently real and severe, to say that the phenomenon is not metaphorical or political.

This said, any attempt to categorize mental illnesses has to be treated with extreme caution if only because there is not one categorization system which is scientifically accepted worldwide. They may be similar, but there are two main systems. There are also many variations on how these two are applied in practice.

Nearly 50 years after Kraepelin published his germinal study, the American Psychiatric Association published the first edition of its *Diagnostic and Statistical Manual of Mental Disorders* (DSM-1, 1952). Now in its fourth edition and moving towards a fifth, this manual grew out of work done by the US army to bring psychiatric care into line with the approach taken by the World Health Organization (WHO). In the sixth edition of the WHO's *International Statistical Classification of Diseases and Related Health Problems*, an edition it published in 1949, it began including mental disorders. This prompted the Americans to try and coordinate the two lists, though this was far from the first American foray into classifying psychopathological states. American statisticians first began collecting information about the mental plight of US citizens in 1840, long before Kraepelin published his work. By the time of the First World War, the American Psychiatric Association had already developed a manual that contained a list of over 20 recognized psychopathological conditions. This was also well before the first DSM, which, as noted above, was not issued until after the Second World War. (The first DSM contained a list of 106 conditions. The current DSM, which is the fourth, contains a list of 296 conditions.)

The DSM requires those who seek to help those who are suffering to choose a classification that fits the symptoms the latter seem to manifest. It invites the helper to locate those suffering with regard to five different "axes". These provide categories that describe clinical symptoms. The first axis highlights clinical factors that include symptoms to do with human development, for example, dementia, substance abuse, mood and anxiety disorders, eating and sleep disorders, phobias and schizophrenias. The second axis highlights personality factors that include disorders that present in terms of symptoms such as narcissism, obsessive-compulsive states, paranoia and mental retardation. The third axis highlights medical conditions like brain injuries and other medical/physical issues like the effects of parasites, diseases caused by the failure of fundamental bodily systems, poisoning and nutritional issues. The fourth axis highlights disorders that are psychosocially and environmentally induced. This axis includes negative life events, communal difficulties, lack of social support, and other inadequacies in terms of the patient's immediate life-world. More specifically, it includes family health problems, divorce or estrangement, neglect, difficulties with acculturation, discrimination or transition to retirement, school issues, housing issues, poverty and finance issues, access to health care issues, arrest and incarceration issues, and exposure to disaster issues, both natural and man-made. The fifth axis involves assessing someone's capacity to cope, whether they happen to be an adult or a child (Morrison, 2009).

The DSM does not in the main explain the syndromes it describes. This is largely because there is not enough knowledge of the pathologies described to allow the DSM's designers to tell its users what is involved. As a consequence, "many of the criteria are highly inferential …" since there are "… few objective measures for assessing their presence or absence …". Critics also note that the "language and concepts employed for describing clinical phenomena" are often not based on theory but are drawn from "commonsense, 'folk-psychological', … [and] protoscientific … understanding" (Poland, Von Eckardt and Spaulding, 1994, p. 240).

It is, in short, qualitative. Consequently, it encourages helpers to see human complaints as medical ones. This leads not only to mental illness being progressively trivialized but to a rise in the unnecessary use of medications. A simple case of sadness, for example, that might be best dealt with by human empathy is rapidly turned by the DSM into a mental illness like depression and, moreover, one that requires treatment in the form of drugs (Szasz, 1974, p. 34).

The DSM does not provide the "detailed, multi-level, multidomain, longitudinal, and cross-situational" understanding that proper analysis requires, not least because it collects data in an "emotionally charged setting in which power relations are highly salient and hidden agendas abound". This would seem to obtain particularly where the DSM moves beyond physical causes into the fourth axis disorders, that is, the psychosocial ones (Poland, Von Eckardt and Spaulding, 1994, pp. 246–247).

As such, the DSM fails to address the key issue of normality versus abnormality. It also fails to address the key issue of what is functional as opposed to what is dysfunctional. This makes it radically unreliable as well as difficult to defend as a valid summary of psychopathological states (Poland, Von Eckardt and Spaulding, 1994, p. 239).

Nor does the DSM address the emphasis it places on the psychopathology of individuals and its failure to confront the fact of social psychopathology. It does not, for example, adequately address those instances where stress symptoms are manifest by whole groups. It was noted in the Introduction that psychopathologists are often uncomfortable with talking about whole cultures, countries or societies in psychopathological terms. However, it was also argued that in the case of modernist cultures, countries or societies it is possible to aggregate the extent of individual mental illness to get a collectivist result, while in the case of pre-modernist cultures, countries and societies it is possible to assess the mental condition of their members to get a communal result.

More generally, it is to ignore the extent to which the DSM is an artifact of the modernist science that underpins its assumptions and the extent to which the DSM helps promote those assumptions in the guise of objective analysis. The descriptions it provides are not culturally qualified in any way despite their culturally loaded character. This makes non-Euro-American alternatives to these descriptions seem partial and wrong and the DSM's descriptions seem universal and right. The point here is that non-Euro-American perspectives on psychopathology are not in the main included in the DSM, while those nods in this direction are not acknowledged as such or very well understood.

This is supported by the tendency to prioritize treatment regimes that use psychoactive drugs. This in turn reflects not only a medical model of how best to deal with those considered unwell, but also the rise of the pharmaceutical companies and the large, profit-making industry they represent. It is one thing, for example, for a people to self-medicate by turning to alcohol in order to deal with the effects of trauma or anxiety. It is quite another to dispense powerful psychotropic substances because of the esteem afforded the medical model and the notion that sanity can only come in capsule form.

The WHO list that the DSM ostensibly parallels provides the same mix of organically- or physically-caused and mentally- or psychologically-caused disorders. It begins by listing those cerebral disorders that arise as the result of different forms of dementia and organic malfunction. It then lists those mental and behavioral disorders caused by the abuse of psychoactive substances. Next, it lists schizophrenias and delusional disorders, a list it follows with another one on mood disorders like depression and mania. Next come the phobias and then the various anxiety, trauma and obsessive-compulsive syndromes. This is followed by behavioral syndromes like those associated with physiological and physical conditions such as *anorexia nervosa*, sleep disorders and sexual disorders. Then there are the disorders expressive of an individual's lifestyle and relational patterns — disorders that include paranoia, a disregard for social obligations, emotional instability, a penchant for histrionics, for pathological stealing, for fire-setting and for psychopathological issues to do with gender-identity. These are followed by such conditions as mental retardation, the diverse disorders that arise during the process of mental development, and the behavioral and emotional disorders that have their onset in childhood and adolescence (WHO, 2007).

Like the DSM list, the WHO list does not in the main explain the syndromes it describes. Again, this is largely because there is not enough scientific knowledge to allow the list's designers to tell its users with authority what is involved. The WHO also fails to address the issue of normality versus abnormality and functionality as opposed to dysfunctionality.

Nor does the WHO question the emphasis it places on the psychopathology of individuals and its unwillingness to confront social psychopathology, that is, those instances where such suffering is manifest by whole cultures, countries and societies. In modernist contexts there is the aggregation of individual psychopathologies to get a collectivist result. In pre-modernist contexts there is the communalist manifestation of psychopathology on the part of the whole culture, country or society concerned.

More to the point, the WHO approach is an artifact of modernist science, which means that it relies on assumptions that promote an objectifying mind-gaze. Indeed, the descriptions it provides are not culturally qualified in any way, which makes non-Euro-American alternatives to these descriptions, as in the case of the DSM, seem partial and wrong and only the WHO's descriptions seem universal and right. Few non-Euro-American psychopathologies are included in the WHO list, despite its ostensibly global remit, while the implications of those non-Euro-American psychopathologies that could be suitable to list are not considered as such. As in the case of the DSM, the WHO's approach also promotes the use of drugs. This is a similar reflection, in part, of the rise of the pharmaceutical industry and the capitalist corporations that constitute this industry.

Why have classification systems like these had such an impact on psychopathological approaches to mental suffering? Why do they continue to be used when they have such self-evident shortcomings?

Firstly, they provide a sense of certainty where ambiguity would otherwise prevail. Human beings are "inveterate classifier[s]" (Page, 1975, p. 23). Faced with the diversity of human behavior, they try to render the confusion comprehensible by mapping it in some way. The result will inevitably be culture-specific and the culture-specificity will lead to diversity in itself as the various attempts to map behavior types compete to define and diagnose what people do and how best to help them. Even where societies agree to use a common system, like the DSM or the WHO lists, the way in which the classifications are applied tend to differ from cultural context to cultural context. This is hardly surprising given the diversity of the subject matter and the differing degrees of mental distress that are manifest worldwide. The outcome is equivalent to stuffing jellyfish into pigeon-holes, which does not prevent analysts making the attempt, but does help explain why the outcome might lack rigor.

Secondly, classification systems provide for political control at both an institutional level and a whole cultural level. The ability to call large numbers of people schizophrenic, for example, despite the difficulty of defining this concept with any great degree of scientific precision, allows those so-called to be consigned to an underclass deemed "ill". This has significant political implications, particularly where personal wellness is seen as the basic condition for political responsibility, as modernist/liberalist societies like the US deem it to be.

The success of such systems in contradicting those who critique them is evidence in itself of the need for certainty and superiority, a need that was demonstrated a quarter of a century ago in an experiment conducted by a professor of psychology and law at Stanford University. This experiment generated a heated debate at the time about its particular design, not least because those taking part were told to lie. This was said to radically compromise the validity of the conclusions since false information undermines diagnosis of any kind. The experiment did tell a cautionary tale, however.

The professor who conducted the experiment decided to try and test if sanity and insanity existed and if so, how we might know what these concepts mean (Rosenhan, 1973, pp. 250–258). He subsequently organized the admission of a number of people who had never suffered any psychopathological symptoms before to various hospitals to see if they were subsequently found to be sane, and if so, why. If these "pseudo-patients", as he called them, were subsequently identified as such, under the "blind" conditions set up by his experiment, then there was at least a superficial case for seeing the distinction between sanity and insanity as being relatively useless in psychiatric terms. If they were not identified as pseudo-patients, this would suggest that the mindset of the psychiatrists and the medical setting provided by the hospital were more important than the actual condition of those who presented for medical consideration. The "pseudo-patients" included a graduate student, three psychologists, a pediatrician, a psychiatrist, a painter and a housewife. Twelve different hospitals in five different American states were targeted. Admission was initially gained on the basis that each individual claimed to be hearing unfamiliar, somewhat "hollow" voices, of the same sex as the pseudo-patient. In all other respects, the pseudo-patients presented themselves and their life-histories in factual terms. Moreover, immediately after admission, the pseudo-patients stopped professing all symptoms of abnormality. Significantly, despite stopping the experiment and otherwise presenting in a normal fashion, all were given psychotropic drugs and were treated in a depersonalized manner that rendered them powerless and that deprived them of basic rights like the right to freedom of movement and the right to privacy. Not one of them was deemed sane, except — significantly — by other patients. All except one was diagnosed as schizophrenic. They were all ultimately discharged, on average after 19 days, but only as schizophrenics in remission.

He followed up his initial experiment with another one at a hospital that heard of the first ruse and believed that it could not be fooled. He asked the staff at this hospital to assess, over a three-month period, whether patients who presented or who were already inmates happened to be pseudo-patients or not. Assessments were subsequently made on 193 patients. Forty-one of these were said to be definitely pseudo-patients by at least one staff member. Twenty-three of these were said to be probably a pseudo-patient by at least one psychiatrist. Nineteen of these were said to be probably a pseudo-patient by one psychiatrist and one other staff member. In fact, he put no pseudo-patients forward during this time period. Were the practitioners erring on the side of caution by calling ostensibly insane people sane? Or was the diagnostic process they were using so unreliable that they were able to make at least 19 misdiagnoses? The experimenter suggests the latter.

Despite the findings above, lists like the DSM and WHO ones are far from useless. The concept of mental illness is, after all, relatively recent and is still being developed. Nor are those who use these lists inhumane, though they may still be learning how best to bring a scientific perspective to bear in daily practice. Categorizing people as physically unwell does allow those who use these lists to eschew such diagnoses as spiritual possession, which in one respect is a radical step forward (Rosenhan, 1973, p. 254). These lists also help systematize a field that would otherwise resemble mental minestrone. The categories they include are viable enough to hold the attention of entire professions and to assist those who work within these professions to sort and share data about mental health. There is, as noted already, widespread agreement about what constitutes an extreme case of psychopathology even though more moderate cases may allow scope for misinterpretation.

The usefulness of the DSM and WHO lists is also apparent in the light of critiques of the experiment described above that outline, in tongue-in-cheek fashion, admissions interviews like the following:

Diagnostician:	Tell me what is wrong with you.
Patient:	I often hear voices that say "hollow", "empty", and "thud".
Diagnostician:	Are you hearing the voices now?
Patient:	No.
Diagnostician:	Good. There is nothing wrong with you. Go home.

(Weiner, 1975, p. 40; see also Spitzer, 1975)

The key issue is the way contemporary diagnostic listings encourage one-dimensional diagnoses and how this fails to do justice, despite the existence of one dimension of the DSM-IV committed to doing so, to the complexities of politico-social behavior. This is highlighted by transcultural differences in diagnosis and treatment. Though modernist descriptions of mental states may be seen as more scientific than traditional alternatives, the "folk" diagnosis of mental disorders can require the satisfaction of several criteria rather than just one. A delusion like hearing voices would never have been enough in the region of Laos that Westermeyer and Wintrob worked in, for example, to result in a diagnosis of abnormality or dysfunctionality. It would have been accompanied by an assessment of the amount of socially inappropriate behavior, the level of social isolation, the ability to work and the risk of violence to the self (Westermeyer and Wintrob, 1979, p. 759).

Mental or Psychological Causes

In turning from organic and physical to mental and psychological causes, we turn to those "events" and "circumstances" that are external to individuals or societies that are sufficiently serious to inhibit their capacity to adapt to their environment. Organic and psychological conditions can result in the same kind of psychopathological symptoms, but the ultimate cause and the appropriate intervention can be very different. Where the ultimate cause is psychological, for example, the affected individuals or societies are less likely to respond to medication, except as a placebo. They do, however, have the potential to respond to psychotherapy of some other kind (Davis, 1984, p. 1; Frank, 2006, pp. 59–75).

Consider the traumatic onset of depression (van der Kolk, McFarlane and Weisaeth, 1996; Bracken, 2002). This can be described not only in organic but also in psychological terms. From the physical perspective, traumatized and depressed people are seen as suffering from an imbalance in their brain biochemistry. The emphasis is then on breaking the self-defeating spiral the organism is suffering. This might be done with electro-convulsive shock therapy or the intake of the appropriate drugs. From the mental or psychological perspective, however, people like these are seen as suffering from an untenable emotional environment, one which has robbed them of a sense of meaning or one which they feel obliged to respond to by closing down every emotional response. The "absence of basic trust …", for example, can be responsible for the "most severe forms of psychopathology, including … depressive states in adults" (Brothers, 1995, pp. 18, 148). People will present with similar symptoms in both cases. It is not likely, in the second instance, that individuals will be helped by the administration of drugs. Rather, an attempt will have to be made by themselves to bring about a radical change in their personal world or their interpersonal or social environment (deVries, 1996; Bracken, 2002).

Now consider anxiety (Freud, 1936; Bracken, 2002). From the organic perspective, this is seen as above as resulting from a lack of balance in the brain's chemistry and as requiring a calming compound of some kind. From the psychological perspective, however, it may be seen as a response to a danger of some kind. "An anxious person … is in suspense, waiting for information to clarify the situation …". They are "watchful and alert, often excessively alert" and as a consequence they are "over-reacting to a wide range of stimuli". Whole societies can feel like this, that is, "helpless in the face of dangers which, although … [seemingly] imminent, cannot be identified or communicated". Such societies are likely to exhibit the sense that they do not know (Davis, 1984, pp. 23, 46). One psychological prescription for such anxiety, among a battery that cognitive psychology provides, is to meet the need for information about the dangers faced and to clarify how realistic the feelings of uncertainty happen to be.

Reference like this to trauma and the depression it can cause or anxiety and the over-reaction it can cause suggests that any assessment of the root of any kind of psychopathology is likely to require a broad range of diagnostic skills. It means a capacity to assess both physical and psychological factors.

However, when assessing psychopathology as it applies to whole societies, the appropriate skills are likely to be psychological rather than physical. While whole societies may manifest psychopathological symptoms that suggest a physical cause, the symptoms are ultimately likely to be the result of disturbing events and mentally confronting circumstances.

Since the present work focuses not only on individuals but also on whole groups and societies, it focuses on the psychological dimension to psychopathology as well. It acknowledges the organic or physical basis of mental illness, but it tends to talk in mental or psychological terms because of the relevance of the latter to those cases where individuals constitute communities or collectivities and where the resulting groups and societies manifest the symptoms of sustained denial or delusion.

Psychologists themselves remain ambivalent about the "status of mental phenomena, and [indeed] of the 'mind' itself ...". They are not sure whether they are trying to systematize the study of "mental life" or of human "behavior" (Frosch, 1989, p. 11).

Those who do look at the mental life of the mind include the followers of theorists like Sigmund Freud, the father of psychoanalysis. Freud trained as a neurologist and never relinquished that perspective. In due course, however, he came to put the mind before the brain in a way that had never been done before. He came to contest the dominant approach, which was an organicist/physicalist one, in order to provide a "psychology for neurologists", as it was subsequently called (Gay, 1988, pp. 122–123; Gay, 1990, pp. 74–94).

Psychoanalysis highlights the life of the mind and how particular ideas can be "actively repressed", that is, made "unconscious" or "preconscious" (Moore and Fine, 1995; Makari, 2008; Davis, 1984, p. 60; Holzman, 1970; Freud, 1957 [1915]). This is not to posit a secondary kind of consciousness. It is to posit mental events of which people are not directly aware (Gardner, 1993, p. 42).

A romantic like Lawrence describes events like these as no more than a synonym for life, but this is to ignore the specificity of the conclusions that Freud and those who followed him were able to come to (Lawrence, 1960 [1921], p. 42). It is to ignore the potential of psychoanalysis to provide what is arguably the "richest systematic description of inner experience that the Western world has produced" to date — a description that covers concerns as diverse as "sex, love, and death; childhood, parenting, and family; cruelty, fear, jealousy, envy, and hate; identity, conscience, and character; desire and mourning ..." (Makari, 2008, p. 483).

Psychoanalysts see the symptoms of mental abnormality and dysfunctionality as most meaningful in terms of the "ideas and feelings" that come from "experience ...". They also see talk about those experiences that are particularly traumatic, or are particularly prone to induce anxiety, as capable of resulting in feelings of release and relief potent enough to alleviate the psychopathology involved (Davis, 1984, pp. 144–145).

Though Freud originally subscribed to the idea of repression and the benefits to be achieved by effecting the release of pent-up feelings and emotions, he subsequently argued that repressed material becomes mentally autonomous and is only accessible to more indirect and subtle forms of search. He began seeking this more radical kind of search using hypnosis. He finally settled, however, upon "free association" as the best way to access the experiences involved. It was this, he came to believe, that would best allow him to bypass the various forms of resistance and to attempt to effect the recall of the traumas and anxieties he sought to alleviate (Nobus and Quinn, 2005, p. 29).

By giving thoughts and feelings free expression, in an environment free from distraction, Freud came to see the person who presented with psychopathological symptoms as being afforded step-by-step access to their past. The outcome was ultimately meant to transform their abnormal and dysfunctional mental plight in the present. As Freud himself said: "Every time we meet with a symptom we may conclude that definite unconscious activities which contain the meaning of the symptom are present in the ... mind ...". Moreover, "... as soon as the unconscious processes involved are made conscious the symptom must vanish". This was the opportunity he believed that his approach provided — as a way to effect a psychotherapeutic intervention. This was the "opening for therapy" that psychoanalysis conferred. This was the way he thought he could make symptoms "disappear" (Freud, 1935, p. 247).

Despite a level of success in this regard, psychoanalysis rested on analytic foundations that were compromised from the start. People came to practitioners like Freud with physical symptoms that only seemed to be amenable to psychological explanations. Their abnormal or dysfunctional modes of behavior seemed to be the result not of diseases of the brain but of states of mind. However, why did states of mind result in such overt physical effects? This was the puzzle that Freud and others like him confronted. And it was a puzzle, because on the one hand a physical approach did not allow for psychological understanding, while on the other hand a psychological approach did not allow for the kind of hypothetico-deductive precision that a physical one did. What was to be done? Freud responded to this puzzle by positing what he saw as the beginnings of a new science of the psyche. The psyche itself he saw in terms of the brain/mind, that is, in terms of an entity that incorporated both physical and psychological dimensions. He tried to see the brain/mind as "both subjective and embodied", that is, as a reality that lay "between the physical and mental realms ..." (Gomez, 2005, p. 9). Since there was no language with which to talk about such a reality, and since such an entity was not, except under particular and usually rather extreme circumstances, reducible to language of the physical or psychological kind, Freud had to develop a language of his own. This he set about doing and at considerable length. Viewed as a physical entity, the psyche could be explained in physical terms. Viewed as a psychological entity, the psyche could be explained in hermeneutic terms. Viewed as both, however, the psyche seemed to acquire a "psychophysical" status that the two preceding ways of knowing and being seemed to preclude. Freud's approach was to ignore this dichotomy and to strike out in a new direction. In so doing he seemed to have perpetrated at best a puzzle of his own and at worst an intellectual sleight-of-mind. He presented as scientific what was really hermeneutic. There is no simple way of resolving the debates that ensued (Gomez, 2005, p. 10).

Psychoanalysis as a form of psychotherapy was itself fraught. Those seeking assistance were apt, Freud found, to transfer their mindset to the person conducting the psychoanalytic sessions. This "transference" was either negative and "defiant" or positive and "compliant" (Freud, 1935, pp. 300, 384–386; Freud, 1949, p. 32). Nor was the person conducting the psychoanalytic sessions immune from this side-effect. Hence the much more active recognition by later psychoanalysts of the phenomenon of "counter-transference", that is, the imposition of the psychoanalyst's own feelings and ideas upon those seeking assistance. Indeed, it was the transference/counter-transference relationship itself that became, in due course, the point of the exploration. "Freud supposed that what was recalled during psychoanalysis had been stored in memory more or less intact ... This supposition ... [was ultimately] abandoned [however] as the recognition ... [grew] that what purport to be memories are versions of past events which have been reconstructed in the light of contemporary attitudes ...". This meant that treatment had to be redefined. It became not a matter of "lifting [the] amnesia" induced by bad experiences, but rather the "opening up [of] communication ..." within the context of a relationship characterized by transference and counter-transference (Davis, 1984, pp. 146–148).

Changes in Freudian thinking were also reflected in another aspect of his approach. Freud originally emphasized physical instincts like the sexual drive, that is, the will to manifest one's libido and the way these instincts result in dysfunctional behavior when they are frustrated or distorted (Freud, 1949, p. 12; Freud, 1935, p. 303). Later, however, we find Freud's erstwhile followers highlighting a will-to-power instead (Adler, 1928) and even a will-to-meaning (Frankl, 1984). The latter clearly raised existential issues. It highlighted psychological and social causes and the way these could result in dysfunctional behavior as well (Davis, 1984, p. 149).

The brief summary above makes Freud's thinking look more linear and logical than it was. Despite his genius and his ingenuity, his work was more of an "exegetical" rather than an "observational" science. Psychology tries to deal with the "facts of behavior". This makes it, as a discipline, an example of the latter. However, psychoanalysis deals with the "relationships of meaning". This makes it more of an example of the former. The psychoanalyst interprets more than he or she observes (Ricoeur, 1970, pp. 359, 365). This is why Jaspers can argue that, while Freud's psychoanalysis exposed a "bourgeois world which lived without faith ...", his exposure was "no less false" than the world it revealed (Jaspers, 1972 [1913], p. 360; Fromm, 1970, p. 30).

Rather less generously, Dufresne argues that Freud's legacy is a "serious menace". He says it is based on a "top-heavy theoretical edifice, faulty premises, circular and self-validating arguments, methodological laxity, motivated self-deception, bad faith and lies piled upon lies ..." (Dufresne, 2003, p. 37).

Less extreme but no less critical are those who insist on an empirically grounded account of the psychological phenomena at the heart of psychoanalysis. They take issue with theorists like Ricoeur who depict psychoanalysis in hermeneutical terms. They highlight Freud's own desire to contribute to the natural sciences and they hold him to the experimental standards that natural science sets. They therefore critique psychoanalysts for "flawed reasoning" and a "failure to seek appropriate ... observational opportunities to evaluate their assertions" (Holzman, 1993, pp. xx–xxi). To quote one leading critic: "Freud's massive elaboration of clinical observations ... still cries out for ... careful scrutiny". Even this critic, however, is prepared to admit that psychoanalytic concepts like "repression, denial, rationalization ... reaction formation, and projection" are cogent and useful (Grunbaum, 1993, pp. 3, 46).

The above also suggests that Freud invented the concept of the unconscious when he did not. Though he made it a feature of his psychoanalytic approach, it has an extensive history that has been documented in detail (Whyte, 1978).

Moreover, the above plays down the distance that quickly arose between psychoanalysts themselves (Makari, 2008) and the distance that quickly came to exist between psychoanalysts and non-psychoanalysts, that is, between psychoanalysts who thought that psychoanalysis did do something even if they could not demonstrate scientifically if it was good, as opposed to those who thought that it did something bad or those who simply looked elsewhere for other forms of therapeutic intervention. Then there are those who think that psychoanalysis works only if it is "done properly", as well as those who are "genuinely agnostic" but continue to do psychoanalysis as a way of earning a living (Frosch, 1997, pp. 78–79; Ricoeur, 1970).

Finally, there are those who see psychoanalysis as starting out as a searching and emancipatory approach, who then accuse it of becoming predictable and conformist, as its practitioners tried to make their profession more respectable (Fromm, 1970, p. 5). Freud himself was a modernist/liberal who promoted the idea of the relevant forms of freedom. He did not consider competing accounts of the modernist project, nor did he question modernist culture *per se* (Fromm, 1970, p. 30; Webster, 1995, p. 503). As a consequence, there are those who question Freud's politics, arguing that he saw the mind as manifesting a "social hierarchy" where "classes are engaged in a civil war for the power to determine the actions of the individual as a whole". In turning the mind in upon itself, he defined truth in terms of the free expression of concealed "intentions, wishes and fears". This gave ideas of power and emancipation a new meaning (Brunner, 1995, pp. 80, 88). It also, however, helped promote modernism/liberalism as the preferred form of world politics.

Criticisms like these make it sound as if Freud discounted the role that social contexts play in what traumatizes people (Everly and Lating, 1995; Williams and Sommer, 1994) or makes them anxious (Freud, 1935, pp. 341–356), which is not the case, though he certainly did downplay the significance of cultural context. Early critics like Karen Horney, for example, noted the importance of environmental factors as well as instinctual drives and came to criticize Freud for failing to place sufficient weight on the cultural as opposed to the biological conditions of mental life. More specifically, she accused

Freud of making the mistake of ascribing to biology "[those] trends prevailing in the middle-class neurotic of western civilization" and of regarding these as "inherent in 'human nature'" (Horney, 1939, pp. 9, 40, 169). She had a particular interest in Freud's preoccupation with men and his misunderstanding of women (Horney, 1939, pp. 101–119; Horney, 1967). Later feminists were to pursue these concerns in great depth and detail (Kurzweil, 1995; Buhle, 1998).

Freud saw people as trying to deal with their instinctual drives. He was basically interested in how these drives manifest psychologically. More controversially, he developed a model of the mind that helped him do so, one that highlighted what he called the "id", the "ego", and the "super-ego" (Storr, 1989, pp. 43–53). Defenders of Freud argued that in developing this model he never forgot that social reality is a causative force (Holzman, 1970, p. 144) and that people have personal life-histories (Jaspers, 1972 [1913], p. 361). Critics say that this was never really the case.

Psychoanalysis continues to highlight the importance of paying attention to seemingly insignificant modes of expression like gestures, actions, forms of speech and dreams. Though the significance of these modes are not scientifically attested (indeed, their significance are arguably not scientifically attestable), this does not mean that they do not have meaning. All analysis takes place in the "field of speech", which means that everything analyzable has to be approached using a language different from ordinary speech. This other language includes gestures and forms of speech and as such, has to be "deciphered" in terms of its "meaningful effects ..." if it is to be understood (Ricoeur, 1970, pp. 366–367). Indeed, the unconscious itself may be structured like a language, in which case it, too, has to be deciphered if it is ever to be understood (Lacan, 2008).

Chapter
2

Psychopathology and World Politics

The subject matter of this chapter can be approached from the perspective of world politics or the perspective of psychopathology. That is, we can begin by looking at world politics, examining some of the abnormal or dysfunctional human behavior manifest there (both individual and collective/communal) and how such behavior might be described and explained in psychiatric, psychological or psychoanalytical terms; or we can begin by looking at psychopathology, i.e., by highlighting some of the key concepts that describe and explain world affairs.

The first approach is the one Lasswell took. He profiled the mental condition of the sorts of people who involve themselves in politics in order to ascertain why they behave the way they do. This would seem to be particularly appropriate when this behavior is abnormal or dysfunctional. Lasswell thought that it might be possible to go beyond case studies like these to ascertain what — in psychopathological terms — makes whole systems work. Why, for example, is it possible for paranoid leaders to create totalitarian or police states or corrupt relatively democratic ones? What makes a whole population so narcissistic or hysterical that it ends up becoming fascist? How does phallocentrism prevent us from seeing the limits and distortions of a world that promotes and protects masculinist concerns?

The second approach involves looking at key psychiatric, psychological and psychoanalytical concepts that might contribute to an understanding of global affairs. Why is political paranoia so pervasive, for example, and how have particular leaders used it to structure whole state systems? What causes the narcissism that seems to underpin an extreme form of nationalism like fascism? How do whole societies become hysterical? Why is the phallocentrism of world affairs not more obvious given how highly gendered these affairs happen to be and the extent to which masculinism manages to define what is deemed "normal" there?

Psychopathological Approaches as Reductionist

The first approach is often critiqued for being reductionist since the world's political systems are strategic (military and diplomatic), economic and social, as well as cultural and spiritual. To think that all these dimensions to human experience can be summarized by mentally profiling global leaders is seemingly absurd. It appears to be a travesty of what should arguably be included in a comprehensive analysis of world affairs. To see why that might be the case, it is enough to step away mentally from what is happening to contemplate the "succession of generations", the individual's place in this succession, and the group dynamics individuals unconsciously enact (Kilminster, 2007, p. 247).

This is to miss the point, however. Highlighting the relationship between psychopathology and world politics is not to deny the relationship between diplomatic or military analyses and world politics, or market analyses and world politics, or analyses of the civic self and world politics. Nor is it to deny the significance for world affairs of class analyses, social movements, patriotism, environmentalism, post-colonialism, or attempts to articulate the causes of indigenous peoples and the poor. Nor is it to deny the significance of the auto-critiques of the rationalist context to global politics that were mentioned in the Preface, namely, post-modernism, post-structuralism, romanticism and phenomenology, and the critiques mounted by those who not only prioritize reason but continue to meditate or pray. It is possible to acknowledge all of these aspects of world politics while at the same time accepting that a psychopathological perspective is necessary to complete the analytic picture. Having accepted such an argument, in other words, it is still possible to say that the discipline deserves to have the disciplinary gap filled that a psychopathological perspective represents.

The second approach is commonly critiqued for being reductionist, too. How could a set of psychiatric, psychological and psychoanalytical concepts provide a meaningful account of mainstream world affairs?

This is to miss the point as well. Descriptions and explanations of world politics are based on the assumption that practitioners and even whole peoples act rationally. Psychopathologists suggest that this is not always the case. Their studies of the self and of the collectives and communities that selves constitute suggest that international political behavior is the result of motives that are, at least in part, unconscious ones. As such, they are not necessarily rationalistic ones either.

To the extent that psychopathologists are correct in arguing that better understanding of the unconscious dimension to the mental burdens that particular individuals, collectives or communities bear may help in alleviating these burdens, they are identifying a potential role for the analysis of this dimension. Such an understanding might be used, for example, to expedite negotiations between ethnic, national or religious groups with regard to the conflicts that might have created the mental burdens involved in the first place. Many Native American families, for instance, suffer from "alcoholism ... learned helplessness and dependence, violence, and the breakdown of values that correlate with healthy living" because of the historical, inter-generational trauma induced by Euro-American imperialism in all of its (often highly violent) forms (Duran, Duran and Brave Heart, 1998, p. 61). This trauma is ongoing. It is characterized by "racism, oppression, and genocide", all of which are exacerbated by the failure of the world community to acknowledge the Native American holocaust and the pain this continues to inflict on those involved (Duran, Duran and Brave Heart, 1998, pp. 65, 66). Moreover, treating this trauma in a context where Native American epistemologies as well as Euro-American ones obtain is seen as a superior response to one that relies on the latter alone. This post-colonial response is combined with "healing rituals" like "communal memorialization" to provide the kind of "catharsis ... group sharing ... and communal mourning" that is deemed necessary to deal with the inter-generational group psychopathology involved (Duran, Duran and Brave Heart, 1998, pp. 70–74).

Psychopathological Approaches as Not Reductionist

Highlighting the psychopathological aspect of world politics does not, therefore, mean downplaying its sociological, economic or strategic dimensions. The latter have well-recognized parts to play in world affairs. A psychopathological perspective means introducing into the analytic equation an awareness of how the unconscious mind works and how motives can be hidden from the modernist/rationalist perspective — motives that require consideration in their own right if their contribution is to be assessed with regard to what it is that causes conflict, for example, or prevents the protagonists of a conflict from being reconciled.

The example above of a conflict within a state can be complemented by reference to conflict between states. Why is it that those who inhabit some states feel more fearful of the world than those who inhabit comparable states elsewhere, when by all accounts the former have no more reason to feel that way than the latter? What unconscious causes help explain what the usual array of politico-strategic, -economic, -social and -cultural factors seemingly does not?

More than the usual mainstream analysis would seem to be required to explain such a stance. Psychopathologists would concur. They would look to the unconscious component to what Australians feel as a national collective for evidence of this anxiety. They would look in that place also for an analysis of its cause.

The Modernist Project Again

To appreciate the significance of putting world politics in the context of psychopathology, it is necessary to return once more to the

Enlightenment project and the modernist/rationalist mind-move mentioned in the Preface. The success of this project and the success, therefore, of the mental revolution that made it possible are undeniable. The ensuing revolution in scientific knowledge and its technological outcomes are convincing evidence of this dynamic result. The rationalist revolution was not only applied to the natural universe, however. It was applied to the human universe as well. The global population is surrounded with articulations of rationalism as applied to world affairs. These articulations are nearly all predicated upon particular assumptions about human nature and human nurturing practices. Consequently, they are each a partial account rather than the whole account of world affairs since a whole account would only be possible from a perspective of total objectivity. This is not a perspective a human being could achieve unless endowed with divine luminous wisdom, and there are few of those. Analysts and practitioners reach in this direction but fail to grasp the grail of absolute detachment. The results of their attempts to reach in this direction are the various articulations they provide.

The Enlightenment project was carried forward in the New World (North America) by those who thought that it had not been carried far enough in the Old World (Europe). They believed that the only reliable conclusions were those that resulted from using the hypothetico-deductive method.

In due course, however, the Enlightenment project was ultimately turned back upon itself. Once rationalist analysts began to ask what reasons there might be for prioritizing reason as an end in itself, it became possible to see modernist culture in a new light.

This — the post-modernist mind-move — helped create thinking and speaking spaces for those marginalized by the grand narratives of the rationalist project. By challenging the grand narratives of the modernist project, it helped open up thinking and speaking spaces for feminists, environmentalists, indigenous peoples, post-colonials and the poor.

A similarly reflexive approach was also made to question the discourses used to talk about the results of rationalist analysis and the values built in to the way these discourses are structured.

This — basically post-structuralist — perspective helped open up thinking and speaking spaces for the same groups marginalized by the grand narratives of rationalist analysis that post-modernism highlighted.

In addition to the above, there were those who preferred to know about the world in an emotionalist rather than a rationalist way. These basically romantic analysts sought the truth about world affairs by getting close to listen to them or by taking part in them and documenting the results in literary, musical and other artistic forms.

Then there were those who preferred to bracket off the objectifying use of reason in order to seek the truth about world affairs as a thing itself and by intuiting the primal mental categories of their own minds. They saw these categories as intending the world they previously thought they had been attending to.

Finally there were those who decided to relinquish the rationalist perspective altogether in favor of the opportunities the mind offers to those who would meditate or pray. Rationalism was originally set up in opposition to spiritual beliefs like these. In eschewing the objectifying perspective, neo-sacralists re-embed rationalism in a concept of what the mind is capable of doing when it is used not only in irrationalist but in anti-rationalist ways. They see rationalism as only one aspect of what the mind can do and only one aspect of what it needs to do to know what is true.

The psychopathological approach is one way in which rationalists have historically become critical of their own rationalism. Concerned with mental motivations that limit and distort the quality of their reasoning, they seek to understand these motivations in order to compensate for them. Among these motivations are the unconscious dimensions of the mind. These dimensions craft what seem to be rational analyses and policies and they do so without the analyst or practitioner being aware of the irrational source of their rationality.

World politics analysts and practitioners tend to remain wary of psychopathological insights, in part because they see these insights as asking them to come to terms with forms of behavior they would rather not confront. They also do this because these insights seem to provide little practical help when it comes to dealing with intra-state or inter-state affairs. They see them as applicable to individuals and not to societies or states.

Is this a legitimate response? Can psychopathology be dismissed this readily?

With regard to the traumas that inhibit "reconciliation" between conflicting groups within particular states, for example, or with regard to the anxieties that promote inter-state "dependence" on the part of small and middle powers, psychopathology can and does help explain the unconscious mental mechanisms at work and how the resulting symptoms might best be mitigated. In other words, there is considerably more to a psychopathological approach to world politics than mere "rationalization, displacement, [or] projection ..." (Volkan, 2005, p. 525). Without an understanding of mental abnormality, there is arguably no understanding of world affairs at all.

Psychopathology as a set of research methodologies and research findings offers maps of the mental world that are arguably unparalleled (Makari, 2008, p. 483). Claims for success in alleviating psychopathological symptoms by using such maps continue to be modest, but this is not to say that there has been no such success at all. There has been success, for example, in identifying when leaders are no longer mentally competent to wield state power. There has also been success in applying a wide range of psychopathological concepts, at both the individual and the group level, to world affairs (e.g., Volkan, Montville and Julius, 1990 and 1991, vols. 1 and 2).

Global Conflict

Consider, for example, global conflict. This is an issue that remains endemic in world affairs, both within and between states.

When Albert Einstein was asked how humankind might be delivered from the menace of war, given that scientific advances had made this question one of life and death on a planetary scale, he turned to Freud for an answer. He saw Freud as someone more used to seeking out insights in the "dark places of human will and feeling" than he was himself (Einstein and Freud, 1933, p. 12).

Einstein recommended the construction of an international institution to deal with global conflicts, though he also recognized that
"strong psychological factors" would continue to stand in the way of
any effort to get nations to surrender the sovereignty required to sustain such a body. Einstein thought that it was the human "lust" for
"hatred and destruction" that informed these psychological factors
(Einstein and Freud, 1933, pp. 15–16, 18). He was also aware that
humankind's "aggressive instinct" was to be found at work in both
civil and international conflicts.

Freud concurred. Originally, he said he thought force invariably
prevailed in human society, though he could see that brute force
might be suppressed by larger communal alliances. He concluded,
therefore, that "[t]here is but one sure way of ending war and that is
the establishment, by common consent, of a central control which
shall have the last word in every conflict of interests". However, like
Einstein, he agreed that humankind has an "active instinct for hatred
and destruction", and that this instinct would subvert any attempt to
implement a centralized form of global government (Einstein and
Freud, 1933, pp. 36, 40). He referred in the process to his own
attempt to envisage a dichotomy between a "death-instinct" that
sought to destroy (Einstein and Freud, 1933, p. 45) and a "[l]ove"
instinct that sought to conserve (Freud, 1975 [1930], pp. 54–59).
The death-instinct, Freud argued, precluded any notion that our
aggressiveness could ever be suppressed. As a consequence, the best
we could do, he said, is to divert this instinct by fostering community
and identity — a diversion that might even require fostering the
dependence of the led upon those who lead them (Einstein and
Freud, 1933, pp. 48–49).

Einstein and Freud are not the only analysts to have written about
this issue. Though the literature on psychopathology and world politics is not widely acknowledged as such, this is not to say that there is
none of it at all.

Vamik Volkan, one-time president of the International Society of
Political Psychology, has discussed at length the human need to have
enemies and allies. He moves in his work from discussions of clinical
practice to discussions of international relationships. He concludes in

the process that while it would be reductionist to account for nuclear weapons in terms of our "aggressive drives" alone and Freud's death instinct is not one that can be "proved or disproved by clinical observation ...", that we can hold our human nature to some extent "responsible" in this regard and Freud's conclusions about such an instinct are probably correct (Volkan, 1988, p. 260).

Global Conflict and the Unconscious

Conflict occurs both within states and between them. Unconscious factors exacerbate both.

With regard to domestic affairs, Edkins highlights the way "[s]overeign power produces and is itself produced by trauma: it provokes wars, genocides and famines". At the same time, sovereign power works by "concealing its involvement ... rewriting these traumas into a linear narrative of national heroism ...". The state "conceals" the trauma that it "necessarily" produces. Moreover, any resistance to this "re-scripting ... constitutes resistance to sovereign power" (Edkins, 2003, p. xv).

More specifically, one can highlight the way historic grievances get transmitted from one generation to the next so that the group "other" can be demonized as the enemy, the group "self" can be construed as the victim, and violence can continue to ensue. Psychoanalysts document in a similar fashion how aggression arises from the inability to mourn (Volkan, 1979, pp. xii–xviii; Volkan, 1997), a phenomenon manifest at a group level as well as at an individual one.

With regard to international affairs, what follows highlights delusion and denial. It examines what unconscious factors might be at work that cause these mental disorders and carry them over into world politics.

With regard to denial, for example, Freud talked of group psychology with reference to heightened feelings, a reduced capacity for intellectual insight, and a profound sense of the presence of the "primal father". The latter he saw as the "group ideal, which governs the ego in the place of the ego ideal" (Freud, 1949 [1922], p. 100). In this light, it is possible to talk of sovereign state denial as the result of group infantilism. Those in denial may perpetuate global conflict by urging leaders to act as state "parents". They may refuse to face the truths that resolving violence might require. As a result they collude in circumstances that are psychopathological (Foulkes and Anthony, 1957, p. 121; Foulkes, 1990).

Whether this psychoanalytic account is the only one possible or the most convincing one possible is not the issue. The point is that Freud is offering a coherent account of a key psychopathological disorder that can have important world political outcomes. It is one place to start in exploring the mental underside to rationalist accounts of world affairs.

International Politicians and Psychopathology

The most obvious example of the relationship between psychopathology and world affairs is the one where an individual with a large amount of political power, such as an important state leader, becomes sufficiently mentally ill to cause a significant loss of human life. The reason for the leader's abnormal or dysfunctional behavior can be either physical or psychological.

Less obvious are those instances where psychopathology does not result in the large-scale loss of life but still has an adverse effect on a state leader's performance. Davidson, Connor and Swartz, for example, conclude from a review of biographical sources from 1776 to 1974 that just less than half of America's presidents suffered from a major mental illness of some kind and that just over one-quarter did so during their term in office. In many of these cases, they say, the president's performance was affected "adversely" (Davidson, Connor and Swartz, 2006, p. 51).

Where the cause of the psychopathology is physical, there is little ambiguity about the nature of the dysfunctionality. The effect on the outcome is usually unambiguous as well.

For example, in the case of the American President Woodrow Wilson, he had high blood pressure at a relatively early age that caused "mild but progressive dementia" and ultimately a "devastating atherosclerotic occlusion" or stroke (Park, 1986, p. 4). This made it difficult for him to think or speak. More specifically, his "cognitive functions" were impaired, his "recent memory" was compromised, and he manifest "emotional responses" that were "disproportionate and inappropriate ..." (Park, 1986, p. 63). While Davidson, Connor and Swartz argue that "no national calamities appear to have occurred due to presidential mental illness" (Davidson, Connor and Swartz, 2006, p. 50), this is hard to reconcile with Wilson's stroke, since the latter prevented him from persuading the US Senate to ratify the League of Nations and from concluding the First World War with a non-punitive peace treaty (Post, 2004, p. 51). France was then able to use the Paris Peace Conference to cripple Germany, which led to the politico-economic and -social conditions that led in turn to the rise of Adolf Hitler.

Hitler himself was beset by a range of psychopathological conditions that included the regular intake of no less than 73 medications. Among these were "sedatives, stimulants, hypnotics, tonics, vitamins and hormones ..." (Post, 2004, pp. 52–53). Under the supervision of his personal physician, Hitler is said to have taken sufficient methamphetamine to seriously affect his decision-making capacity. This was augmented by cocaine in large enough quantities to induce "restlessness, excitement, irritability, impairment of judgment, and frequently paranoid ideas" (Post, 2004, pp. 52–53). Hitler's paranoia resulted in a determined attempt to cleanse an imagined Aryan nation of polluted "blood" and the destruction of an estimated ten million European lives. This included the infamous Holocaust. Hitler also suffered from Parkinson's disease, arguably induced by "psychomotor epilepsy" of the "temporal lobe". This, too, can produce changes in behavior such as "emotionality, evangelistic and messianic zeal, a sense of personal destiny, altered sexual interest, aggressiveness, and periods of poorly controlled rage alternating with overt paranoia" (Park, 1986, pp. 160–161).

Ironically, at the Yalta Conference convened in February 1945 to discuss the reorganization of Europe after the Second World War, the capacity of the American President who attended that conference (Theodore Roosevelt) is said to have been radically compromised as well. In this case it was a combination of hypertension, arteriosclerosis and congestive heart failure. Roosevelt died a mere two months later (Post, 2004, pp. 52–53). Nor was he alone in attending Yalta in ill-health. Winston Churchill, the Prime Minister bargaining on behalf of the British, was by this time prone to bouts of bipolar depression, though how significant these were remains contested (Post, 2004, p. 55; Owen, 2008b, p. 42).

One of the post-World War Two US Presidents, Ronald Reagan, eventually succumbed to Alzheimer's disease, though this seems to have happened after he left office. While in office, he did have surgery for colon cancer. This was in the first year of his second term. He resumed the powers of his office on the same day but was still recovering from the operation. At that time he signed an authorization to send arms to Iran in exchange for hostages, an authorization that subsequently played a key part in what came to be called the Iran-Contra scandal. Reagan later said he could not recall providing such an authorization and under the circumstances, this may well have been the case (Post, 2004, pp. 57–58).

Another post-war US president who was plagued with physical illnesses that were sufficiently serious to have impinged upon his mental capacity to function effectively was John F. Kennedy. As a teenager, Kennedy had suffered from colitis. He later developed osteoporosis and a degenerative back disease. He was also diagnosed as suffering from Addison's disease, a rare endocrine disorder. He became president in 1961, though by the mid-1950s he was already taking a range of powerful medications including "narcotic[s] ... the stimulant Ritalin, barbiturates for sleep, and ... major ... and minor ... tranquillizers for tension and anxiety" (Post, 2004, pp. 59–62). How significant these disabilities and treatment regimes were in terms of his capacity to perform his presidential duties remains a matter for speculation. Kennedy is not usually seen as having been psychopathologically impaired, however.

Where the cause of a leader's psychopathology is not obviously physical but psychological, there is a considerable degree of ambiguity about how dysfunctional the condition is and its probable effects. Deciding whether a leader is acting abnormally for psychological reasons requires looking at the pattern of his or her behavior over time, rather than at a particular neurological episode, such as Wilson's stroke.

Nonetheless, there are important examples of psychopathology that are not only unmistakable in that they indicate non-physical causes but also in the contribution they make to the practice of world affairs. In cases like these, it is important not to rush to judgment since what to one analyst is psychopathology may be legitimate mental motivation to another. However, this does not mean that no judgment can be made at all.

The other key leader who attended the Yalta Conference was Joseph Stalin. Once inside the Kremlin, Stalin's naturally suspicious nature flowered into full-blown paranoia. He used a steady stream of assassinations to eliminate the people he assumed were plotting against him. The ultimate cost in lives was between 20 to 40 million. The last of these perceived plots was an ostensible conspiracy by Jewish doctors to assassinate Soviet leaders. Only a cerebral hemorrhage prevented Stalin from killing the practitioners concerned (Post, 2004, p. 55).

Stalin brought his paranoia to the Yalta Conference, insisting on a post-war sphere of Soviet influence that included all of Eastern Europe. World War Two seemed to have made Stalin's paranoia justifiable, at least in foreign policy terms. Behind his insistence on a Soviet sphere of influence was a security strategy designed to build a bulwark between the Soviet Union and the West. This was most clearly manifest in the case of Poland, which Stalin saw as having been used by the Germans twice in 30 years to march on Russia. He consequently considered the need to control that corridor as a matter of life and death.

Stalin had fought the Second World War against another paranoid personality, Adolf Hitler. As well as being the victim of a polypharmaceutical onslaught, as noted previously, Hitler is said to have been an "odd, awkward man, full of rage and hatred" (Bromberg and Small, 1983, p. ix).

Despite his awkwardness, Hitler was able to channel his emotions in a way that was sufficiently charismatic to enthrall an otherwise civilized nation and inspire it to dominate Europe. The problem is that he was mentally paranoid throughout and to an abnormal degree. This was manifest not least in the way he sought to annihilate millions of people he deemed unfit to live simply because they were Jews, gypsies, communists, homosexuals, or anything else he considered deviant or undesirable (Langer, 1973; Waite, 1977; Bromberg and Small, 1983).

Richard Nixon

Among post-World War Two US presidents, one president stands out as being psychologically paranoid, namely, Richard Nixon. Though not the victim of any notable physical affliction, Nixon is said to have suffered from mental, that is, emotional abnormalities serious enough in terms of his subsequent behavior for his conduct to be seen as the same as someone "physically defective" (Abrahamsen, 1976, p. 234). Abrahamsen, for example, believes that "long years of inner struggle" resulted in Nixon succumbing to delusions of grandeur. Because of his status as the symbol of American law and order, Nixon came to think that he was above the Constitution (Abrahamsen, 1976, p. x).

What brought about this extraordinary state of mind in someone who was, after all, ostensibly sane? How could a trained lawyer end up placing himself above his country's legal superstructure?

Nixon's father was "unruly and violent" while his mother was extremely stubborn and believed in "total self-reliance in an unfriendly world". Nixon was caught between the two. Because of the family structure, everything he did was underpinned by a sense of being "cheated out of love ..." (Abrahamsen, 1976, pp. 29, 17, 25). Of his two parents, Nixon was much closer to his mother. Not coincidentally he tended to absorb her particular qualities, though his home environment was never an affectionate one.

Abrahamsen therefore argues that Nixon's emotional development was "stunted", and that he did not develop beyond what Freud called the oral and anal phases. Because of his orality Nixon was ambitious, willful, and often felt suspicious and rejected. Because of his anality he was manipulative, self-righteous, and often felt impatient and afraid of making mistakes.

In moderate cases, such an outcome does not indicate psychopathology. Indeed, it can even be seen as advantageous.

In extreme cases, however, it can be "self-destructive". Nixon always saw politics in personal terms and as a consequence, he could not distinguish between "disagreement and disloyalty". He ultimately installed taping systems in the Oval Office, the Executive Office Building of the President, and the Cabinet Room. Abrahamsen sees this as the final outcome of his deviousness and his destructiveness. It was the most telling outcome of his psychopathology (Abrahamsen, 1976, pp. 26, 169, 184, 221).

Was Nixon as president able to play this political role rationally? Abrahamsen holds the view that we do not ultimately know when he was acting appropriately and when he was manifesting "deeply ingrained instinctual drives ...". Nevertheless, the general pattern his behavior provides suggests "all the signs of a paranoid personality" (Abrahamsen, 1976, pp. 224–226).

Nixon himself has pointed out that the presidency is "not a finishing school. It is a magnifying glass ..." (Nixon, 1978, p. 1078). This should be kept in mind when the question is raised of deciding upon a president's capacity to perform his duties.

However, as Abrahamsen argues: "[i]t is a matter of great public importance when a President or any high government official suffers from a psychiatric disorder which influences his decision-making capacity. People who are intrinsically unhappy, hostile, and therefore depressed, are a threat, to themselves and others — and of course can prove most dangerous when they occupy a powerful public position". Abrahamsen thinks that Nixon belongs in the latter category, having "deviated from the norm ...", and indeed, having been emotionally ill (Abrahamsen, 1976, pp. 228, 232).

Nixon's inner struggle is corroborated by William Chafe, who says that there seemed to be a war going on within Nixon between the "bold statesman and the vindictive politician", between the man who regarded himself as a "spiritual and moral leader" and the "insecure loner who always thought people were looking down on him or out to get him ...". Before he resigned as president, speculation was rife in the White House about his mental state. He had started drinking heavily. He had begun making "strange phone calls while inebriated ...". He was generally acting "irrationally" (Chafe, 2005, pp. 289, 291). Was this mental illness or undue stress? Abrahamsen would say it was the emotional time-bomb implanted in Nixon's mind that was finally going off. But this still does not answer Abrahamsen's question: what is to be done when a president malfunctions? When should the strategic clause in the American Constitution be invoked that relieves a president of his power?

Though not a paranoid personality, a similar sense of strategic inviolability characterized the 20th century's greatest mass murderer, Mao Tse-tung. A pitiless politician, Mao discovered early in himself a love of "bloodthirsty thuggery ... [a] gut enjoyment, which verged on sadism ...". It is said that Mao did not come to violence "via theory". Rather, the propensity was a result of who he was (Chang and Halliday, 2005, p. 41).

Mao caused the deaths, in a time of peace and not war, of over 70 million people (Chang and Halliday, 2005, p. 3). He is said to have loved his mother more intensely than he did anyone else and to have hated his father, a man he fought against, often to victorious effect (Chang and Halliday, 2005, pp. 5–6). Yet these family relationships hardly seem sufficient reason to have caused the deaths of so many people. It is also known that Mao was an insomniac, which inhibited his capacity to work. It is why he is said to have ranked the inventor of sleeping pills "alongside Marx" (Chang and Halliday, 2005, p. 39). But again, this hardly seems sufficient to explain why he was prepared to sanction so many deaths.

Whatever mental abnormality Mao manifest was evident largely in terms of his love for himself and his love for political power (Chang and Halliday, 2005, p. 654). These affections seem to have had, in Mao's particular case, the status of a natural force. He is said to have had the moral sense of the true brute. Imbued with this sense, he seemed to have found it necessary to cause more people to die than any other leader before him or since.

Woodrow Wilson

Wilson is the only major leader to have attracted the attention of Sigmund Freud, who wrote a "psychological" study of him together with William Bullitt (Freud and Bullitt, 1999 [1966]). Ostensibly a friend of Freud's, Bullitt had been psychoanalyzed by him in Vienna in the 1920s. When Bullitt told Freud he was working on a study of the principal political protagonists of the Paris Peace Conference, Freud expressed an interest in working on a collaborative study of Woodrow Wilson.

Bullitt was not an objective analyst with regard to such a subject. He had worked for Wilson as a supporter of his liberal internationalist platform and had subsequently traveled to Moscow in an attempt to establish relations with the Bolshevik regime. However, he was not able to persuade Wilson to support the latter initiative. The lack of Wilson's support turned him against the Treaty of Versailles and he testified to the US Senate to this effect.

Freud had a very different agenda, which was to elaborate, in this particular case, his theory of the psyche and of the unconscious libidinal force that underpins the love of the self ("narcissism") and the love of objects. Rather than read Wilson's psychopathology in physical and organic terms, as many came to do later, he read it exclusively in the psychoanalytical terms that he had devised as a way of understanding why a person might behave in an abnormal or dysfunctional fashion.

The book begins with a concise summary of Freud's ideas about the libido and its effects. As to love of the self, Freud saw everybody as having both feminine and masculine components. Our feminine component he saw as being characterized by the need to be loved and to submit. Our masculine component he saw as being characterized by the need to love and to dominate. As to our love of objects, the first are a child's mother and father or their substitutes. Initially the child is passive, though later he or she becomes active. In a son, this leads to a particular kind of complex — the Oedipus complex. He wants to kill his father, Freud said, while at the same time seeking to submit to him. He ultimately resolves this complex by identifying with his father. His negative and positive emotions then become his super-ego, or as it is otherwise known, his conscience.

"We cannot estimate accurately the magnitude of ... [Wilson's] libido", said Freud, but "...Wilson's father was his great love-object ... In comparison his mother was a very small figure indeed ..."

(Freud and Bullitt, 1999 [1966], pp. 36–40, 51, 54). Wilson's father was "… overpowering … a strong, handsome … [man] who lectured him incessantly, kissed him, hugged him, preached to him and dominated him as the representative of God on earth …". This, Freud thought, was the root of Wilson's mental problems. In making such a man into his super-ego, Wilson came to walk a "thin ridge up the mountain of greatness balancing precariously between the abyss of neurosis on the one side and the abyss of psychosis on the other". Such a man is lucky, Freud said, if before he dies "he does not fall …". Not accidentally, Wilson "… slipped many times toward neurosis …". Toward the end of his career, Freud said, "he nearly plunged into psychosis" (Freud and Bullitt, 1999 [1966], pp. 59, 63).

According to Freud, Wilson was able to get away with being overwhelmed by his father because he was born in America. In Europe he would have had to deal much more directly with his internal conflicts and with his passivity with regard to the power of this parent. In America he had a "screen of rationalizations" to hide behind in the form of ideals inherited from "Wyclif, Calvin and Wesley" (Freud and Bullitt, 1999 [1966], p. 71). As a consequence, he spent three of the ten years of his young manhood in his father's manse unable to become a man.

In due course Wilson did strike out on his own and was able to succeed; however, in due course he also failed. He succeeded in part because of the "demands of his time", though Freud thought that this success was also due to the "excessive" nature of the "reaction-formation" against his passivity towards his father. The narcissism he subsequently manifest made him "unattractive" as a human being, though it also made it possible for him to use everything he had to advance his career. His super-ego, Freud said, "tortured him by demanding impossible achievements", though it did drive him to "considerable accomplishments …". The "qualities of his defects" can be seen as having "raised him to power …". At the same time, these same defects made him a "fiasco …". They ultimately destroyed him, or more accurately, in Freud's parlance, he was destroyed by the same "incomparable father" who had created him (Freud and Bullitt, 1999 [1966], pp. 81, 85, 130–131, 291).

Freud's analysis remains controversial in that it reduces Wilson to a textbook example of Freud's own reading of psychoanalysis (Waite, 1977, p. xiii). However, some of Freud's conclusions did receive corroboration from a later analysis by George and George. This analysis argued that power for Wilson was a "compensatory value, a means of restoring the self-esteem damaged in childhood ..." (George and George, 1964 [1956], p. 320). Evidence for this was to be found, they said, in Wilson's private papers, which apparently testified to a "consuming inner difficulty" for which Wilson was ultimately to pay a "terrible price" (George and George, 1964 [1956], p. xx). It was also to be found, they said, in Wilson's behavior. For example, he refused ever to countenance interference, resisting any challenge to his authority — "... a characteristic", they believed, "that might well have represented a rebellion against the domination of his father, whose authority he had never dared openly to challenge ..." (George and George, 1964 [1956], p. 11). They did concede the tentative nature of any such conclusion. Yet, having considered Wilson's career as a whole, they claimed to be able to observe repeated forms of the same kind of behavior. His desire to dominate, for example, was "so strong that nothing — except, on occasion, the lure of higher office — could overcome his determination to bring his opponents to heel" (George and George, 1964 [1956], p. 12). It seems, in short, that there was much more to Wilson than his final, incapacitating stroke. He had struggled psychologically all of his adult life.

Adolf Hitler

The world leader who has stimulated the most psychopathological interest is Adolf Hitler. His evil genius still hovers over the attempt by political and social analysts to understand how, in the heart of modernist Europe, pre-modernist barbarism should have occurred on such an extraordinary scale and in such a distinctive form. How could such an advanced and seemingly civilized culture have accepted such levels of media control, such a high degree of mass mobilization, such extraordinary destructiveness, and such a lust for racial hatred and mass genocide? Was Hitler no more than an opportunist or a

con-artist? Did he have a clear and premeditated plan? Was he a capitalist stooge? Or was he simply mentally deranged? In which case,
why did so many Germans follow a pathological person "into the
abyss" (Kershaw, 1998, p. xxii)?

In reminiscing on his childhood, Hitler does not cite anything of
particular note. He honored his father but loved his mother, he says
(Hitler, 1992 [1925–1926], p. 17). So far so good. His father was a
civil servant who wanted his son to follow in his footsteps, while
Hitler himself wanted to be an artist, a painter. This brought him into
direct conflict with his father, but it hardly justifies the statement he
makes a few pages later in his autobiography that "... by defending
myself against the Jew, I am fighting for the work of the Lord"
(Hitler, 1992 [1925–1926], p. 60). Nor does it justify the conclusion
he offers in the penultimate sentence to the same work that "... [a]
state which in this age of racial poisoning dedicates itself to the care
of its best racial elements must one day become lord of the earth"
(Hitler, 1992 [1925–1926], p. 628).

Analysts who have reviewed the evidence concerning Hitler's
health conclude that he was mentally well before World War Two and
for the first two years of the war itself (Redlich, 1999, p. 197). But
how is it possible to reconcile the fact that he seemed to know what
he was doing and that he did what he did with such pride and enthu-
siasm, they say, with the way he became so destructive and so
paranoid (Redlich, 1999, pp. 335, 339)?

He had issues to do with aggression and willfulness and with self-
destructiveness and anxiety, but these did not seem to impinge in the
beginning. He also had phobias like hypochondria, depression, shame
and guilt, narcissism, ambivalence about his identity, paranoid delusions, and problems with his sense of reality and judgment. Redlich
sees the last as having been Hitler's "most significant" psychopathological issue, and given his claims about a racially "pure" state
becoming the "lord of the earth", this conclusion would certainly
seem justified (Redlich, 1999, p. 293).

How well was he, then? Was he as radically disturbed at the start
as he later came to be? Can we argue, as Robert Waite does, that the
"inadequacy of traditional historical methods ... in dealing with so

patently pathological a subject as Adolf Hitler ... [is that] they ignore one historical fact of overriding importance about their subject: he was mentally ill" (Langer, 1973 [1943], p. 220)? Was he, in a word, certifiable? Or did he remain close enough to the human norm for psycho-historians to conclude that he was no more than an extreme fascist? His health was certainly compromised by physical insults like Parkinson's disease and too many drugs. But is it legitimate to conclude, as Ralph Mannheim does after translating *Mein Kampf,* that the analytic logic of this work is a psychological one, and that Hitler fought persecutors in a "dream-world" that he specifically created to augment his sense of self-worth (Hitler, 1992 [1925–1926], p. vii)? How legitimate is it for D. Cameron Watt, in the introduction to this same translation, to conclude that Hitler used transference to hate the Hapsburg state that his father served because he hated the memory of his father, and that we should therefore remain, in a much larger sense, forever alert to other such "enemies of peace in power ..." (Hitler, 1992 [1925–1926], pp. xviii, lxi)?

In an attempt to resolve this issue, it is possible to turn first to the earliest attempt to understand Hitler in psychopathological terms (Langer, 1973 [1943]). In the midst of World War Two the Americans commissioned a secret assessment of Hitler's mental health and, what is more, of the German people he sought to lead to victory. The report thought that Hitler appealed to a specific part of the German personality that was profoundly repressed. More particularly, it concluded that in many German men, there was what Freud would have described as a feminine-masochistic component that was largely masked by the male propensity to favor men's masculine-sadistic side. German men were usually oblivious to this side of themselves. Indeed, they typically denied having one, even when confronted with the fact of its existence. Nonetheless, it was manifest in such telling forms of behavior as submission, self-sacrifice and self-discipline. It was this part of German men, the report concluded, that Hitler used to inspire support and to deal with his own inner demons. In the process, a large number of individual Germans ceased to think critically. Hitler gave them what they wanted, in the process becoming integrated into the mental structure of his followers in such a way as to be able to assert absolute dominance over them. The result, in the short-term, was a connection between a leader and his led that was immune to rationalist critique or intellectual scrutiny. The result, in the longer term, was also of significance for the German people since it meant that after the war, a basic overhaul of their culture was necessary before they were fit to act creatively within world affairs again (Langer, 1973 [1943]).

Twenty-five years later we find Robert Waite arguing for a non-facile use of the psychological approach in order to understand a man that the typical biography tends to misunderstand. "Common sense", Waite says, "tends to assume that people act rationally". Hitler, however, behaved irrationally. With Hitler, Waite says, the outcome of an inquiry not biased by common-sense rationalism is to see simultaneously a "consummately skillful political leader of high intelligence ..." and someone "mentally deranged" (Waite, 1977, pp. xiii, xvi).

Waite is tentative about talking in terms of psychopathology. After all, Hitler is no longer available for direct analysis. Diagnostic labels of this kind are also imprecise and once labeled like this, an individual may be assumed to be the same as others who are characterized likewise (Waite, 1977, p. 349).

Waite also acknowledges the importance of external issues like the economic Depression and the fact that without this crisis, Hitler would probably not have come to power. "[D]esperate times demanded desperate measures", with the times in this case being dominated by financial stress, and the measures mooted to meet this stress being the sacrifice of German freedom for the promise of German salvation (Waite, 1977, p. 327). Hitler stepped into the political arena at just the right moment to offer national salvation.

Nevertheless, Waite does see Hitler as deranged. His disorders were compound ones and he was, says Waite, certifiable. Thus, Waite documents Hitler's childishness, humorlessness, feelings of unworthiness, fears and obsessions. The latter alone included neuroses to do with time, death, decapitation, food, drink, wolves, and his own messianic status (Waite, 1977, pp. 5–48).

Waite notes that successful statesmen often use their mental disorders as "assets", projecting them onto a nation as what its citizens should prefer (Waite, 1977, p. 348). "Hitler's private life and public career show [just] this process at work ...", he says. Hitler wanted war. Once in power, he had a modernist state with modernist weapons at his disposal. The problem is that he was also a "deeply split borderline personality ... [who] externalized his own inner confusion by projecting a view of the world that was dangerous and threatening: the Jews in particular had organized an international conspiracy against him ... the Jews and their allies in Russia and the West [who] were attempting to destroy the Motherland. He must defend her" (Waite, 1977, p. 387). He must promise a utopia that redeemed his nation. He must compensate in the process for the failures he felt he had suffered in his earlier years.

Other analysts are more forthcoming in their assessment of Hitler's mental state. Bromberg and Small, for example, are quite categorical. Hitler was a *"narcissistic personality* with *paranoid* features ...", they say, who functioned at a *"borderline ...* level" (Bromberg and Small, 1983, p. 8).

More particularly, they see him as having suffered from a wide range of the symptoms of this mental illness. He suffered, they say, from general, non-specific anxiety, poor impulse control (which meant he could be "neither reasoned with nor interrupted"), a weak ego (hence his temper tantrums), anger, hatred and cruelty, grandiosity and omnipotence (hence his disinclination to tolerate any doubt as to his infallibility), megalomania (hence his sense of himself as unquestionable), an extreme willingness to take risks, an insatiable desire for praise (hence his hunger for recognition and admiration), hypochondria (hence his preoccupation with his bodily functions), neuroses (hence his compulsive hand-washing and diverse phobias), exhibitionism and voyeurism (hence his attention to the "stagecraft" of political meetings as well as to the "big buttocks of women farm-workers bent over their tasks in the fields"), envy, contrived kindness, a failure to enjoy life, low self-esteem, self-contradictions ("[h]e boasted of being the greatest German ... [y]et his favorite films were *King Kong* and Disney's *Snow White and the Seven Dwarfs*"), primitive denial ("[h]e demanded and exercised absolute power ... but proclaimed he was not a dictator"), projection and paranoia, poor relationships (he was self-centered, demanding, arrogant, angry, suspicious and demeaning), an under-developed and distorted super-ego or conscience, depression, and various sexual perversions (Bromberg and Small, 1983, pp. 160–243). Little wonder he ultimately brought the Third Reich to its knees.

Psychopathology and International Politicians

The emphasis above upon profoundly dysfunctional world leaders should not obscure the significance of psychopathology as it pertains to whole cultures, countries and societies. All these leaders would not have been able to influence world affairs to the extent that they did without carrying large numbers of other people with them, often in similarly dysfunctional ways.

Indeed, psychopathology can apply to entire peoples and not just those who lead them. As was suggested in the case of Native Americans, the historical transgenerational trauma they have suffered and continue to suffer is shared by whole Native American communities. It is not an isolated individual event. In the case of modernist peoples, the dysfunctionality is manifest when an assessment is made of the collective state of mind of the society involved. It is not an isolated individual event.

Having briefly considered how the mental condition of particular state leaders might impinge upon world politics, the next step is to reverse our analytic perspective and consider key psychiatric, psychological and psychoanalytical concepts that might contribute to an understanding of global affairs. How might world politics be described, explained and prescribed for in the light of such psychopathological concepts as paranoia, narcissism, hysteria or phallocentrism? What might transference, counter-transference, unconscious fantasies, dreams, identity, object relations, resistance or somatization have to say about the way the world works?

All of these concepts — and there are many more — deserve works in themselves. The range of potential analysis they present is extremely challenging and broad.

For practical reasons, the discussion here will be confined to a brief analysis of paranoia, narcissism, hysteria and phallocentrism. It will not consider any of the other concepts that it could have done. This is not, it must be emphasized at once, because these other concepts are unimportant. It is simply that in one work there is not room to do justice to the range of issues that psychopathology raises with regard to world affairs.

It is also hoped that the two case-studies that constitute the four chapters that follow will help compensate for the limited nature of the discussion of psychopathology and world politics introduced in this chapter. In providing detailed accounts of two particular psychopathological concepts, that is, denial and delusion, an attempt will subsequently be made to illustrate in greater detail what the relationship between psychopathology and world politics might be.

Paranoia

Paranoia is not about feeling picked upon — a feeling that, depending on the circumstances, can be completely justified. Where feeling picked upon is justified, then paranoia is a synonym for a benign mental state where people are not sure what to feel and consequently treat the environment or other people as potentially dangerous or deserving of distrust. This can be a very healthy response and as such can even help secure the survival of the individual or the group.

However, if a person or people feel seriously paranoid and the feeling is not justified, then the condition is malignant. Without an independent and legitimate reason for such a feeling, it is abnormal or dysfunctional and a form of mental illness.

The cause of malignant paranoia can be physical or psychological (Robins and Post, 1997, pp. 4–5). As such, it can manifest in an active or passive form. The active paranoid is suspicious, hostile, "untrusting ... quarrelsome, litigious, quick to take offence, intensely suspicious and sometimes violent". The passive paranoid is submissive, humble and vulnerable, that is, someone who bows to what is seen to be inevitable (Oyebode, 2008, p. 404).

Malignant paranoia is known in all cultures and in all ages. Its key element is that of "self-reference" (Oyebode, 2008, p. 404).

It was the father of modern psychiatry, Emil Kraepelin, who first defined paranoia in systematic terms. Kraepelin's place in the pantheon of psychopathology was discussed in Chapter 1. Suffice to say here that he used paranoia to denote a relatively uncommon complaint in which a "fixed delusional system" develops "insidiously" and "without hallucinations" alongside "normal thinking ..." (Robins and Post, 1997, pp. 4–5).

With regard to world politics, paranoia entails a sense of persecution (Robins and Post, 1997, pp. 4–5). The precise point at which a benign sense of persecution tips over into a malignant one and hence into mental illness is very hard to specify. There is no unambiguous way to say, for example, when the level of suspicion appropriate in an ungoverned state system (where constant vigilance and self-help are the norm) has become neurotic or even psychotic. After the event, there are attitudes and forms of political behavior that may be identifiable as such. Before the event, however, given the anarchic state of world affairs, they may not seem to be so. Should Sino-American relations, for example, be characterized as mutually paranoid, as some analysts say they should be (Sinha, 2003)? Or are they just the relations of two countries having to cope with each other in an ungoverned world?

Political analysts and practitioners of the so-called "realist" persuasion are particularly prone to paranoia since they are essentially pessimistic about human nature. They interpret all of world politics in the light of this particular assumption. Their strategic/diplomatic stance tends therefore to be offensive ("peace is only ever a lull between wars"). Their economic stance tends to be mercantilist ("national markets must be protected from international exploitation and depredation"). And their social stance tends to be nationalistic ("having a sense of a motherland or a fatherland is central to state autonomy"). Taken to extremes, "realism" manifests all the symptoms of political paranoia — suspiciousness most fundamentally, but also self-centeredness, "fear of loss of autonomy", and "delusional thinking" (Robins and Post, 1997, p. 7). As realists become more radical, they become more militaristic and aggressive. They tend to control their currencies and impose high tariff or non-tariff barriers, and they tend to foster patriotic fervor to a potentially fascist extent. It does not matter how much the liberalist argues for the reciprocal benefits to be had from cooperation and a more calculative, less competitive approach to world affairs. Nor does it matter how much the globalist wants a hail-fellow-well-met perspective instead. To the radical realist, world politics is fundamentally dangerous. As such, it contains only potential enemies. It does not contain potential allies or potential friends and any assumption to the contrary is seen as a snare and a delusion. This, radical realists argue, is also the whole truth about how world affairs work. It is not a part truth. War is only ever actual or imminent. Free trade or investments are only ever an opportunity for others to cross state borders and extract profits. The failure to foster patriotic fervor can only ever result in national fragmentation.

If suspiciousness is the most characteristic symptom of paranoia, "projection" is its most "fundamental mechanism" (Robins and Post, 1997, p. 12). Paranoids tend to see their paranoia as due not to themselves but to other people. They protect their sense of themselves by projecting their paranoia onto everyone else. This in turn reinforces their sense of paranoia. Rather than confront their mental fears, they choose to live with a heightened sense of persecution instead.

In the same way that dishonest people feel justified in being dishonest because they expect other people to treat them dishonestly, paranoid people feel justified in being paranoid because they expect other people to persecute them. In other words, everybody else is blamed for what paranoids feel but do not acknowledge feeling. As such, projection is a form of psychological defense. It is a form of denial.

As an example of direct relevance to the political domain, Robins and Post cite how competing peoples view each other not only as potential enemies but also as bigger and better armed than is often the case. When they are sufficiently serious, sentiments like these can become delusions, that is, "false beliefs" that continue to be held despite "strong contradictory evidence". This is the "fixed, crystallized extremity of projective thinking" (Robins and Post, 1997, p. 12).

Projection was a key part of Hitler's attempt to purge the German body politic by killing its "contaminant", which was mainly seen as Jews. Hitler is said to have projected those aspects of himself that he hated onto the Jews so that he could then attack them. As such, he is said to have exemplified a classic case of political paranoia (Robins and Post, 1997, p. 17).

The Hitlers of this world, like the Stalins or the Pol Pots, are relatively rare. Delusions that are as extreme as the ones these leaders exhibited are relatively uncommon.

More common are those leaders whose delusions are "borderline". Leaders like these can seem relatively normal. Richard Nixon's political paranoia, for example, was as "complex as Nixon himself", being a mixture of "active and reactive prudence based on hard experience shading onto provocative actions against imagined enemies that produced genuine enemies" (Robins and Post, 1997, pp. 19, 29). Like Nixon, most paranoid leaders suffer from delusions that are not psychotic. They may be neurotic, but their neuroses remain anchored in the real world rather than in their own minds. They are not manifestly insane.

Paranoia does not pertain to state leaders alone since it can be seen as pertaining to whole countries and societies. This is particularly so where the peoples concerned feel that they are being picked on by the international community at large or by a dominant domestic component of a particular population.

There is also cultural specificity in this regard. How paranoia is manifest and how comprehensively it pertains to a particular country or society will differ depending on the country or society. While paranoia in its pathological form is manifest worldwide, how it is described and explained and what is seen as the preferred way to deal with it will depend on the cultural context. A modernist country, for example, may be seen as suffering from mass hysteria and as requiring radical changes in the dissemination of its dominant ideology if it is to recover. A traditionalist community may be seen as suffering from transgenerational trauma and as requiring particular healing rituals and specific healing knowledge to improve its members' mental health.

Narcissism

Narcissism is a personality disorder characterized by intense love of the individual, collective or communal self. It manifests as an exaggerated form of false pride, that is, as a "grandiose sense" of personal or group importance (Oyebode, 2008, p. 411). It is said to be "inextricably linked with power". It is also said to be related to "adult attention deficit/hyperactivity disorder (ADHD), substance abuse … hypomania, bipolar disorder, [and] paranoid personality disorder …" and to be caused by "genetically co-determined" factors that predispose personality traits like these (Owen, 2008a, pp. 428, 431).

Technically, narcissism denotes a "symptom … not a condition". Its lack of precision also makes it difficult to use with precision and without seeming to offer offence (Oyebode, 2008, p. 267).

When used with care, however, it makes a valuable contribution to what is known not only about an individual's mental state but also about a group one. Narcissism can manifest in collective or communal form as group indifference and aggression towards other groups. As such, it is readily identifiable in terms of a sense of ethnic superiority or hyper-nationalism, that is, fascism.

Freud saw narcissism as a fundamental part of any person's psychology (Freud, 1957 [1914]). He saw it as tantamount to the desire to survive. In its more benign form, narcissism is part of the capacity to give self-love to others. It allows people to feel a certain degree of autonomy and significance. In its more extreme form, however, it prevents people from looking outwards. Withdrawn in this way, narcissists become megalomaniacs. As such, they tend to overrate their own capacities while exhibiting a heightened need for entitlement and recognition. They tend to cease empathizing with others while exploiting them to their own ends. Extreme narcissists also deny that this is what they do. They rationalize their feelings in terms of the attention they feel they deserve.

How might this concept apply to world affairs? In what way is global politics characterized by narcissism and does it do so in a benign or a malignant form?

Leaders who suffer from extreme narcissism do not usually last long, though they can be extraordinarily destructive before their condition causes them to self-destruct (Kernberg, 1975, p. 108). There are many instances of narcissistic leaders since the political profession seems to attract them. It is not clear why some leaders succumb and others do not, though the stress of a sustained period in power may be what ultimately triggers predisposing features. What is clear is that narcissism can present a "greater threat" than "conventional illness" to the "quality of leadership and ... proper government of ... [the] world" (Owen, 2008a, p. 432).

What if we look beyond leaders, however? Contemporary global politics, as noted previously, is part of the modernist project. This project is predicated upon an objectifying way of knowing which requires detaching the individual from his or her social context. This in turn exacerbates the individual's sense of self. It is no surprise, therefore, to find modernist culture promoting a certain amount of narcissism. The whole culture fosters autonomy and self-aggrandizement rather than humility and a sense of communal responsibility. How else are modernists to learn to put the social and natural worlds at a mental distance? How else are they to discourse rationally about such worlds in the meta-society of the mind? Not all cultures accept the presumptive principles of modernity. Many prefer to remain communalist, for example. Nonetheless, if they want to enjoy the benefits of the modernist project, they have to at least do a cultural deal with that project. They have to at least accept a hybrid alternative to the way they have lived before.

In a modest form, the modernist project is the basis for the scientific perspective that makes contemporary industry and technology possible. In this form, alienation is the price that modernists of any cultural persuasion have to pay for the knowledge that proliferates daily. It is pervasive, but it is more like a low-grade infection than a life-threatening disease.

In its extreme form, however, modernity is the basis for the conclusion that the universe can only be understood in terms of an absolutely detached sense of self, one that makes only the hypothetico-deductive method the source of reliable knowing. In this form, alienation is so acute that it results in nihilism. This is a much more serious condition. When the only knowledge deemed worth having is objectifying knowledge, life as such no longer has a subjective purpose or meaning. Scientism, when carried far enough, results in a highly subjectified form of life that floats above its cosmic context, rendering it objectively valueless. Christopher Lasch calls this the "culture of narcissism", by which he means the "coexistence of hyper-rationalization and a widespread revolt against rationality ...". Both phenomena he sees as stemming from the same source, namely, the alienation identified above with its feelings of "homelessness and displacement ..." and the growing gap it creates between the desire to "have it all" and the knowledge that this is not possible (Lasch, 1979, p. 248).

The modernist project is articulated in very particular ways. Unalloyed rationalism is only possible for someone who is completely detached. Since the mortals who analyze world affairs are not completely detached, they make assumptions about human nature and nurturing practices. They subsequently describe and explain (and prescribe for) world affairs in this light.

Rationalists/liberals, for example, see human beings as basically calculating. Their concept of narcissism is characterized by the voting, shopping, rights-claiming individuals who promote international law, international organizations, consumerist capitalism and universal concepts of human rights and human responsibilities.

In its benign form, this amounts to a desire to promote and protect democratic principles, free markets, and a respect for global values. It is the shining face of the hegemonic political project of the last century or so. It might result in a little "agency panic", as rationalists/liberals seek to protect their political integrity, but little more than that (Melley, 2000, p. 37).

In its malignant form, however, it involves the creation of a world system and society that favors its founders, the psychological manipulation of human needs by an entire industry ("advertising") to ensure that the products of industrial mass-production are purchased in sufficient quantities to sustain economic growth, and the attempt to impose values defined in terms of someone who does not exist (i.e., the a-social/individuated individual) upon the entire planetary population in the guise of doctrines like those of human rights and democracy. This is a controversial set of projects that realists, mercantilists, nationalists, globalists, socialists and international collectivists all contest.

Modernists/nationalists see human beings as basically competitive. They tend to see narcissism in terms of ethnocentricity.

Again, in its benign form, this is patriotism. It is the sense that those who inhabit a particular state have a common heritage and share a common destiny.

In its malignant form, however, it leads to psychopathological intolerance that results in hatred, conflict, and even genocide. Avner Falk points out how group narcissism underpins nationalism; how there can be an "unconscious attachment to the motherland as an early mother figure"; how the "unconscious need for enemies" is a repository of "unconscious splitting, projection and externalization"; and how the Israeli-Palestinian conflict, for example, is represented not only by the "objective reality" of that conflict but also by its "emotional perception and distortion". Both Israeli Jews and Palestinian Arabs, he says, suffer from "deep narcissistic injuries ...". Moreover, it is extremely difficult, he says, for such enemies to empathize with each other. Nonetheless, he concludes that empathy is the "only way" to prevent more violence (Falk, 2004, pp. 3, 90).

Hysteria

Hysteria refers to either sympathetically transmitted manifestations of abnormal behavior or responses to extreme fear or shock. It would seem to be instinctual, whether it involves frivolous practices like dance manias, horticultural fashions, the use of catchphrases, stock exchange behavior or dueling practices (Gruenberg, 1957, pp. 204, 206–207), or whether it involves minds acting upon bodies faced with a sudden and serious threat.

Originally, hysteria was seen as a physical phenomenon. However, Freud saw it as the physical manifestation of a condition that had a psychological cause. This helped reverse the tendency to attribute it to biology (Freud, 1922).

The symptoms of hysteria are culturally diverse and were historically associated with women (Oyebode, 2008, p. 278). Since the late 20th century, an effort has been made to be more precise and less sexist and, as a consequence, hysteria is now formally known as "conversion disorder" or "dissociative disorder" (Oyebode, 2008, p. 261).

Hysteria pertains to world politics mostly in its epidemic forms. Its sympathetic transmission can lead to forms of abnormal behavior that sweep the global sphere, swamping leaders and their led with fear and shock so severe as to cause mental disorder.

For example, there are those occasions when groups turn on each other, or one group turns on another, to sudden and highly confrontational effect, thinking and acting in ways they would not likely do if they were alone or meeting in a non-political context (Gruenberg, 1957). After steeping the self in a group perspective, the result can be a form of regression sufficiently psychopathological to result in barbarism (Abse and Ulman, 1977, pp. 44–45; Freud, 1922). The outcome can be hysterical violence and hysterical responses to that violence.

Then there are those cases where hysterical behavior spreads rapidly across the world because of economic stress. One result of the fear and shock this can induce is the emergence of charismatic leaders who promise short-term and long-term relief. The regular financial crises that inflict the global political economy are one example. So is the immediate search for economic saviors that then ensues. Charismatic leadership cannot be understood without considering the "psychology of the alienated ..." (Wilner, 1984, p. 262; see also Tucker, 1965). Psychotic saviors tend to blend their (paranoid and/or narcissistic) desire for power with the hysterical desire on the part of peoples to be saved. Under these circumstances the leader saves the people, at least in the short-term, but the people save the leader, at least in the short-term too (Abse and Ulman, 1977, p. 50).

Phallocentrism

Phallocentrism refers to the way the masculine is privileged in the construction of all forms of human meaning. This includes the construction of meaning as manifest in all dimensions to world affairs. World affairs are radically gendered in that men, not women, dominate every aspect of its study and practice. Though women do work as world affairs analysts and practitioners and do play many roles there, their presence is usually made marginal or invisible or restricted to the performance of support tasks (Enloe, 1989).

In its modest form, phallocentrism refers to the way world affairs represents an arena where stereotypically masculine behavior is promoted and feminine behavior is demoted, whether on the part of a woman or a man. World politicians tend to be assertive and to exhibit the desire to dominate. They tend, in the process, to marginalize the need for compromise and the desire to submit.

In its extreme form, phallocentrism is psychopathological. It denotes masculinist assertiveness and domination carried to an insane extreme, at the expense of the feminist capacity to listen and care.

There are many ways in which the phallocentrism of world affairs might be demonstrated, but one of the most telling is the account provided by Carol Cohn of the year-long period she spent observing nuclear strategic analysts, initially as a participant in a course taught by leading strategic thinkers. Her analysis will be considered in the following chapter. Suffice to say here that Cohn was fascinated and appalled by the detached way these thinkers talked about nuclear war. It was immediately apparent to her that the mental milieu she had entered was almost completely male. This was initially manifest in the way nuclear war was articulated in a highly technical and acronym-ridden discourse that made it possible for those concerned to remain detached from the subject of their discussions. Euphemisms and abstractions were rife, indeed, so much so that they were the strategic reality of all concerned (Cohn, 1987, p. 690). Never once was it noted that nuclear weapons caused "mass murder, mangled bodies, and unspeakable human suffering" (Cohn, 1987, p. 691). This led to a truly astonishing gap, Cohn found, between the strategic imagery being used and the strategic reality being discussed (Cohn, 1987, p. 692). Part of this imagery was also explicitly sexual. At one point in the course, for example, program members were invited to board a nuclear submarine and to put their hands through a hole in a bulkhead in order to stroke a missile (Cohn, 1987, p. 695). Another part of the imagery evidenced a male desire to appropriate the female capacity to create life (Cohn, 1987, p. 702). The whole "bomb project" was underpinned, Cohn found, by notions of "male birth" (Cohn, 1987, p. 699). In due course, Cohn found her own consciousness being colonized by the masculinist version of rationalism that underpinned the strategic perspective. She admits to finding it difficult in the end to extricate herself from this particular milieu.

Though Cohn does not say so, she is talking much of the time about extreme phallocentrism since, in strict psychiatric terms, nuclear strategists of the kind she describes are clinically insane. As noted in the next chapter, anyone who is able to contemplate the destruction of most or all of the people on the planet and who is not appalled at that prospect is suffering from a form of denial so dire that it is psychopathological. The issue is worse than the issue of epistemology or ontology that Cohn highlights in her conclusion. It is one of psychopathology as well (Pettman, 1989).

Conclusion

In discussing how psychopathological concepts pertain to world politics, it is important to emphasize that they apply not only to global leaders but also to the global led. Concepts like these apply to individual politicians, but they also apply to whole cultures, countries and societies. They can be used to characterize the mental state of individual statesmen and women, but they can also be used to characterize the mental state of the collectivities or communities that these individuals represent.

Moreover, these are real people with real minds. Psychopathology is not speculative. The unconscious dimension to world affairs is not a metaphor. It is an international relations fact and one that calls into question what analysts and practitioners think they are doing when they describe and explain world affairs, or prescribe policies for world affairs, in rationalistic terms.

Denial

Denial has been described in general terms as an "amazing human phenomenon, largely unexplained and often inexplicable ...". As such, it can be seen as a product of the sheer complexity of our emotional, linguistic, moral and intellectual lives (Cohen, 2001, p. 50).

In more particular terms, it is the mental defense mechanism otherwise known as disavowal. It is one way in which psychopathology is manifest in world affairs.

Forms of Denial

Denial can be conscious or unconscious, passive or active, realistic or fantastic, a response to internal threats or external ones, neurotic or psychotic. It can be used to delete "the total existence of the precept to be defended against" or it can be used to erase the "impact, the meaning or the affective meaningfulness" of such a threat by discrediting or renaming or justifying it (Moses, 1989, p. 287; Taylor, 2008, pp. xiii–xiv; Cohen, 2001, p. xi).

As such, it can result in statements that assert that something either did not happen or does not exist (Cohen, 2001, p. 3). It can therefore be shown to be untrue in the light of available evidence. If the denial is unconscious, however, this will not result in the acceptance of that evidence or recognition of what is true.

When leaders lie, the denial may be deliberate and intentional. Here, the light of truth and the use of appropriate evidence may be more efficacious.

In between there are "states of mind, or even whole cultures", where we "know and don't know at the same time". Under these circumstances, it seems that the unconscious sets up a barrier which "prevents ... thought[s] from reaching conscious knowledge ..." (Cohen, 2001, pp. 4–5). These are the "blanks in experience hidden by holes in vocabulary" that Goleman talks about (Goleman, 1985, p. 15). These are where the mind maneuvers to hide from awareness an otherwise painful reality so that it "hear[s] no evil, see[s] no evil, and hence feel[s] ... no confusion". Thus, it does not have to face reality or think differently. Nor does it have to confront why individuals or their governments act as they do or what prompts their behavior (Milburn and Conrad, 1996, pp. 1–2).

In protecting consciousness from anxiety by diminishing awareness, denial creates blind spots at the level of both the individual and whole societies. "The collective mind", says Goleman, "is as vulnerable to self-deceit as the individual mind ... The areas of experience blanked out in the most individual minds will be the darkest zones for the group as a whole" (Goleman, 1985, pp. 22, 226). Or as Milburn and Conrad put it: "... our official life as a nation is built on a shared denial of painful realities and the suffering they engender" (Milburn and Conrad, 1996, p. 3).

Benign denial

Denial is not necessarily pathological. Indeed, it is used on a daily basis to make life circumstances more supportable by reducing discomfort and levels of anxiety (Taylor, 2008, p. vii).

As such, it allows people to habituate to and cope with negative stimuli, particularly where these do not change. If humans could not do this, they could not attend to new stimuli when these presented themselves. Because they can do this, issues like those that nuclear weapons or global warming present, for example, "simply sink into the background. They are part of the ground rather than the figure ...". This, in turn, "makes it very difficult to keep them in mind" (Frank, 1982, p. 631).

Pathological denial

This said, denial can indeed be pathological. There is "nothing positive about a society denying it has an AIDS problem", for example, "or the failure of the international community to recognize early warning signs of genocide and other mass disasters" (Cohen, 2001, p. 278). Steadfastly substituting a false view of the world for one that is patently true means misrepresenting or distorting world affairs in order to meet personal or group psychological needs or to serve personal or group political needs (Taylor, 2008, pp. vii–viii).

Pathological denial requires the repression of unwanted responses and the suppression of contradictory evidence along with the refutation of the cogency of competing claims. Consider, for example, prejudice and bigotry. This is a response that can range from the relatively restrained to the radically violent (Taylor, 2008, pp. x–xi). Prejudice is a pre-judgment. It does not allow for alternative views. Indeed, the prejudiced are typically driven to more intense responses the more alternative views are presented as viable ones.

Taylor sees denial specifically in terms of individual or group prejudice. As such, he sees it in terms of a belief in the "wickedness of others, the infallibility of the self ... the supremacy of right-minded authority; vindictive attacks on supporters of opposing points of view; obsessive fear, to the point of neuroticism ...; stubborn refusal to believe widely accepted rational explanations for past events; defence ... through action that, at worst, may include violence, and, at least, may include a vexatious form of litigation; re-emphasis on the strength of ... beliefs while rationalizing away rebuttals in order to cope with contradictions in ... [self]convictions; and overweening egotism combined with an inability to see ... [selves] as others see them" (Taylor, 2008, p. xv).

The Psychoanalytic Concept of Denial

As a mental disorder, denial was first described by Freud in the context of his psychoanalytic model of the mind (Cohen, 2001, pp. 25–37). More particularly, he described it in terms of the need to be innocent of a "troubling recognition" (Cohen, 2001, p. 25) of some kind. Dealing with such a recognition led to one of two mental mechanisms that he called repression and projection.

Denial as repression was a symptom, in the first instance, of the failure to fully understand the significance of reality. More particularly, it was a symptom manifest by little boys who, thinking girls have a penis and facing the prospect that they could be castrated themselves, find this too difficult to accept. Hence, denial (Milburn and Conrad, 1996, p. 13).

As noted earlier, Freud described the mind in terms of three basic drives. The first drive, the id, was the drive to survive and reproduce. The second drive, the ego, was the drive to assess costs and benefits, to accept losses contingent on later gains, and to strategize in ways the id did not allow. The third drive, the super-ego, consisted of the drive to make moral judgments and determine behavior with regard to ideas about right and wrong. The tension between these three drives, Freud said, resulted in anxiety. However, the super-ego was able to create defense mechanisms that helped repress this tension. Denial was another such repressive mechanism.

Freud also saw denial as stemming from an awareness that the cosmos is running down. Biological life is counter-entropic but only for a limited period. The death wish that Freud saw paralleling cosmic entropy begets its own mental response, which he saw as denial. This kind of repression was evident, Wangh says, in Freud's own behavior (Wangh, 1989, pp. 6–7).

Finally, Freud saw denial in terms of mental disorders like fetishism. In cases like these, the unconscious mind saw what was real but the mind repressed the truth in order to preserve a false but more comfortable sense of the world. The result was a mental split where the denial was either so effective that the conscious perception of reality never impinged or where it was partial. Awareness of the truth was completely controlled in the first case. It was only partly so in the second. In either case, as Freud put it in an oft-cited conclusion, the unconscious did not contain a "no" (Freud, 1961 [1925], p. 239).

The other mental mechanism Freud discussed — namely, projection — describes the displacement onto others of the emotions and drives that animate the society or the self. Those "in denial", for example, may see aggression in others where they themselves are the ones being aggressive. Or they may feel paranoid and that others are "out to get them", when it may be they themselves who are "out to get the other" by affirming their sense of self or their social solidarity (Taylor, 2008, p. xiii).

Freud's approach was revised and elaborated by that of his daughter, who analyzed in detail the defense mechanisms people use to deal with their anxiety (Freud, 1968 [1946]). Later analysts came to their own conclusions as to its ultimate cause. For example, Milburn and Conrad saw it in terms of punitive parenting. This they saw as resulting in unresolved negative emotions like fear, anger and helplessness, that were then available to be exploited by national leaders (Milburn and Conrad, 1996).

Though denial cushions the effect of mental trauma, it cannot change how the world is. Taken to extremes, it becomes psychopathological. However, given its mentally protective significance, what constitutes "extremity" in this regard is far from being self-evident.

Someone faced with a life-threatening disease, for example, who lives refusing to acknowledge that fact, can be said to be in a state of extreme denial. But is their mental condition psychopathological, especially if that denial makes it possible for them to spend their last days in relative mental and emotional comfort? In one sense, failing to confront the fact of a terminal illness is psychopathological. In another sense, it can make what remains of a life more tolerable. The psychopathological refusal to acknowledge the fact begins, under circumstances like these, to look more like a blessing than a curse. It begins to look notably less psychopathological. This is consistent with the clinical observation that, despite being a culture of "doers" and one that therefore tends to look down on those who behave otherwise, denial presents in so many ways that to cast it in a negative light is arguably "unfair" (Edelstein, Nathanson and Stone, 1989, p. ix).

By the same token, by denying death, for example, the death so denied can be made more certain for those doing the denying. In not facing the fact of their imminent demise, those concerned can conspire to promote their individual or group extinction. Here the example of the 400,000 Jews confined by the Nazis to the Warsaw Ghetto is regularly cited as a case in point. Instead of ignoring news of Jews being murdered in Ponary, Vilna and Chelmno, Wangh says (citing Laqueur, 1980, pp. 125–130), the Warsaw Jews thought that only communists were being killed there. They chose "massive denial" over mass rebellion. As a consequence they were murdered as well (Wangh, 1989, p. 14).

This said, blaming the victim (a practice often said to be associated with guilt) does not do justice to a number of mitigating factors. The Jews who were put in ghettos like these were isolated and as such were not always able to get reliable information. What is more, the Nazis actively deceived them as to the extent of the genocide they were carrying out. Escape was also made a near-impossibility. So was physical resistance, though a significant amount of physical resistance did also take place.

The desire, post-Holocaust, to avoid "traumatic reexperiencing" has to be seen in this light. So does the time it took for survivors to start to talk and societies to start to listen (Davidson, 1989, pp. 310, 314, 319).

Beyond the Psychoanalytic Concept of Denial

Since Freud started using the term, denial has acquired a meaning less closely attached to psychoanalysis. It has come to be used to describe the reduction of anxiety that results by refusing to acknowledge facts or thoughts or feelings deemed mentally intolerable. It is used when intellectual implications are avoided and normal feelings are repressed, thereby resulting in dazed, "constricted", amnesiac, even fanciful forms of disavowal (Goleman, 1985, pp. 52–53).

Everyone is capable of turning a "blind eye" to something they find disconcerting. However, in its most radical form, denial denotes subconscious repression. Not thinking or feeling about something means living without the suffering that the stress of thinking or feeling about it causes, which is why it can be preferred to confronting "the truth" about, for example, the millions of civilians killed mostly by their own governments since World War Two, or the millions more who have been maimed or forced to flee or killed by preventable diseases and lack of food, clean water and adequate sanitation.

Repression like this is manifest in the form of circumlocutions of a number of different kinds. These are the signs that subconscious disavowal is at work. "Just as the hull of a Gothic church is held up by buttresses, so denial in order to be sustainable is often buttressed by means of positive, substitutive images, by 'dreams of glory' ... by dreams of the might of, and identification with, fairy-tale figures, and more often than not, by solid appearing rationalizations, or [even] by [the] religious consolations of [an] afterlife" (Wangh, 1989, p. 12).

Anxiety is ostensibly reduced by confronting the truth, on the assumption that denial stops individuals or societies from dealing as well as they might have done with particular threats (Moses, 1989, p. 295). "When we speak of denial", however, we "assume we know what the truth is ...". In practice, though, "... [w]e can only state ... [what this might be] from our own, relative vantage point ..." (Wurmser, 1989, p. 278).

The anxiety that is manifest in the form of denial can also, as Freud argued, be reduced by projecting the painful consequences of what is true — whatever these might be — onto somebody else. By blaming others, it is possible to avoid accepting the responsibility that the individual, group or society concerned incurs. For example, denial can be used to describe and explain those who continue to plan for nuclear war. Planners like these typically refuse to face the appalling reality that their work entails, namely, the danger of thermonuclear conflict and species decimation or even species suicide. Or they may face that reality but refuse to allow the fact of it to affect what they do. Or they may face that reality and the fact of potential catastrophe while displacing their admission onto the planners who work for their adversaries. Whatever it is that is seen as being the likely effects of a large-scale exchange of nuclear weapons, it remains the case that their use is unimaginable. Mental disavowal, if not directly addressed, is psychopathological. In strict medical terms, that is, planners like these are insane.

Denial like this can cause others to behave in ways that make them complicit or prevent them from dealing with issues as directly as they might otherwise do. As will be discussed in more detail below, this makes it more difficult to acknowledge the danger that nuclear weapons represent, for example, and to bring about nuclear disarmament in a conscious and measured way. "Although we know that denial serves to relieve us of anxiety", says Wangh, "and [that] such relief is necessary for living, we must renounce its comfort to remain alert to the danger to our whole biosphere that a 'nuclear winter' brought about by a nuclear war holds out for our planet Earth" (Wangh, 1989, p. 14).

Denial is also used as an unconscious defense mechanism to avoid confronting the fact of industrially induced global warming, the fact that this is occurring, and the fact that humans cause it. There are those who are prepared to admit that global warming is taking place as a result of human activity but who refuse to see the results as overly significant. There are also those who admit that humankind is causing global warming and that the outcome may be catastrophic but who do not think this is something they can mitigate or prevent because of actors elsewhere. Again, the degree of mental disavowal is often such that it can be called psychopathological. In strict medical terms, those involved are insane. As with nuclear weapons, climate change denial can cause others to behave in ways that make them complicit with or prevent them from dealing with the issue as directly as they might. This makes it more difficult to acknowledge the danger the industrial revolution represents and to bring about environmental reforms in a conscious and rational way. Again, while denial relieves anxiety and as such helps people live on a day-to-day basis, it may be necessary to renounce this comfort to remain alert to the danger to the whole biosphere that global warming represents.

Stages of Denial

As a psychological response, denial can be highly personal. Elisabeth Kubler-Ross sees it as the first of a five-step response that helps people survive the loss of a loved one, for example, or shocking news about the circumstances they face. Denial allows people to "pace" what they feel about these circumstances. It is "nature's way", say Kubler-Ross and Kessler, of "letting in" only as much as can be handled. The "letting in" of feelings is the psyche's "protective mechanisms", they conclude (Kubler-Ross and Kessler, 2005, p. 10).

The DSM-IV has a seven-step scale that ranges from the kind of dissociation and repression that keeps mental threats at bay to maladaptive behavior it calls "defensive dysregulation". The latter involves perceptions of reality that are discernibly different from objective ones (DSM-IV, 1994, pp. 751–753).

As a personal response, the questions that denial raises are to a degree "confluent". If they are asked by neurotic persons, for example, "such a defense will tend to be conscious, will be more directed against external rather than internal percepts ... [and] will ... result in the coexistence of different levels of awareness." If they are asked by psychotic persons, however, the denial will likely be directed against "internal percepts — that is, drives and affects" and will likely be viewed as "totally eliminating the threatening stimulus from consciousness" (Moses, 1989, p. 288).

To Moses, it is the "neurotic, adult, normal" kind of denial which is used by people in nations and is evident in the political process (Moses, 1989, p. 289). It is very evident in any country where denial is a daily reality for individual soldiers, who eschew the risks of what they do in order to do it. It is also very evident in those they fight for, who must live with the potential loss of particular loved ones. For Moses: "... the ongoing denial of continuously existing external dangers ... becomes part of the public life of that society. It is part of the political process in that it ... [becomes] part of a pattern of living for the majority of the population. As such, it is usually sanctioned and supported by the powers that be" (Moses, 1989, p. 292).

The Holocaust presents a highly particular phenomenon in this regard. The reality of this episode was exposed at the end of World War Two. However, the enormity of the fact of it was typically not faced for years afterwards, until the stories of the survivors began to be heard, initially by a more immediate audience and then by the next generation of those whose parents were the ones directly involved. By this stage it had to contend with those who argued that the whole appalling episode was a hoax. As such, it had to contend not so much with denial as the opposite of historical truth but denial as part of a long-standing, ostensibly reasonable, extremely widespread, profoundly dishonest and highly political agenda of overt anti-Semitism (Stern, 1993; Taylor, 2008, pp. 38–70).

Returning to the issue of stages, denial is arguably "ubiquitous". Everywhere tragedies "have been — and are being — pushed out of awareness, that is, denied, by people ... all the time". Denial is found wherever and whenever conflicts are found. It is manifest in different forms only because of different "national characteristics" and "external exigencies" (Moses, 1989, p. 293; Klein and Kogan, 1989; Davidson, 1989).

In Kubler-Ross's terms, the psychopathological form of denial is the one that gets stuck at the first stage of numbness and disbelief. A sequence of subsequent steps in the denial process, she says — namely anger, bargaining, depression and ultimately acceptance — provides the tools people need to contextualize what they feel, though not everyone goes through all of these steps and not everyone does so in the particular order nominated above.

As a psychological response, denial can also be institutional. After invading Iraq, for example, US president George W. Bush was faced with a pervasive period of insurgency. However, he refused to acknowledge the implications of this fact. By June 2004 there were 60 attacks a day against the coalition and its Iraqi allies (Woodward, 2006, pp. 267, 327). At the same time, there were senior intelligence officials in his administration who refused to believe that Iraq did not have weapons of mass destruction (Woodward, 2006, p. 282). As Woodward points out: "... the real evidence of just how badly things were going — the data and trends on the violence, the number and the effectiveness of the enemy-initiated attacks — was kept classified, hidden away from the voting public" (Woodward, 2006, p. 327). In his second inaugural speech, delivered on 20 January 2005, Bush was "so sweeping" that one observer felt the Americans seemed on the point of a bid to "colonize Mars" (Woodward, 2006, p. 378). He provided "upbeat talk and optimism". What he failed to tell America, however, was the truth about "what Iraq had become" (Woodward, 2006, p. 491).

The Cultural Component of Denial

Denial has an important cultural component. It is not the same wherever it is manifest. It varies from one society to another.

Wurmser documents this variance firstly in terms of the culture of contemporary treatment. He calls this the *"flight from [psychiatric] patients"*, a flight that he says has now become a "rout" (Wurmser, 1989, p. 277). While some of those who deal with the mentally ill resist this tendency, most, he says, do not.

Secondly, he documents the difference between cultures in terms of the spread of "large-scale institutionalization and bureaucratization ..." (Wurmser, 1989, p. 278). Despite the individuation that modernism involves (with its doctrines of human rights and democracy), it has also led to the use of others as a "means to an end and not as ends in themselves". This in turn has meant denial of the "individuality (hence [the] ... creativity ... originality, and ... privacy)" on which modernism is predicated. Individuals who do not conform to or fit "the system" are subsequently encysted or otherwise eliminated. At the same time, individuals who feel this denial most acutely mount acts of "anarchic rebellion" and "self-sabotage" of the kind that often present in clinical practice. This phenomenon can be found occurring on a more general scale, Wurmser says. As such, it helps explain what would otherwise be "senseless events of mass destruction" (Wurmser, 1989, p. 278).

Thirdly, he documents the difference between cultures in terms of what he calls the *"historical present"*. More particularly, he documents the struggle to extract a reading of the secular today from that of the "true reality of [in the particular case of Judaism] timeless Biblical history ..." (Wurmser, 1989, p. 279).

Finally, he documents the difference between cultures in terms of culture in general and the Jewish and Chinese cultures in particular. He describes China, for example, as a culture where "inner conflict ... is disavowed" and "psychic tension [is] understood as a failure to conform" (Edelstein, Nathanson and Stone, 1989, p. 274). He highlights the significance for both Taoism and Confucianism of the concept of harmony, and he finds the Chinese aversion to an account of psychopathology like psychoanalysis in the society's "deep antipathy" to conflict and especially "inner conflict. In the Chinese worldview", he says, "inner conflict simply does not seem to exist" (Wurmser, 1989, p. 280). He counter-poses this worldview with the modernist one which values above all else "truth", which is (to quote Rorty) "the illusion of something absolute". Such a perspective denies anything and everything that cannot be reduced to "(1) to mathematical physics, (2) to standards of computation and technological control, (3) to numerical and impersonal equality, and (4) to the (physicalistic) balance of forces ..." (Wurmser, 1989, p. 284). Such a perspective radically dehumanizes. It radically occludes "quality and excellence" and a sense of community. It engenders "rage", not least against the attempt to oblige human beings to submit to "quantification and computation" (Wurmser, 1989, p. 285).

The Psychopathology of Nuclear Deterrence

Psychopathology with respect to world affairs is manifest, as noted above, in the form of the denial of the significance of nuclear weapons or such processes as global warming. Here it is the nuclear issue that will be discussed since it is the nuclear issue that arguably presents the most important danger.

The advent of weapons that take the fundamental forces of the physical universe and put them in human hands means that humankind now has the capacity to commit species suicide. The large-scale use of nuclear weapons would not only obliterate large components of the earth's population but would create ecological conditions that would poison the rest. This secondary effect is a matter of continuing debate, but the risk is generally agreed to be both real and grave. The number of nuclear weapons has been reduced by two-thirds since the level it reached during the Cold War; nonetheless, "new scientific research makes it clear that the environmental consequences of nuclear war can still end human history. A series of peer-reviewed studies, performed at several US universities, predict the detonation of even a tiny fraction of the global nuclear arsenal within large urban centers will cause catastrophic disruptions of the global climate and massive destruction of the protective stratospheric ozone layer. A nuclear war fought with several thousand weapons would leave the Earth uninhabitable" (Starr, 2009, pp. 1, 5). Locked up in bolt-holes or lingering in places less affected by fallout or by the ecological consequences of a large-scale nuclear war, some people would live on for a while. They would last as long as their supplies and their sealed environments did. However, all those above ground not killed at once could die quite quickly because of the effects of "nuclear winter" or "nuclear autumn".

This is the worst case scenario. This is why it is argued that the main task for the current century is that of doing away with nuclear weapons. This is why humankind has been accused of "sleepwalking towards disaster ..." (Datan *et al.*, 2007, pp. 1, 14).

Weapons like these could certainly be used without such catastrophic consequences. But with horizontal proliferation, which is the acquisition of the requisite technology and materials by more and more regimes and the growing diversity of nuclear explosives, nuclear accidents as well as the more limited use of nuclear weapons by regional powers or by terrorists have become a distinct and growing possibility. This means a possible repeat of Hiroshima or Nagasaki, which would certainly be salutary since it would serve to remind humankind of the awesome power of these arsenals and what their possession entails.

The death of huge numbers of people and the possibility *in extremis* of species suicide is an appalling prospect. It beggars the imagination to feel the enormity of such a fact, which is why the typical response is avoidance, resignation, or trust in leaders not to commit the species to this fate. However, this can present a danger in itself since it can prevent the weapons involved from being abolished (Thompson, 1985, p. 11). Huge numbers of people have died before and continue to do so today. They have died in war and in times of peace, under ruthless regimes and as the result of widespread poverty or famine or epidemics. There are many episodes in recent times that can be used as a measure of the scale and scope of mass suffering and death. We have nothing, however, with which to compare species suicide. It is an apocalyptic act that could only happen once.

Any behavior that puts humankind at risk like this could be called pathological since psychopathology, as discussed previously, is specifically concerned with the study of behavior that is maladaptive or inappropriate and a source of undue stress or threat to the self or the society at large. Defining what is maladaptive or inappropriate or undue stress or threat means making judgments about human values. In the light of the risk of species suicide, this judgment can be made with respect to the value of all human life itself. This is a basic value and one that could be said to apply regardless of culture. When not ordained by a sacral belief of some kind, it is based on the premise that it is reasonable to prefer life to death if only, as Alice Walker once remarked (Lipton, 1984, p. 31), because life is "less boring and … has fresh peaches in it". Note that by reasonable is meant reason plus emotion. It means neither rational as in the sense of logical nor emotional as in the sense of blind rage (Calder, 1970, p. 278).

There are circumstances where it might be reasonable to prefer death to life. Unless one appeals to spiritual strictures in the light of which life has absolute sanctity, no act or thought or feeling is maladaptive or inappropriate in itself, including that of suicide. Unless divinely inspired, we justify our acts or thoughts or feelings by giving reasons for them and we do so with reference to what we consider valuable. What we hold dear may include one or more such values as freedom, justice, equity and well-being. We trade these off against each other and against our survival, trying to maximize what matters to us most. Sometimes, however, no trade-off seems possible and a hierarchy of values has to be established. In constructing such a hierarchy, survival may not be ultimately preferred. Faced by a lethal dictatorship, for example, we may choose to risk death rather than become its willing victims. That is not unreasonable. There have been enough lethal regimes in immediate times to demonstrate what they can do and what lack of freedom can mean. However, neither of those countries that have large nuclear arsenals could currently be called such a regime. Neither the United States nor the Russian Federation, which are the main contemporary nuclear powers at the moment, advocates exterminating some part or all of its erstwhile opponent, or anyone else for that matter, except in self-defense. This being so, and given the risk of species suicide that nuclear weapons present, is it not legitimate to ask if it is sane to plan for a major nuclear war rather than a policy of "live and let live", up to and including the surrender of either power to the other? How do American and Russian policy-makers, strategists and their respective publics behave in this regard? Does their political demeanor include a defense of the basic value of human life on earth? The nuclear gamble they take is a calculated one that is meant to secure other values. Most would argue that it does. Is this gamble justified, however, given the risk of species suicide?

The risk of species suicide is difficult to quantify. Nevertheless, if the most reliable evidence suggests that it continues to exist, then the debate is obliged to start from that conclusion. If the world still has to live with the prospect of species suicide — and contemporary science continues to say that it does — then decision-makers, strategists and those members of the public who know about this fact can only depict themselves as committed to humanity's welfare if they are appalled at humanity's potential plight. If they are not appalled, then given the absolute nature of the risk and the fact that neither superpower is inherently evil, they are either divine or to some degree less than sane. Few are divine. This leaves the rest. Though less than sane, the latter may in all other respects behave adaptively and appropriately, not unduly distressing themselves or other people. But with regard to species survival, their response is by definition psychopathological since the only sane response to this prospect is extreme panic or utter dismay.

Though talk of psychopathology under such circumstances sounds provocative and even polemical, it is the only response that adequately describes the failure to fully confront the fact that 23,000 nuclear warheads remained on standby long after the Cold War was over. 10,000 of these weapons remained "operationally deployed" and most of them had more destructive power than the ones that demolished Hiroshima and Nagasaki. 2,000 remained on high alert, that is, they could be launched in four to eight minutes. What is more, the nuclear arms race did not stop with the end of the Cold War. The United States continued to develop more reliable and portable nuclear weapons as well as ones that could penetrate bunkers more effectively. The Russians continued to develop a hypersonic delivery system with missiles that could change course in mid-flight. The United Kingdom continues to consider refurbishing its nuclear submarine fleet (Datan *et al.*, 2007, p. 16).

When President Barack Obama came to power in 2009 he announced his determination to push for global nuclear disarmament and to reduce the number of nuclear weapons that are actively deployed. As the only country to have used such weapons, the United States was morally obliged, he argued, not to bolster America's missile defense shields, as George Bush had sought to do, but to work towards getting rid of nuclear weapons altogether. In April 2010 he succeeded in gaining the support of the Russian president, Dmitry Medvedev, for a new Strategic Arms Reduction Treaty. This treaty involved an attempt to cap the American and Russian arsenals at a much reduced level and to bring down the number of weapons to 1,550 each.

The key issue remains, though, as the report for the International Commission on Nuclear Non-proliferation and Disarmament points out, that these are the only weapons with the capacity to "wholly destroy life on this planet ...". By combining their "blast, radiation and potential 'nuclear winter' effects ...", it is still possible to see that they could do this "many times over" (International Commission on Nuclear Non-proliferation and Disarmament, 2009, p. 3). The reductions achieved so far do not contradict this fact. As a consequence, the possibility of species suicide continues to confront humankind, despite ongoing attempts to reduce the risk of this actually taking place. That risk is a fact that humankind can either continue to deal with, or turn away from and choose to deny.

Who is Most "In Denial" Here?

Two arguments have been made that suggest that a negative outcome to the nuclear issue is inescapable. The first states that as products of natural selection, species traits that are supposed to fit humankind to survive no longer do so, that is, they lead humanity down an evolutionary dead-end (Dawkins, 1986, pp. 178–193). It states that the human intellect has over-reached its capacity for co-habitation and that, as a consequence, the species could now fail. In this sense, no-one is to blame. It is contemporary human biology that has bequeathed the species its destiny, and its fate is therefore inescapable regardless of what people might think they can do. The other argument emphasizes not psychophysiology but the conditioning effect of history. To put the issue in Laing's terms, the insane level of denial identified above may be the only sane response to an insane environment. No-one is individually responsible for having built the modern state system with its patterns of power and its insidious security dilemmas. Some may connive and collude in perpetuating this inheritance. Others may rail against its limits and distortions. All, however, must work with what is there.

Humankind lives with the legacy of generations of scientific inventors. Whether actively involved in furthering their knowledge and deploying the bombs and rockets wrought from their equations, or whether merely bearing witness to the mental and material endeavor involved, humankind cannot dis-invent nuclear weapons. In this sense, history really does determine humanity's fate.

At the same time, whatever biological hardwiring humans have in their heads and whatever the historical story, they retain an unparalleled capacity for voluntary action. As Frank argues, "it is perfectly true that in human nervous systems there are programs for violent behavior … [However w]ar is an elaborate social institution which has to be learned afresh by every generation …". Moreover: "[t]o say that because man is biologically aggressive, war is inevitable, is exactly the same as saying that … because man is a meat-eater, cannibalism is inevitable. You cannot jump from the biological to the social. It is well to keep this in mind, because the hopeful side is that social institutions, whatever their source, wither away when they cease to have any useful social function" (Frank, 1982, p. 635).

Humankind inherits an extraordinary capacity for reasoning and imagining. These abilities can always be turned on themselves to mitigate physiological pre-dispositioning. Therefore, determinism of any kind is always a poor excuse. History bequeaths one set of circumstances rather than another and people may feel the inertia of these circumstances bearing down upon them. However, human history is a human story that is written as it is told. People may not be able to pick up the narrative wherever they like, but they can craft the next chapter in a way that is not determined by where they came in. Destiny, to quote Bierce's pithy aphorism, is a "tyrant's authority for crime and a fool's excuse for failure" (Bierce, 1958, p. 31). Fate is the over-dog's defense of the status quo, in other words, and the under-dog's apology for indifference or resignation. Neither human destiny nor human fate is inescapably fixed.

Having dealt with determinism, the question remains: why does psychopathology prevail? Why are state leaders, strategists and publics, particularly those of the two superpowers, not patently appalled? Some clearly are, but why is it not apparent to all that nuclear weapons are insane? Why is the fact of the risk of species suicide not squarely acknowledged by everyone concerned? To answer these questions it is necessary to look at who is involved, namely, the populace at large, those who continue to specialize in planning the deployment and use of nuclear weapons, and finally the decision-makers who implement the nuclear policies that they and their strategists devise.

Publics

When do people feel it is appropriate to behave in a way that by extra-cultural standards seems pathological? When do large numbers of people become so frustrated, for example, or frightened or patriotic or imbued with ideas of what their collective identity represents, or so seemingly detached from what is true in some other way, that they end up sanctioning an unreasonable arms race, a holy war, genocide, or in the case of nuclear proliferation and nuclear deterrence, the risk of species suicide? To identify these occasions it is necessary to have a universalistic measure of psychopathology. The measure taken here is equanimity in the face of humankind's collective demise. How such equanimity is expressed will vary from culture to culture. It has to be disentangled from equanimity due to ignorance, lack of imagination, or sacrally inspired indifference. Nonetheless, it is the key symptom of the psychopathology of nuclear deterrence.

Equanimity due to ignorance is widespread. So is equanimity due to lack of imagination. Many of the citizens of a superpower like the United States would find national destruction in a nuclear war difficult to imagine. If it is the cost the country must pay for keeping others at bay then so be it, they are likely to say. Most people accept the personal risk of a fatal accident whenever they take to the nation's freeways. National risk on the high roads of world politics may seem to be similar given the ungoverned nature of the strategic traffic at that level. Ungoverned, after all, does not mean unregulated. Nuclear weapons have been in existence for a generation and there has been no nuclear war. This may have been more the result of "sheer dumb luck" (Evans and Kawaguchi, 2009) than international planning, but prolonged familiarity with the radical dilemma that having nuclear weapons represents has bred a working acceptance of them and with the ways in which they are arrayed. This has arguably generated apprehension at the prospect of changing these ways — an apprehension clearly expressed by analysts like Deary who sees nothing "mad" at all about nuclear deterrence but rather a benign intention to protect, indeed, a whole "system of protection" that should not be interfered with (Deary, 1986, p. 167).

Considerable imagination is required to conceive of the nothing-at-all that could be the consequence for humankind of nuclear war. It takes some thinking through to appreciate the full force of the argument of reducing arms levels to a limit that would still allow for defense but would reduce the risk of species suicide. Sympathy for adversaries is also required. More typical is the sense that "if we have to go, then why shouldn't everybody else?" A global concern for the species as a whole requires a universalistic awareness that parochial loyalties do not readily allow.

Though lack of imagination *per se* is not pathological, this is a grey area since it is a normal human response not to fret forever about what seemingly cannot be changed and to get on with daily life. This is adaptive in the short-term. However, such a response can be counterproductive in the long-term if it promotes indifference to a life-threatening situation that is not likely to go away unless something is done about it.

Indifference of this sort shades over into the many mechanisms human beings use to deny truths they do not like or cannot readily cope with, mechanisms like "psychic numbing" (Raphael, 1984; Dyer, 1986, p. 3; Lifton, 1982). These are akin to the first stage of disavowal that Kubler-Ross identifies, namely, disbelief.

This denial can be psychopathological; for example, it can be passive. As such, it can manifest as hopelessness. It also provides no emotional hook to hang facts from. As a consequence, they may not catch in the consciousness and may therefore simply fall through. This effect is likely to be worse where the culture is already alienated. Non-scientized cultures are typically subjectifying ones. Their sense of continuity with the cosmos is typically more immediate and close. Scientizing cultures, by contrast, are typically objectifying ones. The cosmos is located outside the self and the self looks back at it and everything else in it. The self is looked at, too, as an aspect of external reality, that is, as part of a natural, objective order; as an object. Alienation then ensues. If there is denial of an important aspect of the objectified cosmos as well, there is alienation "squared", as it were. The individual feels not only apart from the world as an observer of it but apart from something that has arisen from the act of systematic observation itself. In this case, the "something" at issue is a way of waging war so extreme as to portend the possibility of species suicide. Hence, the issue seems to be twice removed. (It is important to note at this point a potential difference between most women and most men. Even in an objectifying, scientizing culture, women are more likely to remain more alive to a subjectifying sense of the cosmos than men and therefore more immune to the alienation just described.)

Psychopathological denial can be active as well. Once the imagination is used, it can induce dismay so powerful that helplessness ensues. More common is the way some more atavistic feeling, such as paranoia, is put in front of people's fears to help them ward them off. In this case, the threat the adversary represents simplifies perceptions to the point where they cease to correspond to fact. The world is seen in terms of "us" versus "them"; good versus bad; right versus wrong. Personal or collective faults are projected onto adversaries, thus absolving "us" of responsibility and making "them" to blame. Nuclear weapons might defend "us", but "they" are the true threat with "theirs". At its crudest, this device stereotypes adversaries and dehumanizes them. Either response makes it easier to imagine harming them and makes more legitimate the need for weapons that can do so, albeit at cost to "us" as well as "them". Destructive omnipotence of this sort can exert its own fascination: a "residue", in the words of one particular psychoanalyst, of the "primitive, omnipotent, psychic world of the young infant ..." and, as such, a world the adult may revert to under stress (Childs, 1984, p. 15).

Another form of active denial, potentially psychopathological, is to keep doing something even though what is done may not be appropriate. This can initiate supposedly threat-reducing behavior that makes matters worse. Such an explanation has been advanced to account for why Americans, for example, continue not to urge the abolition of nuclear weapons despite their awareness of the risks of not doing do. Even if Americans did know how large the nuclear arsenals still are and that no-one could "win" an all-out nuclear war, they are still likely to support their government retaining nuclear weapons. Why do they continue to believe these weapons can increase their security, however? "Perhaps", it has been argued, "... Americans hope to get relief from the overarching and terrible fact that they face an extraordinary threat to their survival and there is nothing they can do about it ... Perhaps the defense the Americans wish the Pentagon to maintain is less a military defense against foreign aggressors than a psychological defense against an awareness that they have not yet assimilated. Of course, if this awareness should take root, the implications would be profound. It could well lead to a greater realization that nuclear weapons, by making the major countries so vulnerable to each other, have altered the systemic features of geopolitical reality" (Kull, 1985, pp. 51–52).

Strategists

One would expect strategists not only to know more than the populace at large but also to have a more vivid awareness of the implications of large-scale nuclear war and to be more appalled by these implications; however, quite the opposite can be true. Strategists typically present a particularly potent form of denial. Those involved are so close to the issues concerned that they ought to manifest acute alarm. In practice, however, their responses seem to be heavily sublimated: "[n]uclear duties impose a cognitive dissonance between the inherent morality of being a good person and the untenable immorality of large-scale destruction", a dissonance which is resolved by denial, or what Thompson calls a sense of "predictive unreality". This response is exacerbated when strategists are trained in ways specifically designed to blunt or diffuse their sense of responsibility, to project immorality onto their ostensible adversaries, and to obey orders (Thompson, 1985, pp. 59–60). The result is behavior that treats mass death as a mere datum. It is not surprising that medical practitioners find such behavior schizoid (Caldicott, 1978).

A number of analysts have documented this mindset in considerable detail. One particularly vivid account was cited earlier and is provided by an American academic who attended a summer lecture series on nuclear strategic doctrine that was taught by a number of eminent civilian strategists (Cohn, 1987). In their professional lives, these men moved freely around America's bureaucratic and intellectual arenas working on ways to control the nuclear arms race, to enhance nuclear deterrence, and to use nuclear weapons expeditiously should they ever be needed. Their work helped shape and make respectable America's nuclear arms policies.

Listening to her lecturers (who were all men), Cohn found herself "aghast, but morbidly fascinated ..." by their "extraordinary abstraction and removal" from what she thought and felt to be the truth of the matter (Cohn, 1987, p. 688). The professional discourse was consistently dispassionate and couched in a special language that was concise, closely argued and utterly devoid of any sense of "horror, urgency, or moral outrage" (Cohn, 1987, p. 690). She was most disconcerted to encounter such a lack of awareness among a group of individuals who she otherwise found charming, funny, clever, decent and concerned.

A conspicuous feature of the strategic discourse was also the abundance of euphemisms (Chilton, 1985). Bland words defuse emotionally fraught concepts, making them seem technical and neutral. Their habitual use leads to the "meaningless of assigns", that is, to less information as well as misleading information (Osgood, 1962). Phrases like "intercontinental ballistic missiles" become "ICBMs" which generate quite a different image from that of state leaders, sitting atop their respective trees, posturing obscenely with their nuclear bananas. Likewise, "collateral damage" or "countervalue attack" fail to provide the same sense as "guts", "blood" or "mangled or burning children and mothers". Euphemisms distort perception to ideological and, in this case, to pathological effect. They make it possible to detach talk about nuclear war from talk for it, which might be admissible if detachment had no policy implications — but it does.

Talk about nuclear strategy is used to craft policy for the use of nuclear weapons on a mass scale, and if the talk is emotionally detached so will be the policy. Again, this might not matter so much if the policy applied to beef quotas, but it applies to potential death and destruction on an awesome scale. The argument for keeping the planning language as close as possible to the policy consequences is very strong. Indeed, it would not be unreasonable to put a signifier on the word "nuclear" whenever it is used before the word "weapon" (Booth, 1987, p. 253). This would help emphasize the fact that nuclear war would not likely be war as conventionally understood since even words like "apocalyptic" or "disaster" or "catastrophe" could not do justice to the events that would constitute the large-scale use of "nuclear" weapons (Booth, 1987, p. 253).

Some of the euphemisms and language that nuclear strategists use is far from bland, however, and this is revealing in itself. Carol Cohn became acutely aware, for example, of the sexual and patriarchal connotations of some of the key images used by the "white men in ties discussing missile size" who were presenting her course (Cohn, 1987, p. 692). She was not so much interested in their motivation. She was more concerned to see how the imagery they used constructed a work-world they felt was tenable. She noted in the process some memorable examples of stereotypically male dominance language, of sexual trivialization, and of male creation fantasies. She also found that by domesticating nuclear weapons and by finding comfortable analogues for them in their minds, that the strategists were able to minimize the lethal meaning that rockets and bombs actually have. Human qualities were brought into the technocratic realm to make it livable. Here the self-deception was obvious. However cozy this realm was made, it was not friendly and familiar. It was a place of inhuman calculation meant to wreak appalling havoc. The strategists made their key concepts and abbreviations technically precise, ideologically compelling, even enjoyable to use. But the work involved the possibility of species suicide. Consequently, it is legitimate to ask whether what in some other context would be natural, normal, or endearing was not psychopathological.

Specialized language provides a feeling of competence and control that is ego-gratifying. This feeling can define a sense of what is true in itself. Divorced from the world, it is supposed to describe and explain, as well as prescribe policy for, language like this can be manipulated at will. Like the coteries of those who follow modern art, those who speak the appropriate language fluently form a group apart, applauding particularly clever displays and innovations and patronizing those who do not understand. They waft aloft, looking down, discussing in this case how best to protect people. In looking down, they tend to feel immune from what might actually take place. That is the danger of detachment: it exacerbates denial.

Cohn also draws attention to the religious imagery that pervades strategic thinking, at least in the West. Some strategists, she notes, have even been known to refer to themselves collectively as a religious order. It is hard, she says, to decide what is more extraordinary here: "the easy arrogance" of the claim to manifest the "virtues and supernatural power of the priesthood"; the "tacit admission (*never* spoken directly) that rather than being unflinching, hard-nosed, objective, empirically minded scientific describers of reality, they are really the creators of dogma"; or the "implicit statement about who, or rather what, has become god" (Cohn, 1987, p. 702).

The language and imagery of strategists is therefore not neutral. It may sound neutral because of its rationalist underpinnings, but it articulates a typically realist/nationalist ideology that has potentially earth-shattering implications in human terms. Given the degree of acceptance that this language and imagery has found, particularly among American strategists, it is conceivable that nuclear war could now occur not because it serves a human purpose but because it fits the logic of strategic discourse alone. The "incentive" for such a war would be the affirmation of the weapons themselves, "not human lives, [and] not even states and state power" (Cohn, 1987, p. 711).

Incentives defined in terms of broader human purposes tend in strategic discourse to sound "inexpert, unprofessional" and "irrelevant to the business at hand". As a consequence, strategists talk about nuclear weapons and how they are meant to protect nation-states and peoples without seeming to ask if the weapons can actually do so or if they are "the best *way* to do ... [so]" (Cohn, 1987, p. 712). Where these are acknowledged as valid questions, they tend to be seen as quite separate ones, along with questions about morality and ethics.

This might not matter except that strategic intellectuals like these continue to shape the nuclear policies of the nuclear superpowers, and it is their military mindset that is most notable even though in America for the first 20 years of the nuclear age military professionals were largely excluded from the policy process by civilian experts (Kolkowicz, 1987, p. 19). As political parties of varied stance and style came and went, it was interlinked groups of economists, mathematicians, physicists, social scientists, and eventually scholars trained within the strategic studies discipline itself, who largely formulated the models that defined nuclear policy in the abstract. These models were quantified where possible and dedicated to managing the dire risks nuclear weapons represented.

In Russia, nuclear policy continues to be crafted by military officers under the general aegis of the party command. Initially this was the communist one, but after the end of the Cold War a less coherent and quasi-democratic control structure emerged.

What remains unchanged is the fact that the risks the Russians run are as high as species suicide. Nuclear weapons remain, as they did during the Cold War, potentially an all-or-nothing threat. This dramatically affects any military advantage they confer.

On the basis of the same logic that says to children that if they do not eat their greens it will be necessary to destroy the house, strategists have built complex systems that analyze, legitimate, socialize and proselytize (Booth, 1987, pp. 259–262). These systems have achieved near hegemonic status. They represent highly privileged realms of authoritative discourse which makes them highly resistant to criticism. The nuclear threat system remains a deeply entrenched one. At its worst, in 1984–1985, it involved 70,000 weapons. Despite American and Russian leaders committing their countries to radical amounts of disarmament since then; despite the post-Cold War decommissioning of thousands of warheads, a process which continues to this day; despite unilateral cuts in the nuclear arsenals of all the major nuclear powers; and despite a broad range of initiatives by other states that demonstrates their desire to reduce the nuclear risk (South Africa gave up its nuclear weapons program in the early 1990s, as did Belarus, Kazakhstan, Ukraine, Argentina and Brazil); the world is still a nuclear one and the risk of species suicide is still real.

More disturbing is the extent to which strategists may be implicated in exacerbating the very security dilemmas they are supposed to resolve. Not only do these security dilemmas help justify an international armaments culture that is highly profitable and cynically oblivious to human need, but its strategic proponents also talk of world politics as anarchic and then proclaim themselves to be uniquely qualified to manage them.

Most disturbing of all is the propensity of strategists to form groups of supportive, affirmative, nurturing peers. Might this not have something to do with the impoverished sense of personal importance each one feels, as well as the need to share ideas with others so as to refine and elaborate them? In other words, as well as the conscious process of elaborating concepts and hypotheses and pointing out their strategic significance, there appears to be an unconscious need to keep the demons of existential despair at bay.

Decision-makers

States-persons seek first and foremost sovereign "security". Their military forces and bureaucracies, their police forces and judicial systems, are supposed to support them as they strive for this goal.

The leaders of capitalist/democratic America, for example, tend to fear non-capitalist/non-democratic "others". This fear is what they use to rationalize the defense of their realm. The leaders of communist/capitalist China, by contrast, tend to fear non-communist/non-capitalist "others". This fear is what they use to rationalize the defense of their realm. And so on.

All these statesmen (and they *are* mostly men) are not ideologically neutral. They cannot be since they cannot be completely objective. They mostly articulate the modernist project, and they do so with regard to the assumptions they make about human nature and nurturing practices.

They are also highly competitive. They cannot lead without acknowledging the need to defend state autonomy.

As members of the larger human project, they may also favor cooperation. America's President Obama uses liberal internationalist rhetoric to argue for a reduction in the number of nuclear weapons overall and in the number actively deployed regardless of his commitment to his country's sovereign autonomy.

The state system remains, however, a realist, dog-eat-dog, Wild West one, and the collective consequence of such competition is aggravated apprehension. In the post-World War Two period, this led to a runaway arms race with a potentially apocalyptic finishing line. The species did not cross this line and could even be said to have drawn back from it. The line remains there, though, as appalling and as preposterous as it ever was — a fact acknowledged on 4 January 2007 by four leading US statesmen in the *Wall Street Journal* who shared an attempt to argue that nuclear weapons have ceased to serve any useful strategic purpose and that the dire risks they represent require their outright abolition (Shultz, Kissinger, Perry and Nunn, 2007, p. A15).

It is impossible to describe how dramatic an abdication of the ordinary duty to conserve human life a nuclear apocalypse would be. Words pale into insignificance in the face of such a fact.

This said, the use of a medical term like insanity to describe the decision-makers involved might still seem inappropriate. Leaders may be irrational or foolish, but are they insane? Insanity denotes severe mental illness, whether organic or psychological. Surely using such a medical term in this context obscures its significance and its seriousness. Surely it does not reveal a new dimension to what is true and real.

This said, talk of insanity in this context can be seen to be entirely legitimate. The medical meaning of psychopathology is directly applicable to those statesmen (and the odd stateswomen) who face the world in a state of acute denial and behave accordingly.

There have been many suggestions as to how to deal with this mind-state. For example, Roger Fisher once suggested that the code the American President needs to launch his country's nuclear weapons, instead of being carried near him in an attache case, should be implanted in a man's chest. Fisher said that friends in the Pentagon were horrified at this suggestion. "That's terrible", they exclaimed, since having to kill someone might alter the President's judgment. He might never press the button (Dyer, 1986, p. 3). Fisher's suggestion was a satirical one, but it does give pause for thought. What is to be done when the distance between unleashing extreme violence and facing the consequences of doing so is so great and when the effort of imagination required to bridge that distance is so great, too? Any way of reminding those who command the great nuclear arsenals of the human stakes involved in using them would certainly seem salutary.

How Sane are State Leaders?

While the motives of state leaders are patently political, they are also psychological. Lasswell argues that a high proportion of such leaders displace their private feelings upon public institutions, feelings that they then rationalize in terms of the common good (Lasswell, 1960 [1930], Ch. 10). However, rationalization is psychopathological when it is evidence of uni-dimensionality, that is, when it tokens a psyche that is fixed (Lasswell, 1960 [1930], p. 16). One form of such fixity is when a mind does not mature, that is, when an adult mind is only partly adult. The political consequences can be serious when such a mind makes its way into a position of power.

Frank cites evidence that 75 chiefs of state in the last 400 years have led countries "for a total of several centuries while suffering from severe mental disturbance" (Frank, 1967, p. 59). He finds nothing surprising in this given that rule for much of that time was by birthright and many of the key families, in Europe at any rate, were highly inbred. Democratic methods of selecting leaders arguably exclude complete idiots from office, but it cannot ensure that those elected are or will remain sane.

A culture like the modernist one that imparts to its members a keen sense of their individual selves also fosters feelings of alienation, that is, of separateness and relative insignificance. The human response is typically to move through these feelings towards more creative ones. Work and relationships are sought that do not threaten individual integrity but still allow meaningful expression of the emotions and the intellect. If this movement is frustrated or seems too difficult, however, then we may go the other way, into personal resignation or mental surrender. In the latter case, individual integrity may be traded for a collective identity that grants psychic comfort. This solution is, in principle, a solution found "in all neurotic phenomena. It assuages an unbearable anxiety and makes life possible by avoiding panic; yet it does not *solve* the underlying problem and is paid for by a kind of life that often consists only of automatic or compulsive activities" (Fromm, 1984, p. 121).

Considering the leaders of the great states (as well as their strategic advisers), it is not far-fetched to describe their behavior as neurotic and even psychotic in this regard. Even a cursory reading of the relevant American or Russian record reveals an inordinate amount of "automatic or compulsive" speech and prose. There is a remote quality to what is said and written. The political posturing and the strategic idea-systems seem to have assembled themselves, without human agency. However, decision-makers *are* human beings, and without psychoanalyzing each and every one of them, it is legitimate to wonder why so many speak and write in this way.

Masochism and Sadism

It is not necessary to delve too far into the mental mechanics of masochistic submission or sadistic domination to find apt descriptions of important aspects of strategic policy. The deterrence relationship between the superpowers is a highly dependent one. Each side uses the other to define and sustain itself. Under such conditions, which are mutually antagonistic but very close, aberrant and even pathological behavior is common. To an outsider, reviewing in retrospect what the policymakers of the superpowers and their strategists plan, it almost seems as if they are following advice "given them by an enemy", advice that says "behave in such a way as to be most detrimental ..." (Fromm, 1984, p. 123). Might this not be psychopathologically masochistic? Rationalized as loyalty, it is certainly consistent with the neurotic syndrome that masochism describes. The sense of martyred necessity that pervades strategic thinking and how our plight is seen to be "entirely due to unchangeable circumstances" (Fromm, 1984, p. 123) is consistent with masochism, too.

Psychopathologically sadistic propensities are also apparent in a rationalized and highly aggressive form, for example, in the doctrine that by striking first it might be possible to provide a defense against the chance of harm (Fromm, 1984, p. 124). As Fromm says: "there is no greater power over another person than that of inflicting pain on him, to force him to undergo suffering without his being able to defend himself" (Fromm, 1984, p. 135).

The great strategic arsenals were augmented in no small part because of the competitive attempt by each side to dominate the other. This competitive drive has been explained as an instinct common to all human beings and part of their nature. To dominate is to feel safe and to get whatever else is gratifying in life, and to many political theorists and psychoanalysts alike, the pursuit of power has seemed an autonomous instinct or drive. Whether the dominance behavior that power-seeking produces is innate or not is debatable. Sadistic domination behavior is common in world affairs, however, and even the most cursory acquaintance with strategic decision-making in general and the techno-strategic literature in particular reveals concepts like that of "counter-value punishment". These concepts sound extremely sadistic in their total disregard for the human suffering they imply.

The excitement and satisfaction derived from being made to feel painfully weak and helpless is masochism. The excitement and satisfaction had by humiliating or hurting others, even if this can only be had symbolically or by anticipating such consequences rather than by actually inflicting them, is sadism.

These are emotions from which policymakers and their strategic advisers, like any human being, are not immune. The extreme pain that nuclear weapons would inflict may well attract the particularly perverse, who, despite their rational mien, find in strategic thought and policy-planning an opportunity to experience irrational, even psychopathological, emotions of an equally extreme sort. The experience has to be sublimated. The basic impulse is translated into a highly respectable social activity and one that is well-rewarded. This might even heighten the vicarious pleasure involved. Since the respectability of strategic studies and strategic bargaining is beyond reproach, discreet power perverts can pass undetected. Only systematic and sustained therapeutic study on an individual basis is likely to find them.

The neurotic quality of much strategic policy thinking is palpable even without delving into the unconscious. It is manifest in the way those involved seem to act compulsively and in an "essentially … negative" way in order to escape an "unbearable" situation. "The strivings tend in a direction which only fictitiously is a solution. Actually the result is contradictory to what the person wants to attain …" (Fromm, 1984, p. 133).

The contradictory quality of nuclear deterrence fits this general assessment very well. National vulnerability is experienced as individual and social anxiety. This prompts a collective effort to deal with the security dilemma involved. These efforts mirror those of one's erstwhile opponents, who are doing the same. However, the inverted pyramids of nuclear power, despite their size and complexity, leave those who deploy them as vulnerable as before.

What is to Be Done?

The psychopathology of nuclear deterrence is not widely discussed. Even to admit that there is such a subject can seem extreme. The superpower strategists are familiar with psychological treatments of their theories (Jervis *et al.*, 1989) and they are generally pleased to think that their work involves rationalistic responses, not irrationalistic ones. However, they are less familiar with the denial, the paranoia and the other forms of unconscious motivation that can characterize the sustained stress that nuclear deterrence induces in both leaders and led.

Professional myopia is compounded by ethnocentrism. The desire to feel stronger than and superior to "them", allied to the assumption that everyone else thinks and feels the same way, leads to a lack of understanding of what "they" actually *do* think and feel. Sunk into wells of respective suspicion, superpower strategists and decision-makers are apt to see no further than the walls of those wells. Failure to acknowledge the closed nature of the debate they then have and the existence of alternative perspectives can become a further form of denial and disavowal. It feeds the ego, both individual and collective, not to have to know that people everywhere may see the world differently and may come to quite different conclusions. To acknowledge the other is to allow the validity of being in ways that are not one's own.

Conclusion

Comprehensive interests of a global sort are difficult to pursue unless they coincide with what state leaders and corporate managers want. A sense of globally shared purpose is hard to find, though it may ultimately be imposed by the threat of ecological ruin or may grow out of the desire to rationalize economic opportunity, as has happened to some extent in Europe with the advent of a shared market and shared finances.

A shared purpose already exists in the threat of species suicide. The common good to be served by alleviating such a threat is understood only with reference to nuclear deterrence and non-proliferation, however, systems that remain highly competitive and that have more to do with hurt than help, with suspicion than care, and with self-defense rather than mutual benefit.

It may be that a threat so dire will bring about its own redemption. Some would see recent initiatives in this light. Pessimism about the prospects of avoiding nuclear war remains a constant factor in world politics, though it is generally assumed that human life in some form will go on. Revising this assumption is a radical task that cannot be completed in a single stroke. Psychopathological dimensions to the whole threat-system have to be exposed first for what they are, and the exposure has to be sustained to allow the absurd and the less-than-sane their time to recover (Oberg, 1988, pp. 36–43).

Whatever else is done to enhance recognition of the risk of omnicide, it will not help to ignore how decision-makers, strategists and publics think and feel. Psychopathological responses like paranoia may even be turned to constructive account as in proposals for measured and multilateral nuclear disarmament.

It does not help to ignore the limits to a psychopathological approach either. Focusing only on unconscious personal or group psychology can be counterproductive if it obscures what is consciously political about humanity's current plight.

Thus, honest recognition of the danger that humankind is in remains paramount. Mutual acknowledgement of the absolute nature of the danger humankind faces would help make the main nuclear powers more willing to consider disarming down to levels that do not promise omnicide and to implement strategies that are built on the principle of "no-first-use".

The mental mechanisms used to avoid the truth become self-sustaining when this recognition is avoided. With technology driving spirals of distrust to psychopathological heights, it becomes very difficult to reverse these spirals so that the basis can be laid for a more mentally healthy response (Hardin, 1986, p. 221).

Perhaps, after all, omnicide can only be faced by not facing it. This is not to promote denial, but perhaps, as Thomas observes, there are some things that human beings can see tangentially, as it were

(Thomas, 1983, p. 12). Perhaps the risk of species suicide is one of these things.

Perhaps the way to proceed is not to belabor the fact but to explore the context in which it sits. There is more to the world than people usually make of it and, on the whole, that fact does continue to please them.

Consider the earth, for example: "We are only now beginning to appreciate how strange and splendid it is, how it catches the breath, the loveliest object ... enclosed in its own blue bubble of atmosphere, manufacturing and breathing its own oxygen, fixing its own nitrogen from the air into its own soil, generating its own weather at the surface of its rainforests, constructing its own carapace from living parts: chalk cliffs, coral reefs, old fossils from earlier forms of life now covered by layers of new life meshed together around the globe, Troy upon Troy ... Seen from the right distance, from the corner of the eye of an extraterrestrial visitor, it must surely seem a single creature, clinging to the round warm stone, turning in the sun" (Thomas, 1983, p. 17). Averting the human gaze for a moment from world affairs might allow the humility that is arguably the proper context for human pride. It might put humanity's preoccupation with its own practical achievements, of which nuclear weapons are one, in its proper context.

Chapter 4

Truth

In the sequence of responses that Kubler-Ross and Kessler outline, denial is ultimately dealt with by mental and emotional acceptance (Kubler-Ross and Kessler, 2005, p. 10). Another way of talking about how to deal with denial is in terms of the admission of what is going on now or has gone on before, that is, the acknowledgement of whatever is the contemporary or historical fact (Cohen, 2001, p. 222).

Valuing acceptance means assuming that bringing denial to an end will be basically beneficial. For example, "[v]irtually all the objectives of Truth Commissions ... have connotations of ... catharsis" (Cohen, 2001, p. 222). ("Truth Commissions", or "truth and reconciliation commissions" as they are also called, are relatively recent institutions designed to find out the facts about a social conflict and determine who was most to blame. They have been used in countries like South Africa, Argentina, Morocco and East Timor to promote discussion about what previous governments did wrong and to formulate and implement policies that allow for mediation between the contending parties. The intention is to reconcile those who were previously adversaries, in part by giving those who were victims a voice, thereby helping prevent the promotion of revisionist versions of state terrorism. Those previously in power may also be indemnified for a relatively complete and honest account of what they did.

Acknowledging what went on in the past pertains as well to what goes on in the present.)

Why assume that acceptance is basically beneficial, however? Why assume that acknowledging that what is true is necessarily best for all concerned?

What Purpose Does Truth-Telling Ostensibly Serve?

Firstly, there is the notion that only the truth can set those involved fully free. Following many years of denial, for example, there can be a very powerful desire to know what precisely took place (Cohen, 2001, p. 225) and to turn it into a public statement of some kind. This is supposed to have an emancipatory outcome at both the individual and the collective level.

Closely connected with the reason given above are the emotions of the victims involved. They may want the truth to come out because they feel that the truth will provide them with a way of dealing more effectively with their feelings.

Finally, there is the urge to prevent what happened in the past from happening again, or to prevent what is happening in the present from happening in the future. This is the desire to ensure that what caused the need for denial is not repeated, or to ensure that what is causing it now is prevented or stopped.

What is Truth?

Before addressing the issues above, it is necessary to ask what "the truth" might be that is supposed to displace denial — no simple question since "truth" is a key concept whose meaning has been debated for millennia (Glanzberg, 2006). The first paragraph to this chapter suggests that the truth is "factual or forensic", though the attempt to deal with the consequences of social conflict using Truth Commissions highlights other forms of truth-telling such as "personal or narrative", "social or 'dialogue'" and "healing and restorative" ones (Cohen, 2001, p. 227). While "factual or forensic" truth attempts to establish what took place or is currently taking place in as detached, objectified and impartial a manner as possible, "personal or narrative" truth allows for the subjective experiences of those who were previously silenced to be given a public hearing, "social or 'dialogue'" truth allows for "discussion and debate", while "healing and restorative" truth validates what those involved feel by acknowledging that their feelings are real and "worthy of attention" (Cohen, 2001, p. 228).

"Truth Commissions" are not the only ways to acknowledge "the truth". There are also criminal trials, the mass disqualification of whole categories of people from government jobs, compensation and reparations, naming and shaming, and the criminalizing of attempts at denial. In addition there are various forms of commemoration and memorialization, expiation and apology, and reconciliation and reconstruction (Cohen, 2001, pp. 228–240). Nor are these mutually exclusive practices. There is, in short, no formula for turning denial into acceptance, a fact that is especially significant when entire peoples "slip into mass denial" — a process that can have appalling consequences for those who find themselves "dislocated from historical time" (Cohen, 2001, p. 242). The reality is that societies use either "selective amnesia" or "regimes of discontinuity" or both to prevent the truth (in any form) from becoming known (Cohen, 2001, p. 243). Meanwhile, to deal with mass denial, entire peoples can go to the other extreme. They can over-compensate by seemingly exaggerating their acceptance of the truth. In this case: "… strong political action … [can be] needed to prevent the virulent forms of over-acknowledging the past from becoming the driving force of political cultures … The litany of memory is endless — martyrs, revenge, feuds, shame, redemption, sacrifice, grudges and the suffering of ghosts. The language of collective denial combines [then] with the rhetoric of 'blood and belonging' to offer two attractions: settling accounts with the past and shaking off any residual restrictions on … brutality [in the present]" (Cohen, 2001, p. 245). All of which is to say that no political organization, "least of all the state", should be allowed to control what and how much the truth entails (Cohen, 2001, p. 247).

Talk of the truth in factual or forensic terms is typical of the attempt that modernist analysts make to reach for the Grail of absolute truth. This attempt entails the pursuit of truth as discussed in the Preface. It involves the prioritization of reason as an end in itself. Bierce calls the truth an "ingenious compound of desirability and appearance" (Bierce, 1958, p. 136). Less ironic accounts talk about a belief being true only if there is an "appropriate entity — a fact — to which it corresponds". Other analysts talk about a belief being true if and only if it is part of a coherent "system of beliefs". Others again talk in pragmatic terms of the "end of inquiry", which can have elements in it of both the "correspondence" and "coherence" approaches noted above (Glanzberg, 2006). In addition there are conceptions of truth as socially constructed, that is, as being what is conventional in historical and cultural terms; as being whatever enjoys a consensus among the whole of humankind in general or a component thereof in particular; and as being profoundly implicated with language, logic and power.

Modernity Yet Again, and Its Various Articulations

Since absolute success in telling all of the truth requires total detachment, and since this is not humanly possible for those who do not manifest divine luminous wisdom, all modernist truth-telling, as noted more than once already, is partial and relative. It is not possible for it to be completely impartial. It is possible to reach in the direction of absolute detachment, thereby providing for greater impartiality than would otherwise be the case. In practice, however, the truth will reflect the assumptions that continue to be made by the modernists concerned. They will then articulate these assumptions in rationalistic terms, thereby promoting their part-truths as whole-truths.

As was also pointed out earlier, the world affairs analysts who are pessimistic about human nature and who are most concerned with the strategic (diplomatic and military) integrity of states will tend to describe and explain world affairs — and prescribe policy there — in terms that assume a dog-eat-dog, competitive, *realpolitik* world. This "realist" approach, so-called, sees the truth in terms of an acknowledgement of the fact that peace is only ever a lull between wars.

By contrast, the world affairs analysts who see human nature as essentially calculating articulate an account of these affairs that assumes a tit-for-tat outcome and highlight as a consequence the potential for international law and international organization. The "liberal internationalist", in other words, sees the truth in terms of an acknowledgement of the fact that as a species we are able to do better than the "realist" says and that historically we regularly manage to do so.

Even more at odds with the "realist" approach are those rationalists who are the most optimistic about human nature and who subsequently describe and explain world affairs in hail-fellow-well-met terms. Their "globalist" approach highlights the potential for global governance and even global government. They see the truth in terms of an acknowledgement of the fact that the species is capable of international behavior that is collaborative and collectivist.

As indicated before, these three basic assumptions about human nature also pertain to the politico-economic and politico-social dimensions to world affairs. Those who are pessimistic about human nature see the truth in terms of an acknowledgement of the fact that state prosperity depends on national autonomy ("mercantilism") and the fact that state sovereignty depends on civic solidarity ("nationalism"). Those who see human nature as essentially calculating see the truth in terms of an acknowledgement of the fact that state prosperity depends on having free markets ("liberalism") and the fact that state democracy depends on the promotion and protection of human rights ("individualism"). Those who are optimistic about human nature see the truth in terms of an acknowledgement of the fact that it is state planning that distributes most equitably the largesse of the industrial revolution ("socialism") and the fact that global social movements can be used by ordinary people to promote their common causes worldwide ("collectivism").

Meanwhile, there are those rationalists who see human beings as what they learn to be rather than what they are born to be. Marxists, for example, see the truth in terms of an acknowledgement of the fact of the material basis to human nurturing practices, the fact of historical modes of production that change by dialectical means, and the fact of capitalist class conflict. Constructivists see the truth in terms of an acknowledgement of the fact of the mental basis to human nurturing practices, the fact of shared values, and the fact of the role that norm entrepreneurs play. Mixed marxists/constructivists see the truth in terms of an acknowledgement of the fact of marxist materialism when combined with that of constructivist mentalism. This mixture is manifest in Gramscian notions like the fact of social hegemony or in Frankfurt School notions like that of the fact of repressive tolerance.

Those marginalized by the modernist project see the truth in ways that articulate their sense of global dispossession. Feminists, for example, see the truth in terms of an acknowledgement of the fact of the masculinist domination of world affairs. Environmentalists see the truth in terms of an acknowledgement of the fact of the current generation's despoliation of the planet at the cost of generations yet to come. Indigenous peoples see the truth in terms of an acknowledgement of the fact of ongoing cultural imperialism. Post-colonials see the truth in terms of an acknowledgement of the fact of the failure of the European empires to relinquish their power. The poor see the truth in terms of an acknowledgement of the fact of the highly exploitative structure of global development.

Those aware of the limits and distortions of the modernist project see the truth in ways that articulate their particular auto-critiques. Post-modernists, for example, see the truth in terms of an acknowledgement of the need to ask "why prioritize reason?" The result is to unsettle the certainty of grand narratives like "realism" that inform the international relations discipline, though taken to extremes, and it results in "ends and means" coming to bear only an "ironical" relationship with each other (Cohen, 2001, p. 278). Post-structuralists see the truth in terms of an acknowledgement of the need to highlight the way language crafts both awareness and identity. This, too, unsettles the certainty of the grand narratives used to articulate world affairs, though it, too, can result in a less-than-benign form of indeterminacy, "epistemic relativism", and an "old-fashioned victory" of "power over truth" (Cohen, 2001, pp. 282–283). Psychopathologists see the truth in terms of the acknowledgement of the unconscious dimension to the mind as one that determines the conscious dimension that is assumed to determine how the world is understood. It argues for self-knowledge of the sort that eschews all forms of psychological defense. Romantics see the truth in terms of the acknowledgement of the emotive dimension to the mind that allows it to feel the world as well as think about it and to express itself accordingly via any of the arts. Phenomenologists see the truth in terms of the acknowledgement of the primal mental categories of the mind that allow it to intuit things-in-themselves and how the mind intends the world in the ways it thinks it attends to it. Sacralists see the truth in terms of the acknowledgement of the spiritual beliefs that rationalism was designed to marginalize metaphysically and the knowledge that these beliefs make available using those dimensions of the mind that can meditate or pray.

All of the above allow their proponents to articulate particular conceptions of power and to "live-outside-the-lie" in their own particular ways (Cohen, 2001, pp. 256–261). All of them can be promoted by force, persuasion and agenda-setting, or by moral appeals that promote and protect what is deemed "politically correct" (Cohen, 2001, pp. 266–277). Where people are met with governments or corporations that deny the effects of policy by rationalizing what those effects happen to be, for example, they can turn (where the judiciary is relatively uncorrupt) to the courts. Their success in countries like the United States in instigating class action suits involving the lethal effects of tobacco, as well as the effects of a range of other noxious substances, has changed the American government's ability to deny the real costs of major industries and the ability of corporations to deny the pernicious effects of polluting practices at home and off-shore. Communal concerns are no longer automatically rendered subordinate to those of politicians or corporate managers and their stockholders (Markowitz and Rosner, 2002, p. 305). In the process, the grand narrative that articulates modernist economic liberalism has been met by critiques that highlight the limits and distortions of such a narrative, thereby making possible more open and emancipatory ways of practising world affairs.

Given the complex character of "the truth", its relationship to denial can be seen as being equally complex. To demonstrate the nature of this relationship, it is helpful to have a case-study at hand. The case-study provided here is that of "Japan" and the "truth" about the perspectives that underpin Japanese approaches to the global issue of conflict resolution.

The "Truth" About "Japan" and Japanese Approaches to Conflict Resolution

Given the multidimensional nature of "the truth", even the most detached perspective that analysts provide, such as the one that constitutes the country called "Japan" or the one that constitutes the global issue of "conflict resolution", will be highly contested. What follows argues that there are Japanese approaches to this global issue. To come to this conclusion, however, it must argue two key points. One is that Japanese culture is a hybrid of modernist and non-modernist traits. As such, it is both like and unlike other cultures. The other is that Japanese culture impinges upon modernity in general and the modernist concept of conflict resolution in particular in ways that are both mainstream and non-mainstream.

What follows also has to be seen in the light of three significant disclaimers. The first disclaimer is the most general. The author is not Japanese. A certain degree of presumption is involved in someone like this attempting to analyze such a question. On the other hand, being non-Japanese does make it possible to see that society and that state "from the outside", as it were. The second disclaimer is more specific. In talking about nationalism, the use of stereotyping, that is, nativist essentialism (which is the obverse of Western universalism), is an issue of constant concern (Littlewood, 1996). This concern is acknowledged as such and an attempt is made to guard against its reductionist implications by locating Japanese approaches in a more general context. The third disclaimer is the most specific of all and is related to the second. Any argument that sees Japan as in any way unique is one that can be appropriated by extreme nationalists to a solidarist and neo-imperialist purpose. The fact that this is the case should not be allowed to preempt the attempt to understand the extent to which there are Japanese approaches which are unique and ones that, unlike extreme nationalism, have a positive contribution to make to an understanding of a global issue like that of conflict resolution.

What is "Japan"?

Japan, or "Wo" as the ancient Chinese called it, first appeared in the latter's chronicles more than 2,000 years ago. At that time it was identified as a tributary collection of more than 100 countries lying off the coast of the colony of "Lo-lang" or modern-day Korea. Emissaries from Japan are known to have visited the Chinese emperor in the year AD 57 and to have been given by him a gold seal. In 1748 this seal was found near Hakata and is now one of Japan's national treasures.

Though unification was a protracted process, Japan had an imperial court in Nara by the end of the first millennium, imperial possessions in southern Korea, and a strong sense as a culture that those who lived in this part of the world were different from those who lived elsewhere. Unity is taken for granted today, but it had to be created out of a disparate and disunited region whose local leaders did not want to succumb to one of their number and who, like the kings of England, Scotland, Ireland and Wales, had to be forced into a single sovereign overcoat by ambitious individuals who faced adversaries at home and competitors from abroad.

It was the Tokugawa warlords who emerged victorious from the unification process. For 250 years they subsequently restricted foreign access to a small island in Nagasaki harbor, because of their fear of falling prey to Euro-American imperialists and the influence of the Christian church.

In 1853 a squadron of American warships commanded by Matthew Perry ended this period of near-absolute seclusion. The dramatic realization that only industrial power equal to that of the Euro-Americans could provide the weapons necessary to prevent colonization inspired the Meiji Restoration. This was followed by a spectacularly successful attempt to assimilate the scientific knowledge that made Western technology and industry and military power possible.

Three important points stand out above. The first is that a sense of Japanese identity is one of relatively long-standing. It is more ancient than that of most contemporary states, many of which only became agents of their cultural destiny after the collapse of the great European empires at the end of World War Two. The second point is that being the agents of their own cultural destiny was reinforced by the decision to consciously cut Japan off from the world for 250 years. One consequence of this isolation was to intensify the opportunity to cultivate a distinctive way of life and one that still prevails. The third point is that the Japanese were and are master modernizers. In one generation they were able to replicate Western industry and the science and technology that made this industry possible. This allowed the Japanese not only to resist Western imperialism but to modernize for themselves and to pursue imperial ambitions of their own.

Less obvious is a fourth point, namely, that the overall result was a culturally hybrid one. As Eisenstadt (2000, pp. 1–2, 24) notes, "actual developments in modernizing societies have refuted the homogenizing and hegemonic assumptions of ... [the Euro-American] program of modernity ... giving rise to multiple institutional and ideological patterns". The best way to understand the contemporary world, he says, is to see it as one where the "continual constitution and reconstitution of a multiplicity of cultural programs" prevails. It is one where the ongoing reassessment of what modernity means results in the dynamic creation of many modernities. This corresponds with the conclusion that identifying a "Japanese" international relations becomes most meaningful only when it is used to decentralize the Western mainstream and to add a new and different perspective to world affairs, that is, when it is used to do more than merely promote a sense of Japanese uniqueness.

As noted earlier, to the extent that cultures become modernist, they promote the prioritization of reason as an end in itself *en masse*. This is what European cultures did during the Enlightenment period. Their subsequent scientific and technological success inspired other cultures, including that of Japan, to emulate them.

However, modernist rationalism is predicated on a sense of self that is an individuated one. It is a sense that is abstracted from its social context. This can be radically at odds with traditionalist ways of living and knowing which are typically communalist. Nonetheless, it is individuation that makes abstract conversations with like-minded selves possible and modernist sciences, both natural and social, possible in turn.

To the extent that cultures remain traditionalist, they remain ambivalent about modernity and its supposedly universalist assumptions and outcomes. The result is a "continuous selection, reinterpretation, and reformulation of ... imported ideas" (Eisenstadt, 2000, p. 15). Traditionalism entails a continuing commitment to communalism and to socially embedded values rather than to individualism and to socially abstracted values. It is also an attempt to dissociate "modernity" from "Westernization", thereby denying Westerners a "monopoly on modernity". It rejects the Western cultural program as modernity's "epitome" (Eisenstadt, 2000, p. 22).

A combination of modernism and traditionalism can be seen as "continual innovation". It can be seen in terms of "... new cultural and political programs emerging" that manifest "novel ideologies and institutional patterns" (Eisenstadt, 2000, p. 15).

In the case of Japan, Eisenstadt argues, the result has been an identity unlike any other. Due to the "conflation" of the "state and civil society", as well as the "weakness of [its] utopian orientations, the absence of principled confrontations with the state among the major movements of protest, and the relative significance of universal and particular components", he sees Japan as unique (Eisenstadt, 2000, pp. 15–16).

What have others made of Japan's hybrid culture? The range of responses varies from rejection of the very concept to its willing acceptance.

Distinctly unimpressed, for example, are analysts like Masaru Tamamoto (1999), who cites Kenzaburo Oe, Japan's Nobel Prize laureate for literature in 1994, as someone who sees the result of this combination in terms of "deep wounds ...". Hybridity creates isolation, Tamamoto says, and an incapacity to engage with other cultures and countries (Tamamoto, 1999, p. 119). The problem, he claims, is that the Japanese lack an authentic tradition of indigenous thought. This means that there is no answer to the question of what the Japanese spirit might be since they do not have one. Nor is there an answer to the question of what the Japanese identity might be since "identity", Tamamoto says, has no equivalent in the Japanese language. For him, the answer to those who ask "who are the Japanese?" is to say "those who ask who are the Japanese" (Tamamoto, 1999, p. 120).

And yet, when Tamamoto talks about the Japanese understanding of "reason", he highlights — with seeming approval — how the "essence of society in Japan is compromise". He lauds the "virtues of Japanese flexibility" (Tamamoto, 1999, p. 122). He even notes how modern Japan has not only succeeded in becoming modernist but how, in the process, it has also been freed to see world history in a way more aware of and more open to cultural differences (Tamamoto, 1999, p. 127). Does this not suggest an authentic tradition of indigenous thought of some kind at least?

More tolerant of the ambiguity that hybridity creates are analysts like Ronald Dore (1969), who notes how describing what it means to be Japanese has long been both a national and an international pastime (Littlewood, 1996). As a sociologist, Dore also notes the difficulties any modernist must face in seeking to assess national character, as well as the difficulties that attend coming to comparative conclusions in this regard. He does think conclusions are possible, though what sort depends on how positive or negative one wants to be. "For each characteristic", he says, "one may choose either the approving or the pejorative terms … as in the declension: 'I am a man of principle, you are obstinate, he is bigoted'." Thus, for Dore (1969, p. 568), the Japanese:

are less self-confident and more neurotically preoccupied with retaining the good opinion of others.	have a keener sense of personal honour and are less complacently self-righteous.
are more imitative.	have a more realistic willingness to learn from others.
are more ambitious.	have a keener desire for self-improvement.
are more slavishly diligent.	are less afraid of hard work.

are more submissive to superiors.	have a more realistic appreciation of the need to co-operate in society.
are less willing to stand up for individual rights.	are less selfish.
are more dishonest and indirect in speech.	are more sensitive to, and less willing to offend, the feelings of others.
are less men of principle.	are more willing to forgo the pleasures of self-assertion in the interests of social harmony.
have less sense of social responsibility to remove abuses in their own society.	are less busybody, with more tolerant willingness to live and let live.
are more childishly naïve.	have more good-humoured cheerfulness.
are more introverted.	are more shy about imposing their views and feelings on strangers.
are more sentimental.	show greater affectionate warmth and quicker emotional responses in intimate relations.

Most accepting of all are analysts like Andrews *et al.* (1996) who see Japanese perspectives as unique but not as inscrutable. Their work is based on the assumption that while Japanese words and phrases that are the key to a colloquial understanding of Japanese culture are not very clear to non-Japanese, they can still be explained to non-Japanese and understood by them. The phrase *wakon yosai*, for example, means "Euro-American learning and knowledge" when used in conformity with "native Japanese cultural traditions". As such, it harks back to an earlier phrase, *wakon kansai* ("Japanese spirit; Chinese knowledge"), that was coined in the 9th century to draw attention to Japan's own cultural heritage and its particular character as a civilization. *Wakon yosai* became current in the Meiji era as Western knowledge and technology began to be adopted on a large scale. It came to exemplify the mixture of traditional Japanese culture and contemporary Euro-American culture via the means of modernist technology. As such, it was used to describe and explain how rationalism and traditionalism were being woven together to make a modern-day hybrid. It was used, that is, to show how hybridity actually works (Andrews *et al.*, 1996, p. 73). Unless Japan is seen as having no cultural characteristics at all, in line with the argument that Tamamoto makes, this phrase provides a graphic account of what being both modernist and traditionalist can mean.

The *"truth"* about Japan as a modernist culture

In line with the description of modernity provided earlier, the extent that the Japanese have become modernist will depend on the extent to which they have learned to valorize the use of reason as an end in itself. It will depend on the extent to which they have learned to abstract themselves from their social context in order to converse with others of their ilk in the meta-society of the mind where the natural and social sciences are made.

Modernist rationalism requires individual detachment. However, as noted before, it is impossible to be totally detached, which is why modernist rationalists articulate assumptions about human nature and human nurturing practices. This is clearly evident in mainstream modernist accounts of international relations as well as in those Japanese accounts of international relations that articulate modernity.

As was also noted before, the dominant modernist discourse about international relations is a politico-strategic one. It articulates either a pessimistic or an optimistic view of human nature or a view of human nature as being fundamentally opportunistic. Modernist analysts articulate each of these approaches in "realist", "liberal internationalist" and "globalist" terms.

Tomoya Kamino argues that the Japanese articulation of international relations realism preceded World War Two. It can be seen in terms of Japan's interest in military strategy and diplomatic history (Kamino, 2008). Diplomatic history as a subject was first taught at a tertiary level at the end of the 19th century by academics like Nagao Ariga and Kiroku Hayashi. The former studied in Germany and Austria and subsequently taught at Waseda University. The latter studied European diplomatic history in France and subsequently taught the subject at Keio University (Kamino, 2008, p. 33). Another pioneer was Jumpei Shinobu, who taught at Waseda University and published works in the post-World War One period about (among other things) the balance of power and international conflict. Realism's military adherents depict international relations in terms of the pursuit of state self-interest in an ungoverned world. After winning a war against China in 1895 and declaring war on Russia in 1904, Japan went to war with Germany and the Austro-Hungarian empire as an ally of Britain. When World War One was over, the US sought peace in the Pacific. The Anglo-Japanese alliance was brought to an end and Japan's ambitions to expand in the region were, for the time being, put on hold. The determination to create a New East Asian Order and then a Greater East Asian Co-prosperity Sphere was revived when the Japanese army occupied Manchuria. This led to attempts to justify Japanese imperialism — attempts that were duly provided (in realist terms) by academics like Masamichi Royama, who was British-trained and a one-time professor at the University of Tokyo. Hikomatsu Kamikawa, who began as a liberal internationalist writing about the League of Nations, also became a realist as Japan moved towards the Pacific War. Kamikawa was, incidentally, the first president of the Japanese Association of International Relations (Kamino, 2008, pp. 35–38).

The Japanese articulation of liberal internationalism similarly preceded World War Two. It can be seen in terms of an interest in international law and international organizations. As with diplomatic history, Japanese academics taught international law from the end of the 19th century and a Japanese Society of International Law was established in 1897. Some academics, like Nagao Ariga, taught both. Others, like Sakuye Takahashi, who taught international law at the University of Tokyo, did so exclusively (Kamino, 2008, p. 32).

The Japanese articulation of globalism is a minority enterprise. It is not one that is widely articulated. While the nation remains determined to join the Security Council of the United Nations and Japanese analysts articulate the reasons why this should be accepted, this is more a liberal internationalist initiative than one that presages a commitment to global governance or global government.

As was also noted earlier, within the modernist rubric there is a second set of discourses, namely, the politico-economic ones. Here there are political economists who are similarly pessimistic or optimistic about human nature. These analysts are, respectively, "economic nationalists" and "socialists". Political economists who see human nature as being essentially opportunistic are "economic liberals".

Modernist Japanese analysts have followed suit. When they needed to replicate the Industrial Revolution, they reviewed what had been written in Europe. Rather than translate the works of the Scottish liberal Adam Smith, however, they translated first the works they thought most relevant to their rapid development, namely, those of the German protectionist Friedrich List. Japan has continued to practice economic nationalism and protectionism up to and including the present day, though economic liberalism did find favor under Prime Minister Junichiro Koizumi. There are also Japanese socialists who articulate their analytical language in line with their optimistic assumptions about human nature, but they are in the minority.

Modernity highlights a third set of discourses as well, namely, the politico-social ones. This includes those students of the global civil society who are pessimistic about human nature and articulate modernity in "nationalist" terms; those who see human nature as being opportunistic and who articulate modernity in "liberal/individualist" terms; and those who are optimistic about human nature and who articulate modernity in "collectivist" terms.

Japan's modernist analysts have followed suit in this regard as well. That is, they articulate the same three discourses.

Japanese nationalists highlight state differences, that is, the importance of having different histories, languages and ways of life. Since this chapter is about truth in the light of denial, it is necessary to note that the extremists in this context foster Japanese fascism. For example, Japanese ultra-nationalists are adamant in their denial of the aggressive and cruel behavior of Japanese troops before and during World War Two. The best known of these events took place in Nanjing at the beginning of 1938 when 100,000–300,000 mainly men, but also women and children, were slaughtered over a period of six weeks. It took several decades for the denial of this mass murder to begin to be formally acknowledged. There were many more atrocities during World War Two, including the systematic use of 80,000–200,000 mostly non-Japanese women as involuntary sex slaves, and the infamous conduct of those who ran Unit 731, a chemical and biological warfare center in Manchuria that involved 3,000 medical personnel and a similar number of patients/victims. The work of the center included biological attacks on the Chinese that are said to have killed up to 400,000 civilians. The Japanese government's reluctance to admit the involuntary nature of the sexual servitude on the part of those forced to work in its military brothels and to accept the heinous nature of what Unit 731 did remains an issue to this day since it suggests that ultra-nationalism is sanctioned still by the Japanese state. The result has been tension between "remembrance and denial" and subsequently "serious heart-searching in Japan, strong official and unofficial protests in China and South Korea, and bewilderment in many Western nations who are puzzled by what they see as Japan's effort to whitewash the more unpleasant parts of its recent history" (Taylor, 2008, p. 73).

Japanese liberal individualists promote such concepts as human rights and democracy and the importance of implementing these concepts at home and abroad. On the basis of an opportunistic view of human nature, they see the chance to arrive at a universalist conception of what is right that is not only rationalistic but also rule-bound.

Japanese optimists argue on behalf of global social movements and their potential to perform good works on a world scale. Japanese members of global social movements have subsequently sought to share their wealth with the under-privileged and to build cooperative relations at both national and individual levels (Kosaka, 1989, p. 73).

As noted earlier, not all modernists make assumptions about human nature. Some think there is no such thing and that we are what we learn to be. Analysts like these highlight the essential nature of human nurturing practices. If that nature is seen in material terms, the analyst is most likely to be a marxist one. If that nature is seen in mental terms, the analyst is most likely to be a constructivist one. If that nature is seen in mixed marxist/constructivist terms, the analyst is most likely to be a Gramscian one or a member of the Frankfurt School.

Modernist Japanese analysts have again followed suit. Japanese marxists describe and explain world affairs in terms of capitalist class struggle. Japanese constructivists promote accounts that highlight norms and values. Japanese Gramscians and Frankfurt School analysts highlight how the ruling class creates a hegemonic culture by every means at its disposal.

More radically, modernity marginalizes those it sees as being insufficiently rationalistic such as women, environmentalists, indigenous peoples, post-colonials and the poor. All of these groups resist their marginalization, asserting their significance using any of the analytic languages just outlined.

This pertains to Japan as it does elsewhere. Women, environmental activists, the indigenous *Ainu*, the impoverished *Burakumin* caste; all use modernist analytical languages to argue their cause. They might promote liberalist/individualist principles, for example, to promote their human rights; or marxist or meta-marxist principles to promote greater awareness of their exploitation; or constructivist principles to promote changes in the societal values and norms that maintain their marginalization. In so doing they critique, as they variously see it, the masculinist, eco-averse, ethnocentric, bourgeois nature of world affairs.

As modernity has matured, its limits have become more apparent. To compensate for the limits and distortions inherent in their way of knowing, modernists have turned rationalism back upon itself to ask what the reasons might be for prioritizing reason. This is post-modernism and Japanese post-modernists follow mainstream Euro-American analysts in this regard. They also ask what the identity of any analytic interrogator might be and what it means to use the language of rationalism, which is the post-structuralist approach and one that Japanese analysts pursue when they ask about identity and language. Meanwhile, there are those modernists who seek to understand the effects of the unconscious on what is a seemingly conscious pursuit. Japanese psychopathologists follow the Euro-American mainstream lead in this regard too. Then there are the modernists who eschew being rationalists in order to become emotivists. These so-called romantics find truth in feeling rather than thinking. There are modernist Japanese who talk about international relations in these terms as there are in the Euro-American mainstream. The same applies to those modernists who bracket-off reason in order to intuit the world as a thing-in-itself. These so-called phenomenologists find truth in intuition rather than in detached reflection. They provide another conceptual opportunity for modernist Japanese analysts. Finally, there are those who seek to explore the sacral alternative to modernist being and knowing. Analysts of this sort relocate rationalism in a more comprehensive mental context, the one that modernists chose to eschew in order to privilege the pursuit of reason as an end in itself. Those modernist Japanese who ask what world affairs might mean in Buddhist terms, for example, would be of this ilk (Pettman, 2004).

The "truth" about Japan as a traditionalist culture

There is more to the Japanese approach than the truths that modernity and its limits and margins provides. There are also the truths that Japanese traditionalism provides.

For example, modernists objectify and reify. Their detachment causes them to see the world from a distance as a thing or things. This includes "the past", which in modernist terms is seemingly another country and, as such, a place of things. Hence, the advent of "museums" as modernity grew apace and with it the notion that "the past" could be visited and looked at in the form of ancient objects. Hence, the advent of a United Nations convention which made possible the listing of architectural and natural "things" said to be of global value (World Heritage Center, 2010).

Traditionalists, by contrast, are non-modernists who subjectify. Their social embeddedness prompts them to see the world in more intimate terms. This includes how they see the past, which for them is a place not of dead things from back there but of living practices that are still here.

The Japanese are modernists. As such, they have built museums like those where culture is reified and commodified, such as in Europe and America.

The Japanese are also traditionalists, however. In this regard they have retained a sense of the significance of their festivals that has often been lost in Europe and America. They have also actively promoted government programs that pay skilled practitioners of traditional crafts to keep doing what they do so that their skills are not lost, as was happening in an economy that was succumbing to mass-production and mass-consumption (Pettman, 2004). In more recent times they have played an active role in ensuring that the United Nations has a convention that not only lists buildings and parks but also lists cultural practices (UNESCO, 2010).

The "truth" about Japan as a hybrid culture

The Japanese combine both modernism and traditionalism in the hybrid, creative way that Eisenstadt anticipated. Kosaka talks in this vein of Japan as a "culturally oriented industrial state" and of Japan as striving to disseminate "creative new styles (or values or norms) of industry, daily life and culture ..." (Kosaka, 1989, p. 14). This dissemination is already taking place. For example, the *juyo mukei bunkazai hojisha* ("important intangible cultural asset-holder") or more simply the *ningen kokyo-ho* ("living national treasures") program that was mentioned above is already held in high esteem by other countries. These countries include France, whose government has copied what Japan has been doing (Pettman, 2004).

It is well-known that Japanese technology is highly advanced. The Japanese understanding of the culture of scientific research is second to none. As a consequence, they are able to make industrial progress at a rate not inferior to that of any other country on earth.

It is less well-known that the country still celebrates the coming-of-age of its adolescents as a national rather than an individual event.

As noted above, the government strives to ensure that local cultural celebrations remain viable and it strives to combine, in a creative way, modernist and traditionalist approaches to contemporary affairs.

If Japan can pursue a universalistic concept of science and a culture-specific arts-and-crafts and festivals policy, at one and the same time, then it is highly likely to be able to think creatively about the global issue of conflict resolution. The question then becomes: what are these thoughts likely to be? What would a "Japanese" approach to the global issue of conflict resolution entail? And more particularly, what possibilities would Japan's cultural hybridity present in this regard?

A "Japanese" approach to the global issue of conflict resolution

Following on from the distinctions made above, a "Japanese" approach to the global issue of conflict resolution would articulate modernist truths, traditionalist truths and hybrid truths that have emergent properties of their own. It would be a complex mix of three main components that are particular to "Japan".

Japanese modernism and the truth about conflict resolution

In their modernist guise, Japanese analysts articulate all of the analytical languages that modernists use to describe and explain world affairs. This means that like their US-European counterparts, Japanese realists talk about conflict as only being resolved once there is an appropriate balance of power. They do not see conflict as being resolved on a permanent basis either, since peace can only, due to the irascible nature of human beings, be a lull between wars. The truth of the matter, as they see it, is that human beings are obliged to live because of who they are in an ungoverned, dog-eat-dog, state-centric world. Like their Western counterparts, Japanese liberal internationalists talk about conflict as being resolved by persuading people to recognize the benefits of the rule of international law. People are calculating, tit-for-tat types, liberal internationalists say, the truth of the matter being the human capacity to see the benefits of behaving reciprocally. Like their Western counterparts, Japanese globalists talk about conflict being resolved on a near-permanent basis by the advent of global governance or even global government. The truth of the matter, as they see it, is the hail-fellow-well-met capacity human beings enjoy and how this makes it possible for them to do notably better than the tit-for-tat world the liberal internationalists describe or the dog-eat-dog world the realists describe.

Like their Western counterparts, Japanese political economists also see the global issue of conflict resolution in different ways. Economic nationalists see global conflict as endemic because of the predatory character of the nations that make it up. The truth of the matter, as they see it, is that economic conflict can only be resolved on a temporary basis by the pursuit of economic protectionism. Economic liberalists see global conflict being resolved in a more opportunistic way as a result of the wealth that results from the free flow of money, goods and labor. The truth of the matter, as they see it, is that global conflicts are constantly being resolved by business leaders so that they can make more money. Economic socialists see global conflict as being resolved by a more fair distribution of the largesse of the Industrial Revolution. The truth of the matter, as they see it, is that it is disparities in wealth that create global conflict and that these can be resolved by planned egalitarianism.

Like their Euro-American counterparts, Japanese students of global civil society see global conflict resolution in pessimistic, opportunistic, and optimistic ways, too. Nationalists, for example, see global conflict as endemic because they are pessimistic about the influence of national differences. The truth of the matter, as they see it, is that international conflict can only be resolved because of these differences on a temporary, often violent basis. Ultra-nationalism in Japan is a notable subset of this discourse, albeit a minority one. As discussed briefly earlier, ultra-nationalists continue to sanction the notion that by going to war, Japan was doing no more than acting in its own defense at a time of Soviet expansion, economic depression, and American and European opposition. The truth from their perspective is that the attempt to establish a Greater East Asia Co-Prosperity Sphere was a strategic and economic necessity (Dower, 2002). They deny the significance of the Nanjing massacre, the creation of involuntary military brothels, and the radical medical perversions practiced by those who worked for Unit 731. They reject the view that any aspect of Japan's historical conduct requires an apology and they endorse what they see as the need to lobby for a more "realist" approach to Japan's capacity to project its power abroad and to command international respect. Liberal individualists, meanwhile, highlight doctrines like those of human rights and democracy, holding out hope for internationally acceptable rules. The truth of the matter, as they see it, is that international conflict can be resolved on a calculated basis using the human capacity for reciprocity. Collectivists see global social movements as weaving a web of beneficial intentions so comprehensive as to allow the world to take conflict resolution largely for granted. The truth of the matter, as they see it, is that international conflicts can be resolved because human beings are basically good enough to resolve them.

In modernist terms, a Japanese approach to the global issue of conflict resolution will account for discourses that articulate assumptions about the essential nature of human nurturing practices as well. As noted earlier, these discourses are materialist (usually marxist), mentalist (constructivist) and mixed materialist/mentalist. Like their Euro-American counterparts, Japanese marxists see global conflict in terms of class struggle. The truth of the matter, as they see it, is the difference between those who own and manage the means of production and those who sell their labor for a wage. They see global conflict resolution in revolutionary terms, that is, in terms of the proletariat overthrowing the bourgeoisie. They see an end to world conflict only once the communist utopia has been attained. Only then will humankind's "species being" finally be manifest. Japanese constructivists, meanwhile, see global conflict in terms of mental norms, highlighting how it is possible to envisage any world one likes, including one where world conflict is resolved. The truth of the matter, as they see it, is that norm entrepreneurs are necessary to change how people think and subsequently behave. Japanese mixed materialist/mentalist thinkers highlight how hegemonic classes make it hard to imagine alternatives to world affairs, including alternatives to patterns of global conflict resolution. The truth of the matter, as they see it, is the need to mount anti-hegemonic ideological initiatives to emancipate the world's working class.

In modernist terms, a Japanese approach to the global issue of conflict resolution includes those discourses that articulate what those marginalized by modernity have to say. Like their Western counterparts, for example, Japanese feminists highlight the global issue of gender conflict and the different ways in which this conflict might be resolved, for instance, by deferring to human rights (liberal individualism) or by defining gender equality and freedom in terms of an end to what is called the world's last colony (feminist marxism). The truth of the matter, as they see it, is that until a more equitable gender balance is established, the global gender conflict will never be brought to an end. Japanese environmentalists highlight the global conflict between the ecological inroads being made on world resources and the stability of the world climate and what future generations as yet unborn will require. The truth of the matter, as environmentalists see it, is the gravity of this contemporary reality and what it portends for those to come. Japan's indigenous peoples continue to struggle for national recognition and to resolve the conflicts this involves. The truth of the matter, as they see it, is their permanent status as national minorities and as highly marginalized ones. The plight of the *burakumin* raises fundamental issues about the inclusiveness of Japanese society and the conflict between this sociological caste and the rest of Japan. Because of the stigma attached to the members of this caste, this results in conflicts that are not likely to be resolved any time soon. The truth of the matter, as this group sees it, is their permanent status as a minority too.

In modernist terms, a Japanese approach to the global issue of conflict resolution includes the auto-critiques of modernity itself. It includes, for example, Japanese post-modernists, for whom the contemporary grand narratives about global conflict resolution (like that of realism) are questionable because of the distorted nature of the modernist rationalism that underpins these narratives. The truth of the matter, as they see it, is that truth itself is relativistic and that those who seek it have to be highly suspicious of those who claim to speak it. Then there are those like the Japanese post-structuralists who talk about global conflict resolution in terms of issues like identity and language. The truth of the matter, as they see it, is similar to the post-modernist sense that truth itself is relativistic and that those who articulate grand narratives about global conflict resolution (like that of realism) are highly suspect. Then there are the Japanese psychopathologists who talk about the global issue of conflict resolution in terms of the non-rational dimensions to the mind. The truth of the matter, as they see it, is that humankind's much vaunted rationalism owes much more to subconscious imperatives than its proponents like to admit. Then there are the Japanese romantics who talk about the global issue of conflict resolution in terms of gut-feeling rather than rationalistic cognition. The truth of the matter, as they see it, is to be found in the emotions as much as in the mind. Then there are the Japanese phenomenologists who talk about the global issue of conflict resolution in terms of gut-thinking. The truth of the matter, as they see it, is the incapacity of rationalism to reveal things-in-themselves and the need to intuit the primal practices of the human mind in order to ascertain how the mind intends the world that it otherwise thinks it is attending to. Finally, there are the Japanese sacralists who talk about the global issue of conflict resolution in terms of spiritual practices like meditation and prayer. The truth of the matter, as they see it, is the failure of modernist rationalism to understand the cosmos in other than secular terms.

Japanese traditionalism and the truth about conflict resolution

A number of key concepts, both creative and destructive, can be used to highlight traditionalist Japanese approaches to the global issue of conflict resolution. They are all highly characteristic of Japanese culture.

First there is *yamoto-damashii* or "Japanese spirit" (Andrews *et al.*, 1996, p. 71), a concept first used 1,000 years ago and revived in the early 1930s in order to foster civic loyalty. At that time, the realists (the "militarists") and the ultra-nationalists (the "fascists") made it the basis of a system of public education. In terms of the global issue of conflict resolution, it served to justify Japanese imperialism. As such, it persuaded Japanese state-makers that "in truth" they had nothing to deny, that is, that there was no need internationally to effect any compromise. This led to conflict stimulation rather than conflict resolution or to conflict resolution of a martial and highly imperial kind.

Then there is *nemawashi* which refers to "prior consultation". This is not a concept unfamiliar to those who live in US-European societies, since "maneuvering behind the scenes to reach a consensus and obtain certain objectives, especially in politics and business" where interests are "potentially in conflict", is not unknown there. It is a high art in Japan, however, and a traditionalist view of what is true would include such a sentiment.

Nemawashi not only makes for consensus and the avoidance of public confrontation, but it also allows the "groundwork for decisions" to be laid "well in advance". Conflicts can then be resolved even before they have arisen (Andrews *et al.*, 1996, p. 129). This is also integral to a traditionalist view of what is most true.

Then there is *amae* or "dependency wishes" or the "desire to depend upon the love, patience, and tolerance of others" (Andrews *et al.*, 1996, p. 93). The Japanese feeling that the individual exists "because of the group" is uncommonly strong and though such sentiments are hardly unique to Japan, the 250-year period it was cut off from other cultures helped make *amae* a core Japanese attribute and one central to what the Japanese consider most true. It is to *amae* that Andrews *et al.* attribute the "somewhat vague notions of subject and object, self and other" that are still evident in Japan, as well as the particular "concepts of privacy and individual rights", the "dislike for cut-and-dried logic ..., the high degree of nonverbal communication", and the "strong aesthetic orientation ..." that are manifest there (Andrews *et al.*, 1996, p. 95).

Amae is usually discussed together with *enryo*, that is, "reserve" or "constraint" (Andrews *et al.*, 1996, p. 95). *Enryo* is said to be a "counterbalance" to *amae*, preventing people from "imposing on or presuming too much of one another". Indeed, it is said that a "considerable degree of social tact" is necessary to realize an "appropriate" relationship between the two (Andrews *et al.*, 1996, p. 97). In terms of traditionalist conceptions of what is true, this is part of the Japanese picture, too.

Tact is also evident with respect to *tatemae* and *honne*. This refers to how stated reasons can differ markedly from real intentions (Andrews *et al.*, 1996, p. 91). With regard to the global issue of conflict resolution, *amae* and *enryo* as well as *tatemae* and *honne* help explain why Japan remains a relatively communalist society where conflict is sublimated rather than encouraged. Japanese people are taught to humble themselves in relation to the society as a whole. Conflicts get dealt with even before they take place because of the truth such an attitude is thought to embody.

This is not to say that humility is not found in other societies because it is. Nor is it to say that to understand the depth and breadth of Japanese conformism, it must be placed in opposition to non-Japanese non-conformism since it can be understood as a thing-in-itself.

This said, societies of the Euro-American sort do tend to be less conformist than that of Japan, even if the difference is relative, not radical. The truth of Japanese sayings like "the nail that sticks up gets hammered down" must be seen in this light (Littlewood, 1996, pp. 52–53).

Japanese hybridity and the truth about conflict resolution

Taken together, modernism and traditionalism result in a synergistic approach to the global issue of conflict resolution. In the case of Japan, this synergistic alternative has its own definitive features and provides its own version of what is true.

Eisenstadt describes Japan's hybrid approach in terms of a strong tendency to minimize the legitimacy of "direct, open confrontations ...". He also highlights what he calls the tendency to minimize the definition of "differences of interests and opinions ..." as well as the tendency to resolve differences in "seemingly informal ways", based on "presumptions of solidarity and harmony ..." (Eisenstadt, 1990, p. 13).

More systematically, Befu describes a characteristically Japanese approach to the global issue of conflict resolution in terms of four different models: a consensus model, a stratification model, a social exchange model and a conflict model (Befu, 1990, p. 213). Each is characteristic of a different aspect of what in the Japanese case is true. The consensus model highlights the conformist character of Japanese culture and traditionalist concepts like *amae, nemawashi, tatemae* and *honne* (Befu, 1990, pp. 213–218). Each is successful in defusing conflict. The stratification model highlights how rewards are "not evenly distributed throughout the population" (Befu, 1990, p. 219). This, he says, is a "likely basis for conflict" and prompts its own resolution responses (Befu, 1990, p. 222). The social exchange model highlights the significance of "gifting" behavior (Befu, 1990, p. 225), a traditionalist practice that is clearly evident in *giri* or "the observance of reciprocity" (Andrews *et al.*, 1996, p. 89). Conflict results when gifting is not reciprocated or when it is not of the appropriate kind. It is resolved, Befu believes, by adequate responses in this regard (Befu, 1990, p. 230). The conflict model highlights the amount of conflict evident throughout Japanese history because of "incompatible goals and interests" and unequal "power, status and reward" (Befu, 1990, p. 233). The first and the third models cast Japan's approach to the global issue of conflict resolution in traditionalist terms. The second and the fourth models do so in modernist terms.

Neither of these conclusions do justice to the creative synergy that Japanese modernism and traditionalism represent, however, when they are brought together. Combining Western rationalism and Japanese traditionalism have arguably made possible new approaches to the global issue of conflict resolution and new ideas about what is true there that are not particular to one or the other.

This "emergence principle" is evident, for example, in the debates that accompany Article 9 of the post-war constitution. This article formally commits Japan to international pacifism.

Realists are cynical about Japanese pacifism. In a dog-eat-dog world, they argue, the truth of the matter is that Japan should have a greater capacity to defend its sovereign integrity and even to project its power abroad.

Liberal internationalists have also argued that the Japanese should eschew their commitment to pacifism in order to become more "normal", that is, in order for them to be able to take part in wars that liberal internationalists deem just. The truth of the matter, they say, is that Japan should be able to join in forceful interventions that serve humane ends (Moses and Iwami, 2009, pp. 80, 82).

By contrast, there are those who see Japan as continuing to have a sense of not being like other countries. The truth of the matter, as they see it, is that "there is a strong case to be made that the ongoing commitment to Article 9 offers a far greater prospect for producing peace in the Asian region (and perhaps even globally)". They believe that the "original reasoning offered … [for its] insertion … remains relevant in the contemporary context". They see the Japanese as potentially becoming coordinators of the global public interest. At the very least, they see Japan as setting an important example to other states in this regard (Moses and Iwami, 2009, p. 83).

Among those who came to see Japan as not like other countries was the Japanese martial artist Morihei Ueshiba. In the 1930s he developed a new approach to interpersonal conflict resolution which he called *aikido*. This approach he found to be uniquely truthful (Ueshiba, 2002).

Ueshiba's art involved neutralizing attack rather than mounting a counter-attack. It resolved conflict in an explicitly non-aggressive way (Pettman, 2010).

It was an art of spiritual harmony rather than physical violence and as such had more than interpersonal significance. Indeed, Japan has been called an "aikido state" (Hook *et al.*, 2001, p. 372) since its policymakers prefer not to initiate conflicts these days but to resolve them by redirecting them. Its "quiet diplomacy" is seen to be no longer dependent on "sheer physical strength". Rather, its policymakers prefer to foster a sense of international cooperation in an "active, yet non-militaristic, way" (Hook *et al.*, 2001, p. 377). In the process, Japan is said to have changed the mainstream understanding of what states can do. It now offers the world a new truth and hence a new kind of foreign policy (Hook *et al.*, 2001, p. 380) — one that does not make, as a realist would see it, for proactive or reactive states of the sovereign-centered kind, but for another kind of international behavior altogether. This behavior promotes foreign policies that offer a different approach to the global issue of conflict resolution, one where states can act in the world system in neither a modernist or traditionalist way (Hook *et al.*, 2001, p. 391).

Realists remain unconvinced of the utility of such an approach, much as those martial artists who prefer physical force remain unconvinced of the utility of Ueshiba's martial art. They see the truth of the "big stick" of brute force as being what will always ultimately prevail.

Acknowledging the efficacy of such an approach comes from the experience of applying it. Hence the importance of eschewing the dominance of the realist approach (and other modernist approaches) long enough to appreciate the truth potential of such an alternative.

This experience has implications for "human security" since it provides a rationale for defining security in these particular terms. Not accidentally, "human security" is very much an "aikidic" approach to world affairs, and not accidentally it is now a prominent feature of Japan's foreign policy (Hsien-Li, 2010). Human security makes it possible for Japan to be active, not passive, while at the same time it preempts the criticism that it is either engaged in "cheque-book diplomacy" or preparing to be neo-imperial again.

Conclusion

Japan is modernist, traditionalist, and both at the same time. As such, it can and does approach a global issue like conflict resolution in terms of its understanding of modernist truths. It can and does approach such an issue in terms of its understanding of traditionalist truths. And it can and does approach such an issue in terms of synergistic truths that are neither modernist nor traditionalist.

To demonstrate what "both at the same time" might mean, it is worth considering how the Japanese people as a whole remain committed to Article 9 and to a pattern of practice that has been characterized as that of an "aikido state". Hybridity like this suggests the possibility of viable alternatives to the constant theme of US-European globalization that dominates the discipline.

Indeed, Euro-American hegemony is being challenged now by new diplomatic practices of which the Japanese experience is only one. Regional examples of this experience could be characterized as "Asian globalism". They represent different ways of organizing world affairs that can no longer be ignored.

In the emerging global context, it may well be that Western hegemony has run its course. Perhaps — as many now suspect — it may be that those who are able to combine modernist science with other cultural perspectives may be coming to prevail.

Perhaps *yosai tokon* ("Euro-American knowledge/Asian spirit") is the most appropriate way to describe the truth today. As a consequence, perhaps the relationship between denial and truth must now be seen in terms of those trees that fall to the "east" rather than those that fall to the "west" (Muhaiyaddeen, 2003b). This said, "there may be some optimal equilibrium between denial and truth. Should all truths be told? Probably not ... [I]n diplomacy ... realities are often handled [best] by artful ambiguity" (Goleman, 1985, p. 245). Yet, "[t]ruths must be told if we are to find our way out ... We need counsel that flows from insight ... [because it is] insight [that is said to have the most] curative [potential]" (Goleman, 1985, p. 248).

Delusion

The Oxford English Dictionary (OED) describes a delusion as "[a]nything that deceives the mind with a false impression ...". By this it means a "fixed false opinion or belief with regard to objective things, especially as a form of mental derangement".

Defining Delusion: The Lay Approach

The above definition articulates what is called the lay account of delusion, an account that highlights how conflicts occur over what is real in the everyday world and how those individuals who are too unconventional or who stray too far from what society at large has to say are in danger of having their beliefs called delusions and themselves declared insane (Heise, 1988, p. 268). The same applies to societies themselves, though here the court of convention is the global community at large and not a particular component thereof (Meerlo, 1968 [1949]; Fridson, 1996 [1841]).

The OED says that the first such usage of this word was in the late 16th century, though Karl Jaspers says that delusion has been considered a key characteristic of insanity since "time immemorial". From his contemporary perspective in the early 20th century, he depicts it as a "primary phenomenon" whereby the deluded mind not only thinks that something that is not real is real but also experiences that reality as a thing in itself (Jaspers, 1972 [1913], p. 93). Meerlo is more specific. He says that it was Francis Bacon who, by contesting the primacy of theory and highlighting the human propensity to see as real what it thinks and feels to be real, was the first to talk about delusion in psychological terms (Meerlo, 1968 [1949], p. 37).

Jaspers sees a delusion as a patently false judgment held with the kind of conviction that survives any attempt to demonstrate otherwise. In other words, he sees it as not being susceptible to other points of view whilst being basically "impossible" in itself (Jaspers, 1972 [1913], pp. 95–96; Maher and Spitzer, 1993, p. 265). By seeing like this he is borrowing (whether the reader knows it or not) from 19th century notions about delusions as exhibiting "symptoms", having "form" as well as "content", being about beliefs that can be tested, resulting from various physical and psychological causes, and manifesting in a number of different ways. Jaspers also accepts — essentially uncritically — the 17th century notion of insanity and delusion as the same thing (Berrios, 1991, pp. 6, 7). He ultimately thinks that delusions are "structurally sound" beliefs whose content is not real. In doing so, Berrios says that Jaspers leads the study of delusion up a "blind alley". In talking of what is non-delusionary in terms of "cognitive morsels of information about the world or the self", he believes that Jaspers obscures the extent to which delusions are "theoretical constructs" in themselves (Berrios, 1991, pp. 8, 6). The influence of Jaspers on contemporary attempts to define delusion remains undimmed, however.

Defining Delusion: The Medical Approach

In turning to the medical literature, there seems to be considerable uncertainty as to what delusion means. There is great unwillingness to define conclusively what it is and to specify its essential characteristics.

In psychiatric practice, delusions are usually described in terms of hallucinations and a strict line is drawn between thoughts and perceptions in this regard. Abnormal perceptions (hallucinations) are seen as different from the mental response to these perceptions (thoughts). Those who have hallucinatory perceptions typically refuse to be persuaded otherwise. They are typically tenacious in their beliefs, and their thoughts reflect that tenacity.

This said, Maher and Spitzer conclude that delusion is one of the "most puzzling phenomena" in the whole field of psychopathology. They quote to this effect a study that identifies 75 disorders that have a delusional aspect. It is no surprise, therefore, that they think that there is no definition of delusion that is "free of problems". There are, they say, simply too many difficulties to do with what it is versus what it is not for them to argue otherwise (Maher and Spitzer, 1993, p. 263).

Blackwood *et al.* (2001) elect to describe delusion in "operational" terms that highlight "false beliefs held with unusual conviction" whose absurdity is obvious to others while being impervious to logic; however, they also note that this description is changing as more phenomenological insights are being brought to bear. They recognize as well how delusions vary and how they respond to "cognitive … interventions" (Blackwood *et al.*, 2001, p. 527).

Munro highlights some of the difficulties of keeping track of key cognate issues by describing how paranoia, for example, disappeared for nearly 60 years, to be confused with schizophrenia. It only reappeared in 1987 as "delusional disorder" (Munro, 1999, p. 7).

Harper, meanwhile, points out the problems associated with assuming that a thing called "delusion" exists and how making lists, like the 7-point one that Oltmanns provides, can result in a sense of certainty that is ultimately inappropriate (Harper, 1992, p. 357; Oltmanns, 1988, p. 5). To quote David: "[d]elusions exist in a world of values, assumptions, prejudices, incorrect inferences, superstitions, wishful-thinking, and paranoia (in the non-technical sense). This is what makes delusions possible … [though it is] also what makes them impossible to pin down" (David, 1999, p. 19). All of which helps demonstrate why delusion is much more likely at the moment to be seen not in singular terms, or in terms of one or more specific components, but as a multi-dimensional phenomenon that lies along a continuum or continua (Blackwood *et al.*, 2001, p. 527) and is socially constructed (Harper, 1992, p. 358).

Uncertainty as to what delusion involves does not mean that the concept has no real-world relevance. Despite the lack of agreement as to what it means, it is used daily to confirm the mental plight of individuals and societies and to define psychosis (David, 1999, p. 17). Individuals, for example, continue to escape their day in court because they are deemed to be deluded. Whole societies may escape moral censure because they are seen to have behaved in the light of a "fixed false opinion" of some kind. More problematically, political non-conformists continue to be punished because their non-conformity is seen not as a political statement but as a psychopathological one (Moor and Tucker, 1979, p. 388).

To see delusion as a concept of political relevance, more would seem to be needed to provide a precise account of it. Which prompts the question: how might a relatively reliable definition be articulated? Should analysts look to clinical practice, for example, to determine precisely what delusion involves? The problem here is whether it is the clinicians whose beliefs are ultimately at issue or those of their patients. Perhaps it is enough to turn to authoritative texts. The problem here, however, is that the definitions these texts provide do not distinguish clearly between the necessary symptoms of delusion and those associated with it (Maher and Spitzer, 1993, p. 264; Oltmanns, 1988).

Most medical definitions highlight the same characteristics that the OED does, namely, falsity and fixity, though they also distinguish between bizarre or abnormal delusions and non-bizarre or non-abnormal ones. The former are seen as patently impossible while the latter are seen as merely improbable (Bell, Halligan and Ellis, 2003).

The DSM-IV, for example, describes a delusion as a false inference about external reality. It also sees a delusion as something that is believed despite all evidence to the contrary and as something that is different from what other members of a society believe (DSM-IV, 1994; Bell, Halligan and Ellis, 2003; Leeser and O'Donohue, 1999, p. 687). At this point, the concerns expressed by Maher and Spitzer apply. Not for nothing does Bortolotti observe that every part of the DSM-IV definition has now been contradicted. What is more, "almost all" of the distinctions that this definition makes are said to be "contentious" (Bortolotti, 2010, p. 23).

Defining Delusion: The Problem with "Falsity"

How appropriate is thinking about delusion in terms of falsity? Maher and Spitzer are unequivocal here, arguing that: "[f]alsity of belief cannot be a satisfactory criterion of delusions ..." because there are delusions where the content is "not empirically falsifiable" or where the content of the delusion is simply "true ..." (Maher and Spitzer, 1993, p. 264). They continue by observing how there can be contradictory evidence with regard to different delusions and there are delusions that can be diagnosed clearly and cogently as opposed to ones where it is not possible to do this at all.

Moor and Tucker concur. They say that if falsity was a "sufficient condition" for identifying those beliefs that are delusions, then "most, if not all of us ... would be delusional ...". This makes it useless as a psychopathological concept, they say. To accuse someone of holding a false belief may mean "nothing more than [that] the person is ignorant", they conclude, or has made a "simple mistake ... [I]t should not be regarded as a defining condition. Otherwise, a physician could rid a patient of paranoia by [merely] persecuting him" (Moor and Tucker, 1979, p. 389).

Harper also concurs. Given that truth can be understood in more than one way, which way should be used to define falsity and unreality? And what about the "interactional and relational context" in which delusions are always found? What, too, of the language used to describe and explain the concepts of belief and delusion and the way this language promotes particular views and not others (Harper, 1992, p. 359)? Is it even possible to talk about delusion when so many different ideas about reality are "plausible and valid" and when reality itself has to be seen in brackets rather than as something separate and abstract? What is the "reality of reality" in this regard and how should it be understood and applied (Harper, 1992, p. 360)?

At this point, it is worth noting that reality is not as absolute as modernist rationalists assume. There are, in other words, competing ways of knowing and being that generate competing facts and truths. Reality ranges from what is experienced using the most familiar of the senses and the material inputs that make sense of these senses, to what is experienced when the universe is "seen" as a mere front for a version of reality that is radically less materialistic. As a consequence, testing a delusion against "the facts" is less straightforward than it might seem, particularly since "the facts" themselves will be, to some extent at any rate, social constructions. To the extent that this is so, what is the right reality for those trying to understand delusion? Would it be realistic, for example, for America to respond to Russia's willingness to surrender nuclear weapons by giving up its own, and vice versa? Given how "realist" world affairs continues to be, this is likely to be deemed highly undesirable by any American or Russian state-maker, however well-disposed he or she might be towards nuclear disarmament. To the extent that a more calculative version of international relations is possible, a reality that allows for negotiated nuclear arms reductions, nuclear non-proliferation, and a comprehensive nuclear weapons ban becomes not only conceivable and achievable but arguably desirable as well. Whether this is the reality that prevails is another matter, however (Heise, 1988, pp. 260, 266).

Given the problems falsity presents, it is common, as noted earlier, to see delusion in terms of a growing number of characteristics or dimensions (Oltmanns, 1988, p. 5) and to place particular delusions along a continuum from the normal to the abnormal (Harper, 1992, p. 363; Garety and Hemsley, 1994, pp. 7, 17, 66). The points along this continuum reflect the available empirical evidence.

Given the range and diversity of the issues involved here, such an approach is likely to be the only one that gets much support. Thus, where there is reliable evidence of a delusion, it is possible to say that a delusion exists. Where there is only sketchy evidence of a delusion, it is much more difficult to argue that it should be considered as such.

Continua of this kind range from those delusions where the empirical evidence is sufficient to establish falsity or reality, to those delusions that are empirically non-falsifiable. The latter is the case, as Maher and Spitzer point out, for all delusions that do not refer to empirical facts. This, they say, includes religious delusions (Maher and Spitzer, 1993, p. 266).

Continua present their own problems, however, since placing individuals or societies along them means assessing individuals and societies as such, and that means not only having assessors to do the assessing but also putting them in positions of authority. Since there is no totally detached ground on which to stand and say what is real, deciding who is deluded inevitably involves the exercise of strategic, economic and social power. What gets promoted as most real is what those with the power to define reality promote as most real.

This sociological insight, Heise says, prompts one to ask: "… what kinds of thinking are … discouraged in the process of judging delusion[?]" Perhaps calling people "mad and their beliefs … delusions" is a way of controlling cognition. Perhaps, in contemporary Euro-American societies in particular, this is a device for protecting "everyday Sensate reality" (Heise, 1988, pp. 268–269).

Given the problem falsity presents, it is also worth noting how the DSM-IV adds to its basic definition by talking not only of fixed, unreal beliefs but also of beliefs that are different from those of everyone else. While this can be entirely appropriate, as in the case of organic disorders, it can be highly misleading in the case of psychological ones.

Consider a society where a scientist comes to a radical conclusion that survives rigorous attempts to test it but who is not believed. This happens more often than those committed to the use of the hypothetico-deductive method like to admit since scientific communities tend to defend their preferred paradigms rather than relinquish them in the light of findings that refute them. Only a plethora of anomalies is likely to cause a radical rethink (Kuhn, 1962). Under these circumstances, it is not the lone scientist who is deluded. It is the whole scientific community (Moor and Tucker, 1979, p. 389).

Societal Delusions

Populations at large, in other words, can also subscribe to delusions. Since it is possible for a majority to be deluded and a minority not to be deluded, then believing in something that others do not is hardly a "promising candidate" for making a definitive determination in this regard (Moor and Tucker, 1979, p. 390). While divergence from what a society believes can be evidence of delusion, so can inter-subjective consensus or mental convergence.

In 1978, for example, nearly a thousand followers of the American utopian socialist, Jim Jones, committed mass suicide by taking cyanide. Jones had earlier moved his community, called the Peoples' Temple Agricultural Project, from the United States to the northwest of Guyana. This "revolutionary suicide", as it was called by its followers (or the "Jonestown massacre" as it was called by the media), was the largest in modern human history. It seems to have been prompted in the main by mass paranoia.

In a world dominated by secular materialism, peoples that believe in god can also seem deluded. Secularists are apt to see no limit to their particular perspective. They are apt to see science, for example, as providing a basically undistorted view of the world. Is this the case, however? Is the version of reality arrived at using the scientific perspective the most reliable version of reality possible and therefore the one to be invariably preferred?

At this point the argument enters highly controversial territory with regard to science and religion as ways of knowing and being. This territory will be revisited below. However, it is necessary to note that particular individuals who declare themselves to be god are likely, in terms of the DSM-IV's definition, to be seen as deluded since they assert a capacity to transcend both scientific and religious perspectives and to compensate personally for the limits and distortions of both.

Again, secularists tend to see such individuals as delusional regardless of what the society believes about god *per se*, though both secularists and sacralists are likely to treat a person like this as insane. There are relatively rare instances of individuals who exhibit attributes that can be characterized as holy. This suggests that it is not enough to conclude, in a blanket fashion, that all prophets are false; however, once more this is conceptual territory that will be revisited below.

Another controversial example with regard to religious as opposed to scientific knowing is that of the Aztecs. The Aztecs believed as a people in the need to sacrifice human beings to ensure that the sun continued to rise and that the life of the world did not stop.

From the perspective of scientific materialism (to say nothing of the Spanish priesthood), this was a delusion that cost thousands of lives every year. Moreover, in scientific terms, this belief was a delusion that could have been tested empirically, thus potentially saving many of these lives.

From the perspective of the Aztecs, the practice of any alternative to their sense of reality was too risky. As a culture they had their own understanding of what worked. Ultimately, they were destroyed by the Spanish and could no longer perform their sacrifices. This hardly predisposed them to accept that their view of the cosmos was unreal and wrong. Indeed, the Spanish invasion led them to a quite different conclusion, namely, one that would have involved more human sacrifice if they had been able to perform it, not less (Heise, 1988, p. 266).

Is Pragmatism the Best Way Forward?

Given the uncertainties described above and the sense evident there that the criteria that define delusions remain "open to dispute" (Maher and Spitzer, 1993, p. 289), the concept is usually deployed in a practical way. If a belief is seen to occasion stress or threaten harm, then it is seen as potentially a delusion. Moreover, as with many other forms of psychopathology, it is not necessary to know what causes a delusion to recognize that a delusion does exist.

Pragmatism like this is most notable when the cause is organic or physical, that is, neuro-chemical or neuro-physiological. Highly specific brain lesions, for example, can result in highly specific mental delusions. This is the case with Capgras syndrome, which was first described in 1923. This particular mental disorder is a specific brain injury that results in the delusional belief that "significant others", such as partners or parents, are imposters (Young, 2000; Stone and Young, 1997).

Pragmatism like this can also be seen in psychological terms, though distinguishing between delusions in organic as opposed to psychological terms is, as noted earlier, arguably outdated. This is because it is widely agreed by now — such being the ubiquity of scientific materialism — that every delusion has a "biological basis", even though in many instances it is not yet possible to specify what that basis might be (Bortolotti, 2010, p. 25).

Despite the ubiquity of biological causes, mental disorders do have psychological manifestations and they can cause considerable harm. "Delusions of grandeur", for example, result in a grossly exaggerated sense of political mission, with persecutory delusions said to be the more distressing ones and those most likely to be acted upon (Freeman and Garety, 2004, p. 4). Adolf Hitler was an individual who exhibited both psychological and physical symptoms in this regard. Even institutions like the United Nations are accused of "delusions of grandeur", though here the argument is an analogical one in that it is an attempt to contest liberal internationalism using competing analytical languages, such as realism or nationalism (Carpenter, 1997). Extreme nationalists articulate internationalist conspiracy theories to critique international organizations. This is a consequence of pessimistic assumptions about human nature and the analytical discourse that pessimism promotes. What sounds in this case like clinical paranoia is more a matter of political rhetoric, though the source of the pessimism remains undetermined. Fascism is part of the modernist project and not part of the attempt by psychopathologists to turn reason back upon itself in the attempt to understand rationality in psychopathological terms. Therefore, fascists may not, in the first instance, be technically insane, though their extreme nationalism can lead them to articulate notions of "racial purity" and the like which are, indeed, delusory and which can be ultimately characterized as neurotic or psychotic.

Pragmatism of the psychological sort has to be read in terms of the "evidential situation". For example, it does not follow that somebody who promotes a particular religious or scientific view is delusional. Indeed, it is widely believed that beliefs that are particular to a specific cultural context are not delusions, though to come to such a conclusion it is necessary to assess people's "experiences, intelligence, and education", and the Jonestown episode remains salutary in this regard (Moor and Tucker, 1979, p. 393).

According to scientific materialists, assessing the evidential situation means concluding that "uniquely unfalsifiable" beliefs are delusional on scientific grounds alone. Scientific materialists are very uncomfortable with beliefs that are promoted in principle or because the believer refuses to acknowledge anything else because of his or her attachment to his or her beliefs (Leeser and O'Donohue, 1999, p. 693). Scientific materialists favor the predictive success of their own beliefs in making such an assessment because of what they see as the superior efficacy of the scientific method. They prefer to insist, where there are inconsistencies, on "simple, testable" explanations where public agreement is more readily forthcoming, rather than on ones that are complicated, hard to assess and where public agreement is difficult to secure. They are also wary of those whose beliefs are supported by "trivial occurrences", or are "interpreted by the subject [or society] as highly unusual, significant, and/or having [only] personal reference" (Leeser and O'Donohue, 1999, p. 693).

The Epistemological Issues that Pragmatism Hides

Despite the resort to pragmatic conclusions in the light of the evidence on hand, there is no way of determining what a delusion might be without coming to an epistemological conclusion of some kind. What is considered practical ultimately reflects what is seen to be the most appropriate way to know.

Since psychopathologists are usually (though not always) scientific materialists, they tend to promote a view of the world that favors the way of knowing that underpins their perspective. Treating those who are seemingly deluded has become more scientized as a consequence. Contemporary psychopathologists tend to promote a view of delusion that is basically materialistic (Young, 2000, p. 47).

This approach is an objectifying and individuating one. By putting the world and those in it at a mental distance, including the psychopathologist him- or herself, it depicts the world and those in it as being made up of organized forms of energy that have emergent outcomes that are ultimately manifest in the form of living beings. It sees delusions in these terms.

It also means eschewing other views of the world. It means, for example, not promoting non-scientific, non-medicalized explanations. It means not promoting a concept of the cosmos as the product of a primal universal power and the consequences this approach might have for ideas about delusion.

Because of the attempt by psychopathologists to eschew non-objectifying views of the world, the question then becomes: have they succeeded? Are they detached and neutral? Or are they, rather, the active proponents of a particular point of view? Modernist rationalists see themselves as trying to be impartial and as not promoting assumptions of any kind (Heise, 1988, p. 269). However, to accept this self-description is to fail to understand the values built into modernist rationalism.

Psychopathologists as modernist rationalists tend to favor the epistemological approach modernist rationalism articulates. This obtains regardless of their religious concerns.

This gives contemporary psychopathologists considerable power. They are supposed to keep a "reasonable balance" between support for the society and a sense of the self. The authority for this project comes from the scientized knowing they articulate. This knowing allows them to say where support for the society is inadequate and where a sense of self has become excessive and even insane.

Power of this kind is also used to define delusion. It is used to exercise medicalized authority in a supposedly detached way, but it is still political power since it determines who gets what and when and how. Hence the argument by social constructivists that "[f]actuality is not part of the diagnostic process; rather, a judgment of falsity is part of the control process — removing authenticity from the patient's [or the society's] reality". Hence the conclusion that it is necessary to consider social context in discussing delusion, not just what specific beliefs entail in themselves and whether they seem real or not (Heise, 1988, p. 270). Hence the conclusion that people should "think socially again" through an "augmented awareness" of their "methods of thinking" and how the "failure to do so constitutes ... [their] tragedy" (Meerlo, 1968 [1949], p. 9).

The Most Radical Epistemological Issue of Them All: The "God Delusion"

The most basic epistemological issue that discussions of delusion raise is the spiritual one. In a work on world politics, consideration of sacral concerns would seem to miss the point. This is supported by the way psychopathologists try and avoid the issue of religion by saying that it is not an empirical one and that delusions that are shared by whole societies are not delusions. Religions (though not their institutional manifestation) tend to be both intangible and widely shared, and in terms of both criteria, psychopathologists say they cannot be considered delusional.

And yet there are religious believers, both individually- and socially-oriented ones, who are patently deluded. As such, they manifest psychiatric symptoms that are "disruptive" and "negative" rather than "enriching" and "positive" (Bortolotti, 2010, pp. 152–153).

Individuals, for example, can assert that they are prophets and yet fail to exhibit any of the empirical attributes of a holy man or woman. This is evidence of delusional behavior. They may be considered holy by their disciples should they have any, but not by those secularists and sacralists concerned with discriminating between what is real and what is not. Thus, a member of a Christian society may be confined to a psychiatric ward despite being certain he is Jesus Christ because he manifests none of the characteristics of a man who was by all accounts a prince among saints. Hence his belief is considered delusional even by those who share the spiritual mores of his culture.

Whole communities can practice spiritual regimes on the basis of what they learn to do even when this is manifestly delusional, too. Social agreement is not enough to discriminate between what is real and what is not in this regard. There is a discernible difference between sharing the mores of a culture, including its spiritual mores, and exhibiting spiritual symptoms that are empirically insane. Asahara Shoko's *Aum Shinrikyo* cult, for example, was prompted in 1995 to attack the Tokyo subway system using sarin gas. The motive was never clear but it was certainly a mentally dysfunctional one.

The sacral context to world politics may have been marginalized by the Enlightenment project, but it remains an important part of the larger picture. Whether by sacral context is meant political conflicts within religions (such as the conflict between the Catholics and Protestants in Northern Ireland or between the Shi'ites and the Sunnis in Iraq); whether by sacral context is meant political conflicts between religions (such as the conflict between Christian Americans and Islamic fundamentalists); or whether by sacral context is meant the relationship between politics and religion (such as the attempt to understand what a religion means and how it relates to world affairs); world politics has never lost its sacral meaning. Modernists argue that religion is only of significance because humans are violent. The radical nature of this claim, however, means it merits consideration in its own right.

The Atheist's Argument

As noted already, the most common criteria used to define delusions are their fixity and falsity. These criteria, however inadequate, allow psychopathologists to objectify what delusion entails and to judge the coherence and meaning of an individual or societal spiritual narrative. Modernists prioritize the use of reason as an end in itself. By objectifying, modernists do not need to assess divinely inspired ideas or attempts to describe the truth in the terms provided by those involved. It is not necessary to go at this point into the history of the world's main religions, the story of the rise of rationalist science, and the various contributions made to that story by Bacon, Descartes, Enlightenment thinkers and the like, to appreciate the mental revolution that no longer accepting a sacral view of what is real involves. It is enough to note here that the modernist sense of what is real is no longer a religious one. It is not one that fosters a sense of a primal universal power greater than the society or the self. It does not sanction the conclusion that there is a power that permeates the cosmos, including all human beings, and that inspires all those who are conscious of it to give to the world rather than take therefrom. It puts all such conclusions at a mental distance as metaphysics at best and as superstition at worst. Such a revolution not only promotes objectivity and impartiality; it sets its own limits to what modernists can reliably know and distorts what the mind can arguably understand.

Fixity and falsity entail, for psychopathologists, a discourse that is modernist and rationalistic. It is not a radically inclusive discourse. It is not one where modernist rationalism is cupped by other ways to know or see the cosmos in a sacral rather than a secular way. It is not an agnostic discourse, either, where religious teachings are neither believed nor not-believed. It eschews as a matter of principle any notion of divinity other than as an object of analysis. It rejects the epistemological influence of any and every religious belief and, indeed, it was historically crafted to serve this purpose. Its most militant proponents decree rejection of this kind as the best evidence of a "healthy mind" (Dawkins, 2006, p. 3).

To support their argument, psychopathologists as scientific materialists cite cases where the proponents of competing religions have instigated violence to promote their particular beliefs. There are any number of such cases suitable for citation. They include the growing number of suicide bombing missions, up to and including the demolition of the Twin Towers in New York, the long-running conflict between the Israelis and the Palestinians, the "troubles" in Northern Ireland, the historic and contemporary persecution of Jews, plus events more far-removed from modern times but no less significant in religious terms, namely, the partition of India, Europe's Thirty Years' War, and the Christian Crusades (Dawkins, 2006, p. 1).

This is to suggest that religious belief is insane, though it may be that human nature is prone to psychopathological violence and that this is manifest in spiritually sanctioned as well as secular forms. In which case, blaming religion alone for how the species behaves is to misplace blame for the cause of human violence and misdirect attempts to investigate that cause.

Defining "god" in a self-serving way

Scientific materialists define god in a very specific way that serves their cause. Thus, Dawkins defines god as a "supernatural creator ..." (Dawkins, 2006, p. 13) or as a discrete entity who transcends the physical world. This is the god of theists and deists. It is god as a "*super*natural creative intelligence" that resides behind the observable universe it created. It either continues to manage cosmic affairs (theism) or it opts out of how they are run (deism) (Dawkins, 2006, pp. 14, 18).

To the extent that psychopathologists are scientific materialists, they subscribe to the same sort of definition. This, however, is to set up a straw man. The anthropomorphic concept of a personal god that is implicit in the concept of a supernatural creative intelligence is a caricature. As such, it is very easy to critique. This is presumably why atheists such as Dawkins like to promote this concept. It depicts god as supernatural, as concrete (a creative intelligence), and from the theist perspective at least, as actively involved in what happens in the universe and on earth. This depiction is very easy to parody. To a scientific materialist there is nothing supernatural, there is no creative intelligence except for that created by the cosmos itself, and there is no "hidden cosmic hand" directing human, including world, affairs.

Defining "god" in a non-self-serving way

What of a different definition that does not offer such an easy target? Much harder to caricature and dismiss is the concept of god as a primal universal power that is neither outside nor inside "nature", indeed, as a process that cannot be described in any way at all, including as a "creative intelligence".

Atheists tend to reject such a definition as too abstruse to have any meaning. This is why they define god in the way they say people have "generally understood it" (Dawkins, 2006, p. 13). And yet, god as a primal universal power is precisely how god is described by many who do say they have understood it.

This said, there are many religious people who agree with Dawkins. They understand god in the way that Dawkins depicts he/she/it/them, which makes them the kind of believers he likes to parody.

Many do not, however, thus making the question: is the more abstruse definition of god to be ignored just because it does not help Dawkins make the case he wants to make? And if it is not to be ignored, how is such a question to be addressed?

Dawkins highlights how traditional concepts of god are readily ridiculed versions of what a supernatural being should be. The god of the Christian Old Testament, he says, is the most "unpleasant character in all fiction: jealous and proud of it; a petty, unjust, unforgiving control-freak; a vindictive, bloodthirsty ethnic cleanser; a misogynistic, homophobic, racist, infanticidal, genocidal, filicidal, pestilential, megalomaniacal, sadomasochistic, capriciously malevolent bully" (Dawkins, 2006, p. 31). The ancient Greek gods (plural in this case) manifest similarly human as well as super-human qualities, as do the ancient Hindu ones.

However, even Dawkins says that it seems hardly fair to take aim at such an "easy target", which is why he does eventually posit what he sees as a more sophisticated one, namely, that there is no transcendental form of awareness that made the cosmos and continues to superintend it since *"any creative intelligence, of sufficient complexity to design anything, comes into existence only as the end product of an extended process of gradual evolution"*. Creative intelligence is manifest only late in cosmic terms, he argues, and as such cannot have made the cosmos. In this sense, he says, any human concept of god is a delusion and a "pernicious" one at that (Dawkins, 2006, p. 31).

How tough-minded is Dawkins' revised concept, though? On what assumptions does it rest and how plausible are these assumptions?

Creative intelligence is clearly manifest as an emergent property of biological evolution. As a species, human beings bear witness to that, and as a biologist Dawkins is well aware of the way natural selection has worked throughout the history of life on earth to make this emergence possible.

This does not preclude the concept of a cosmic agent of a more radical kind, however. Nor does it preclude looking for this agent in other than a scientifically materialist way.

To say that only biological evolution has the answers to the issue of emergence is to ignore evidence that cosmic agency is a feature of the cosmos itself. It is to ignore evidence, for example, that it might be a feature of energy and matter themselves. Dawkins sees the concept of evolution and of "ultimate design" as "close to being irreconcilably different" (Dawkins, 2006, p. 61). He says "close to" here because he cannot completely dismiss the possibility that they are two sides of the same coin. He wants to see reality in terms of one side only, but this may not be the case and he more or less admits that.

The evidence for cosmic agency being a universal feature is inferential. As such, it is not amenable to the experimental testing process that the hypothetico-deductive method entails.

This is not to say that evidence and tests do not exist. Not being scientifically demonstrable renders such evidence scientifically unreliable, but it does not mean that there is no such evidence and that it cannot be accessed.

Bohm's Implicate Order

On the basis of his knowledge of quantum physics, for example, the physicist David Bohm posits an "implicate order" that he sees as being the ground to the way the cosmos works. To think of the cosmos in a fragmented fashion or as made up of separate and independent parts is to think and act accordingly. To see the cosmos as coherent or as an "overall whole that is undivided, unbroken, and without a border" is to think and act likewise. A "proper" view of the latter sort is a fundamental prerequisite, he argues, to a harmonious self and society. Hence the significance of contemporary scientific findings that suggest that the universe does indeed manifest "undivided wholeness" (Bohm, 1980, p. xi). Hence the significance of the quantum conclusion that space is not so much empty as full. Hence the significance of the failure of the human senses to perceive, except inferentially, the immense, multi-dimensional sea of energy that matter rides on like a "small, 'quantized' wavelike excitation" (Bohm, 1980, p. 191). Hence Bohm's ultimate conclusion that there is a "higher-dimensional reality which *projects* into lower-dimensional elements ..." or a "more comprehensive, deeper, and more inward actuality" which is the common ground for both body and mind (Bohm, 1980, p. 209).

In the light of the above, Bohm says that non-scientific cultures that see the "immeasurable" as the "primary reality" are arguably right to do so since measure is a human creation and any reality that is "beyond" humanity or "prior" to humanity cannot be contingent on what is a modernist concept. To suppose that it can be is to suppose that the penchant that modernists exhibit for objectifying and reifying reality is likely to do any more than result in fragmentation and confusion. Bohm's argument is that it cannot and that the prevalence of rationalism today explains why fragmentation and confusion are endemic as well. In other words, "measure", when considered as the essence of reality, is an illusion. Indeed, for Bohm it is the most radical delusion of them all (Bohm, 1980, p. 23).

Is it possible to reach the "immeasurable" when Bohm defines it as a form of awareness where a sense of difference between the self and the cosmos ceases to exist? Are there practices that can provide this result?

Perhaps there are, though Bohm believes that there are no "direct" or "positive" ways to grasp what is so "immensely beyond" what the mind can apprehend. This does not preclude forms of meditation and other such attempts to see the "illusion" of the self and reality as being broken into fragments. The products of meditative insight cannot be rationalist ones, Bohm says. They can, however, help explain both non-rationalism and rationalism (Bohm, 1980, p. 25).

Rees's Six Cosmic Numbers

Another example of the inferential evidence that creative intelligence might be a feature of the cosmos itself is provided by the astronomer, Martin Rees. Out of the mathematical rules that describe how the cosmos works, Rees says, emerge six numbers that define the "basic forces" of the universe. They also define its "size and overall 'texture'", whether it will continue indefinitely, and its most fundamental properties (Rees, 2000, p. 2). The universe is the size it is, for example, because of a number that measures the "strength of the electrical forces that hold atoms together, divided by the force of gravity between them". Any smaller and the cosmos itself would have been small and very short-lived. Life would likely have remained at the level of insects. Another number describes how firmly atomic nuclei are bound together. With a value slightly less or more, the sun (indeed any sun) would not have had the power to turn hydrogen into all of the other atoms, including carbon and oxygen. The third number describes the amount of material in the cosmos and the ratio of gravity to "expansion energy". Too high and the cosmos would have collapsed long before now. Too low and galaxies and stars would never have formed. "The initial expansion speed", says Rees, "seems to have been finely tuned". The fourth number describes how, over "billions of light-years", a form of "cosmic 'anti-gravity'" has worked to control the expansion of the universe. Any larger and like the first and third numbers, it would have prevented galaxies and stars from ever coming into being. The fifth number describes the ratio of two "fundamental energies". Any smaller and the cosmos would have been "inert and structureless", while any larger and it would have been too violent for stars or star systems to form and survive. The sixth number describes the various spatial dimensions. With two or four such dimensions there would have been no life on earth. Three is what is needed, and three is what there is. Time is a fourth dimension, but it is radically different from the other three. Likewise the ten-dimensions that string-theorists say are manifest at a microscopic level and that may have been evident at the time of the Big Bang (Rees, 2000, pp. 2–3). As Rees observes, there may be connections between all of these numbers, but it is currently not possible to predict the value of any one of them from that of the others.

Are the values these numbers present simply a "brute fact", that is, simply a "coincidence" of some kind, or do we have evidence here of the "providence of a benign Creator"? Rees himself thinks neither. This is to say that we exist because we exist, though Rees expresses his dissatisfaction with this conclusion, too (Rees, 2000, p. 164). He thinks that the precise way in which key cosmic numbers are tuned to what makes the universe viable is evidence that our universe is one part of a cosmic "ensemble". He supports the idea of many cosmic environments, one of which resulted in life on earth without the intervention of a cosmic agent or a creative universal intelligence (Rees, 2000, pp. 25, 4).

Though cosmic agency may be too anthropomorphic a concept to appeal to an astronomer like Rees, what of the concept of a primary cosmic power? The numbers Rees provides suggest either a monumental cosmic accident, that is, an equally monumental coincidence, or intention and design of an equally monumental kind

(Rees, 2000, p. 174). Dawkins says Rees is not a theist. He says he is a poetic naturalist (Dawkins, 2006, p. 14). He says a god able to calculate the values just right for life on earth "would have to be at least as improbable as the finely tuned combination of numbers itself ..." (Dawkins, 2006, p. 143).

Rees quotes St. Augustine to the effect that the cosmos was "gifted" with the ability to "transform itself", which does suggest a giver of some kind (Rees, 2000, p. 115). Rees goes on to explicitly eschew such a concept, but he does leave the issue open by asking: "... should we seek other reasons for the providential values" that underpin the cosmos? He tends to favor coincidence as the ultimate explanation and a concept of space as initially "shrunk to a 'point'" and "latent with particles and forces" (Rees, 2000, p. 145). The question of latency remains the rub, however, since it says nothing about what made this particular cosmos possible rather than some other cosmos or none at all. What came before the Big Bang and what caused the Big Bang? What ensured that it took the form that it did? Was all of what subsequently transpired accidental or is there scope for some other explanation? Is it enough to say that everything happened because it happened or are there deeper answers here?

Physicists see themselves as working towards a "theory of everything" that would explain all of Rees's numbers. However, even a theory of everything is unlikely to explain why there is something rather than nothing, which is the most fundamental question of them all.

Taylor's Epiphany

Is there a way of answering the question of cosmic agency in yet another fashion? Is it possible to go beyond the appeal to modernist rationalism to come to convincing conclusions about what animates the whole?

Support for the idea that it is possible to do so comes from an unusual source, namely, an account provided by a Harvard brain scientist of a major stroke that deprived her for years of the capacity to think in a linear, logical way (Taylor, 2008). What Jill Taylor lost in this regard she gained in terms of an awareness of the universe of a non-linear, non-logical kind. And though the experience of one person is at best anecdotal, it can be highly suggestive as to where to look for evidence of an alternative to the scientific certainty that materialists take for granted.

Taylor's stroke was the result of a severe malfunction in her brain's left hemisphere. It was caused by an undiagnosed condition to do with the connections between one of her intra-cranial arteries and one of her intra-cranial veins. The subsequent hemorrhage led to a rapid cascade of highly specific and life-threatening symptoms (Taylor, 2008, pp. 25, 35).

As the language centers of her left hemisphere were rendered silent and Taylor's memories were progressively removed, she was "comforted", she says, by an "expanding sense of grace". Into this "void", where her normal higher cognition and the minutiae of her day-to-day existence used to be, came something else. Her consciousness "soared", she says, "into an all-knowingness, a 'being at *one*' with the universe …". She was puzzled by this phenomenon, but she was curious as well. What did it mean, she wondered? At which point she began thinking: "*I am trillions of cells sharing a common mind. I am here, now, thriving as life … I am cellular life, no … molecular life with manual dexterity and a cognitive mind*", though at that moment a disintegrating one (Taylor, 2008, p. 41).

Taylor's experience is consistent with the findings of Newberg, D'Aquili and Rause (2002). The first two analysts have mapped experimentally, using contemporary brain imaging technology, the way meditation and prayer can reduce activity in the brain's language centers and in the region that allows for "orientation association", that is, the region that allows the brain to tell where in space the self begins and where it ends. As a result of the appropriate forms of meditation and prayer, the self is able to stop perceiving itself as solid and can become one with the cosmos instead (Taylor, 2008, p. 136). Focused spiritual contemplation, in other words, can result in specific changes in the way the brain works that can result in spiritual experiences. These experiences are real, or at least, the perceptions they involve are real. Moreover, these experiences can be documented by scientific means. Those who focus the brain/mind in this way manifest a specific set of neuro-physiological occurrences that can be demonstrated scientifically as such. These occurrences are experienced at the same time as universal harmony. Does this mean that the capacity to experience god is "hardwired" into the brain, regardless of whether or not an individual has had such an experience?

Taylor did not have this experience after meditating or praying. What happened to her was the result of a profound, acute, neuro-physiological trauma.

The consequence of her experience was nonetheless a sense of being part of a "greater structure — an eternal flow of energy ...". Once Taylor recovered all of her left brain functions, they re-asserted her sense of herself as being discrete. At the same time, however, her right brain continued to be aware that she was essentially part of a cosmic whole to which she would ultimately return once her time as a multi-cellular being in a three-dimensional context was at an end. Moreover, she no longer perceived coming to an end as an emotional threat. Quite the contrary, she saw it as a source of tranquility, safety and well-being (Taylor, 2008, p. 16). Taylor subsequently described science as a left-brain activity and as such as failing fully to appreciate what the right brain was able to know and do (Taylor, 2008, p. 169; see also Chadwick, 1992).

Materialists see Taylor's experience, and the experience of those who meditate and pray, as being delusory. They see Taylor's experience as the result of a particular injury and the experience of those who meditate and pray as the result of self-inflicted stress. Regardless of the success scientists have had in mapping the neurological concomitants of these experiences, they see the perception of spiritual transcendence as delusory (Dawkins, 2006, pp. 87–93).

Then there are the materialists who have the experience Taylor had. They talk very differently about what the mind can know.

Is the potential for an epiphany part of the brain's "hard-wiring"?

The conclusion that Newberg, D'Aquili and Rause come to would seem to support the materialist case. All experience, including spiritual experience, must by definition be "brain-based" (Saver and

Rabin, 1997, p. 498). As Newberg, D'Aquili and Rause put it, there is "no other way for God to get into your head except through the brain's neural pathways" (Newberg, D'Aquili and Rause, 2002, p. 37). If there was another way, it would have "little cognitive meaning" without an ability to know about it, that is, without a brain (Newberg, D'Aquili and Rause, 2002, p. 191).

Acknowledging as much does not negate the significance of cosmic experiences, however, since it says nothing about them. It says nothing about whether these experiences reflect the fundamental character of the cosmos or how the mind interprets a particular brain function or malfunction.

All it says is that for those individuals who meditate and pray in a particular way, there are characteristic changes in their experience of their mental functioning and that these changes involve a subjective sense of self-transcendence. As such, they can be mapped objectively using a single photon emission-computed tomography camera.

"In the narrowest scientific view …", analysts like this say, "all spiritual transcendence — from the case of the mildest case of religious uplift, to the profound states of union described by mystics — [can be reduced] to a neurochemical commotion in the brain" (Newberg, D'Aquili and Rause, 2002, p. 146). It seems that experiencing god would seem to involve nothing but a kick in the brain circuitry. Or as Newberg, D'Aquili and Rause put it, "[s]cience has no choice … but to find … natural causes for 'supernatural' events. From a rational point of view, it's hard to imagine that the claims of the mystics could be based on anything other than delusion" (Newberg, D'Aquili and Rause, 2002, pp. 99–100). This is why such claims are said to be "fundamentally confused". It is why they are said to provide a view of the world that is not really real (Newberg, D'Aquili and Rause, 2002, p. 108).

Scientific materialists are reductionists in that they promote science as the only way to know. In the process they completely ignore any necessity to compensate for the limits and distortions of science as a way of knowing. They completely ignore what non-scientific approaches have to contribute to such a compensatory project.

Scientific materialists say that the only reality that is real is the experimental and empirical one. They see their methodology as the only one that results in persuasive conclusions. Describing and explaining metaphysical questions about the ultimate nature of reality is best done, they say, in scientific terms.

In their view, the most real form of reality is the material one and all reality is a manifestation of a materialist approach to the cosmos. Up to a point, Newberg, D'Aquili and Rause seem to concur. While they agree that mapping the brain activity of meditators provides material correlates for mysticism, as a neurological event they also think that this does not constitute proof that there is any absolute spiritual reality (Newberg, D'Aquili and Rause, 2002, p. 126).

From the perspective of the mystic, however, records of brain activity say nothing about what is being recorded. From their point of view, materialist explanations are rationalist and reductionist since they only provide at best a metaphorical rendition of what is real.

Newberg, D'Aquili and Rause are well aware (2002, pp. 113, 170, 173–178) that if they had mapped that part of the brain that receives sensory impulses from the eyes, namely, the visual cortex, they would have found evidence of cortical activity commensurate with the experience of "seeing". Moreover, evidence of such activity is not the experience of "seeing" which is rich and (dare it be said) wonderful. Contemporary technology may be able to document such an experience in the form of patterns of electrical signals in the brain, but it cannot demonstrate what a sunset looks like or what seeing a movie entails.

Similarly, a scientific description and explanation of what happens to the brain when it experiences self-transcendence is scientific evidence that such an experience is taking place; however, it is not that experience. It is not in itself the awareness of being one with the cosmos nor is it the knowledge that this awareness imparts. Hence the willingness of analysts like Newberg, D'Aquili and Rause to conclude that authentic and truly mystical (rather than psychotic and truly insane) experiences can be the consequence of mental events that are not delusional (Saver and Rabin, 1997). Indeed, they say, these experiences can well be the outcome of "sound, healthy minds coherently reacting to perceptions that ... are absolutely real" (Newberg, D'Aquili and Rause, 2002, p. 100).

So: is the sense of self-transcendence that Taylor describes real or is it a delusion? Whatever it is that the brain/mind perceives under these circumstances, does the self really become one with the cosmos or is it "merely" or "nothing but" a side-effect of mental trauma (as in Taylor's case) or of meditation and prayer (as in the case of sacral devotees)?

What we have here are two radically different arguments. One sees mystical experience as nothing but a brain/mind event. The other sees mystical experience as real in its own right and the brain/mind as able to have such an experience.

Scientific materialism can only conduct this argument on its own terms, namely, materialist ones. It cannot accept any other approach because of its commitment to the primacy of materialism and its unwillingness to accept alternative ways of knowing, for example, those ways where the truth is pursued by meditative means. Scientific materialists say that mystical conclusions cannot be verified scientifically, ergo they are false, ergo they are delusory.

What if matter is not as materialistic as scientific materialists suppose, however? What if there is evidence for non-materialist readings of the universe, but that this evidence is only accessible using parts of the brain/mind that scientific materialism does not? What if experimental empiricism is ultimately debilitating in this regard just as (albeit for different reasons) religious dogma is debilitating?

What if, as Newberg, D'Aquili and Rause ultimately suggest, "the mind's machinery of transcendence may in fact be a window through which we can glimpse the ultimate realness of something that is truly divine". At this point Newberg, D'Aquili and Rause note how "[t]ime and time again, people who have experienced intense mystical states insist that these states feel more real than everyday reality. Neurology can neither prove nor disprove this point, but informed speculation tells us that it's possible that AUB [Absolute Unitary Being] is a primary reality, one from which all objective and subjective perspectives of the world are derived ..." (Newberg, D'Aquili and Rause, 2002, pp. 140–141, 178).

A Third Way?

Since science is too materialistic to allow for the spiritual experience of universal one-ness, and since religion is too prone to interpret spiritual experience not as a thing-in-itself but in the terms set by its own dogmas and beliefs, perhaps it is worth looking for an alternative to both. This way would need to be both self-transcendent and allow for empirical tests. The tests in turn would need to be of a non-scientific, non-religious sort of the kind, for example, that the Buddha asked his disciples to carry out. For the Buddha, his teachings needed to be tested in the experimental "laboratory" of meditation and experience. It is this kind of approach that metaphysics suggests might be the most promising when it comes to gaining access to the "mysterious 'holding together' of things" that seems to be such an "integral aspect" of the cosmos (Mathews, 2008, pp. 53–55).

Taylor's epiphany could be seen as an example of this tertiary approach, albeit an involuntary one. Moreover, her conclusions concur with those articulated by renowned mystics, that is, by those throughout history who have had what, by all accounts, seem to have been an authentic experience of one-ness with the cosmos (Armstrong, 1993; Underhill, 1949 [1912]; James, 1929 [1902]; Huxley, 2004 [1945]). Taylor is not alone in having had a radical sense of self-transcendence when her understanding of the material realm was replaced by one of its cosmic context. Many have had similar epiphanies and have come to the same sort of conclusion. Evidence of what god means can only be gleaned, it can be argued, from what these mystics have said. Their accounts of their experience of cosmic consciousness are detailed and consistent and provide an extensive body of evidence of its own kind (Bucke, 1948 [1901]).

Consider, for example, a mystic discourse like the one below. This discourse is an abbreviated compilation of teachings by Bawa Muhaiyaddeen (Webb, 1994; Webb, 2006), a Tamil Sufi who was one of the most luminous of the saints and sages of the 20th century:

"… the world is shown to you as an example", says Bawa, "and clarity manifests in many forms, …

> *Don't touch the world, but like the humming bird, balance above it,
> taking only what you need (the one)!*

… what you see is your own perceptions, your thoughts give energy
to your illusions about yourself, your life is a reflection of what you
perceive and think, and because your mind is the story of your life, it
is the root of all your problems, indeed …

> *Recognise the seven states of consciousness: feeling, awareness, intellect,
> judgment, wisdom, divine analytic wisdom, and divine luminous
> wisdom!*

… what you see outside is what you are inside, …

> *Stay with the one point, the one power, wanting only that!*

… the bad you see outside, for example, is the bad within yourself,
while …

> *See all lives as equal to your own!*

… you are attacked basically because of what your mind and your
desires intend, which is why …

> *Realise that the real you is the one that lies within, buffered by mind
> and desire!*

… it is hard to become a true human being, …

> *Be alone (egoless), hungry (for the one not the world), awake (to the
> one not the world)! Know that there is nothing else but the one that
> is god!*

… you know what your duty is but you cannot do it, and faith shatters
when faced with adversity, so …

> *At any moment of difficulty or distress, happiness or joy, press your one
> point (your divine luminous wisdom) to the one point (the truth)!*

… pray, for prayer, like breath, is a programmed part of the body.

> *Know that science, intellectual learning, language, religion, [even] prayer and meditation come from mind or desire, and therefore cannot be the one! Because the one has no form, being one with the one means having the qualities of the one, and practising those qualities! It means correcting your heart and living a good life!"*

(Muhaiyaddeen, 1980; 1994; 2003a)

The "one" cited above is the primal cosmic power Bawa understands as god. This power, he says, is beyond scientific and religious comprehension. It has no form and is manifest only in the qualities typically associated with holy human beings, namely, wisdom, compassion, truth-telling and the like. In this sense, it is the world that teaches people all they need to know, though it does so only if they are able to get their own thoughts and egos out of the way, which is not easy given how eagerly people engage with the world rather than with what might further their sense of individual agency.

Any number of conclusions by similarly enlightened individuals endorse what Bawa says and world politics can be seen in this light, too (Pettman, 2004). These conclusions represent a body of human experience that is not scientific. It is also at odds with what religions say. Nevertheless, the authority of those who have come to these conclusions makes it difficult to dismiss their conclusions out of hand. The consistency of their experiential findings suggests a body of knowledge that reflects a radically real aspect of human knowledge, though one that emerges only once the workings of the conscious mind are stilled or focused in a mystic way.

The Atheists' Fallback Position

Scientific secularists are wont to articulate an intriguing fallback position. Having set up a concept of god that is an anthropomorphic straw man and having knocked it down, they then make common cause with mystics.

Dawkins has no problem, for example, accepting Einstein's endorsement of Spinoza-style pantheism. Spinoza saw god as a "non-supernatural synonym ... for the Universe, or for the lawfulness that governs its workings" (Dawkins, 2006, p. 18). He saw it in terms of the "orderly harmony" of all that exists. He did not see it in terms of a grandiose entity who monitors what human beings do. Einstein, like Spinoza, accepted that beyond most human experience was "something" both beautiful and sublime that the mind could not directly perceive. This "something" was only knowable, he argued, "as a feeble reflection" of what it was. To be religious was to see the universe in the light of this "feeble reflection" (Dawkins, 2006, p. 19).

Dawkins is prepared to say that, in this sense, he could be called religious too, even though he thinks that this idea of god is so trivial that anyone might endorse it (Dawkins, 2006, p. 153) and that admitting as much is also likely to mislead because of the way the "metaphorical or pantheistic" concept of god that it promotes is so far from the "interventionist, miracle-wreaking, thought-reading, sin-punishing, prayer-answering God of the Bible, of priests, mullahs and rabbis, and of ordinary language". This said, he has no problem endorsing the pantheistic concept of god, perhaps because he sees it as no more than "sexed-up atheism", and as an atheist himself he does not mind appearing to be "sexed-up" (Dawkins, 2006, pp. 18–19).

Dawkins does also admit that "[p]erhaps there are some genuinely profound and meaningful questions" that are "forever beyond the reach of science" and that quantum theory may already be "knocking at the door of the unknowable" (Dawkins, 2006, p. 56). He even says that there may be other ways of knowing besides the scientific one and that knowing god may require "personal ... experience" (Dawkins, 2006, p. 154). His response is to say that if science is not able to reach the answers required here, why should it be assumed that religion can?

The Mystic Rejoinder

What of the metaphysical knowing that is neither scientific nor religious, however? What of the brain/mind's capacity to perceive, albeit indirectly and perhaps "feebly", the ultimate nature of reality?

Newberg, D'Aquili and Rause acknowledge that a materialist might well want to see mystic experience as no more than a delusion caused by the "chemical misfirings of a bundle of nerve cells". They, on the other hand, see another possible conclusion. As noted previously, they see evidence of such activity as evidence of a neurological process that has evolved to enable human beings to "transcend material existence", that is, to find a more fundamental aspect of themselves or even a sense of an "absolute, universal reality" that is able to connect them with "all that is" (Newberg, D'Aquili and Rause, 2002, p. 9). Nor is such an approach inconsistent with one that sees evolution in terms of natural selection and the gradual emergence of a complex account of the whole cosmic environment.

Conclusion

Delusion is a fundamental form of psychopathology. Defining it raises questions about false, fixed and shared belief that are much contested, particularly when the delusion has a psychological rather than an organic cause.

Common sense provides pragmatic alternatives to these definitional debates, but common sense has its own limits. For example, the pragmatism that common sense promotes hides the psychopathological preference for scientific materialism. This is important when considering the so-called "god delusion" that is at the heart of the modernist project, including the psychopathological questioning of that project.

Established religions require specific definitions of god. These definitions are particular to each faith.

Scientific materialists see these definitions as fundamentally delusory. They see them as radically untrue.

The limits and distortions that are intrinsic to scientific materialism (limits and distortions that the proponents of this epistemology refuse to acknowledge since they see science as the most truthful way to know) distort in turn what god is thought to mean. Defined in anthropomorphic terms, god as a concept is easily parodied and pilloried. Defined in mystical terms, however, and god as a concept is rather more challenging. Scientific materialists call the latter concept vacuous. There is evidence, however, that has been tested publically and repeatedly, that it has substance, and that this substance can compensate for the limits and distortions of both science and religion.

Reality

Reality is what exists rather than what appears to exist or is thought to exist. It is what is deemed "real" as opposed to what is deemed "imagined" or "desired". It is what is considered to be the "truth of appearances or phenomena" rather than what appears to be true or is thought to be true (OED). In short, it is what remains once belief and longing are taken away.

As such, it is a 16th-century concept (OED). It came into English as a legal term with the advent of the Enlightenment project, that is, once European cultures began prioritizing the use of reason as an end in itself. This is not to say that there were not equivalent words denoting the same sort of concept before that time. However, reality was the word used to refer to this concept after that time.

Modernity and Reality

To a modernist rationalist, reality is what is "seen" by the objectifying mind, that is, by a mind that has been taught to move away from the world and to look back at the world (and itself in the world) from a detached distance. Such a mind can be taught to talk systematically to other minds similarly detached about what it subsequently sees. The result is science in its natural and social forms.

With the advent of such a perspective, it is no accident that reality should be seen in the same way, namely, as separate from the self. To objectify a view of the world, it is also necessary to individuate. With the advent of such a perspective, it is no accident that reality should also be seen in terms of alienated beings for whom what is real is external and a-social.

Each individual is thrown into the world at birth as a unique genetic experiment. The culture of that individual's life-world then teaches that individual how to think and behave.

In a post-Enlightenment culture, individuals are taught from birth how to push away from their social context. Like a part of a rubber sheet, they learn to pull away from society and to converse intellectually with others similarly constituted.

By the 20th century there was a growing awareness that modernist/rationalist detachment, though hugely productive as a source of new and reliable knowledge and of new and useful technologies and industries, blinded those so imbued at the same time as it enlightened them. In other words, the detachment that emancipated its diverse proponents seemed to incarcerate them as well.

This led to attempts to explore the limits and distortions of the modernist/rationalist perspective. It also led to attempts to compensate for these limits and distortions.

One of these attempts was the post-modernist one. This involved asking what the reasons might conceivably be for prioritizing the use of reason. This resulted in growing humility about how far it was possible to proceed beyond knowing the world as something perceived. It resulted in relativistic notions of what is real as ultimately consensual and the conclusion that reality is what groups of people agree to. Consensus, in other words, is what allows groups to construct what is real for them. Even science can be seen in these terms since no absolutely objective perspective is humanly possible. Despite the self-correcting mechanism that the hypothetico-deductive method provides, scientists promote and protect particular paradigms (Kuhn, 1962). They relinquish these paradigms only once anomalies have accumulated to the point that their preferred paradigm is patently untenable, which in the case of individual scientists may never be.

A second such attempt was the post-structuralist one. This involved asking about reality as constituted linguistically and identity as constituted in these terms too. This resulted in similar conclusions to those the post-modernists came to.

A third attempt sought to explore the limits and distortions of the modernist perspective by eschewing rationalism and articulating emotivism. This was the romantic alternative to rationalist objectivity. It saw reality in what was felt as much as what was thought.

A fourth attempt sought to intuit the primary categories of the mind and how they intended the phenomena that the conscious mind thought it was attending to. This was phenomenology and as such, it was a profoundly subjectifying version of the objectifying perspective (Pettman, 2008).

The final modernist attempt to investigate the limits and distortions of the rationalist perspective was the attempt to study more closely the mind's unconscious dimensions. For example, at the beginning of the 20th century Freud talked, in the terms set by his "psychoanalysis", of a "reality principle", by which he meant how the ego works to control the libido in the latter's pursuit of pleasure. Psychiatrists, as good modernists/rationalists, talk of reality as something it is possible to be "in touch" with. Those who are "out of touch" with it are seen as potentially suffering from schizophrenia. Delusions can be symptoms of such a state, though it is much debated what are "real" delusions in this regard and what are "unreal" ones. These debates are legitimate given the political implications of characterizing individuals or groups as being "out of touch" with a particular notion of what is "real". This does not mean that becoming deluded is not possible and that losing touch with reality does not happen. However, it does make the issue of deciding what the difference is a deeply contested one.

The reality that is completely independent in this regard would be one that transcends all beliefs and perceptions. This would provide the benchmark that modernists/rationalists require.

The problem is that reality of this kind does not exist, at least, for all but the most detached, that is, for all who are not self-evidently divine. This leaves individuals and societies engaged in a perennial debate about what to promote and what to protect as being real.

As noted earlier, at one level of abstraction this results in a debate about the modernist/rationalist project *per se* by those pushed to its margins for being (from the perspective of modernists/rationalists) insufficiently rationalistic. This includes women, environmentalists, indigenous peoples, post-colonials and the poor.

As was also noted earlier, at another level of abstraction it results in a debate within the modernist/rationalist project between those who make different assumptions about human nature and human nurturing practices. In a modernist/rationalist culture, these assumptions are articulated in a modernist/rationalist way. Because there are a finite number of these assumptions, there are a finite number of analytical articulations.

To demonstrate what it means to debate what is real, both from the margins of the Enlightenment project and from within that project itself, the analytic narrative will turn at this point to consider a particular case-study. It will try and show how these debates apply in practice.

It will explore, that is, the political history of the Solomon Islands in both pre-modernist/modernist terms. It will also explore it as a site of contention as to which modernist discourse is most relevant when it comes to describing and explaining — and prescribing policy for — world affairs.

The Solomon Islands

Why the Solomon Islands? Why choose what at first glance is no more than a remnant, or should it be said, an oddment of the one-time British empire? As one of a number of the world's micro-states, the Solomons would seem to represent no more than a footnote to the global political page and a one-line footnote at that (Pettman, 1977, p. 268). As a member of the North American academy argues, it would seem to have significance to "few other than its ... [own] residents" (Papps, 1991, p. 377). Why, then, consider it here?

Constituted of nearly 1,000 equatorial islands — six large ones and many more smaller ones — the Solomon Islands lie in a staggered, one and a half thousand kilometer line that delimits the Coral Sea. It is inhabited by little more than half a million people.

In terms of resources to sell to the world it has timber, copra, fish and gold as well as tourism (McKinnon, Carillet and Starnes, 2008). It has little else. It has no oil or industry, as Papps points out, and despite domestic strife between the inhabitants of two of the major islands that led to armed intervention in 2003, it has not been party to international strife since World War Two. Nor has it become a major site for drug-trafficking, money laundering, arms smuggling, people trafficking or terrorism, despite fears that this might happen with the near-collapse of its government in the lead-up to the intervention.

Hence Papps' argument that "[l]ittle can be meaningfully said" about this part of the world. Hence his opinion of the Solomons as one of a number of little countries that are "politically unimportant ..." and that have "no real prospects for development". States like these do not count, he says, since they inhabit the "backwaters" of the world's great political lakes (Papps, 1991, p. 378).

Is it possible to turn Papps' perspective on its head, however? Is it possible that a relatively remote tropical archipelago like the Solomon Islands can contribute not only to the general fund of knowledge about world affairs but also to questions about what constitutes political reality? The United States is large and difficult to document comprehensively and coherently. The Solomon Islands is small and considerably easier to document comprehensively and coherently. Both states are complex, since small does not mean simple. This is readily apparent once the issues that underpin local politics are directly addressed. The political environment in the Solomons is a relatively intimate one, however, and as such it can be used to illustrate the more abstract findings of modernist social science. This can be used in turn to argue that such a study is particularly revealing.

Reality Construed in Terms of the "West" as Opposed to the "Rest"

Already it seems that there is a Euro-American discourse at work here that involves competing versions of the reality of the state. This discourse involves a dichotomy between the "west" and the "rest".

On the one hand, the Solomon Islands is seen as part of the Euro-American construction of world affairs, that is, as a product of the "west". As such it is seen as one of a large number of small, poor, minimally productive countries who use their sovereignty to vote in assemblies like the United Nations. These votes can be (and are) used collectively to help promote and protect large-state points of view. Micro-states play a role as pawns in regional or global power games and pawns, particularly in combination with more significant pieces, have been known to checkmate kings (Pettman, 1977, p. 268). The raw materials at the command of micro-states like the Solomons are also seen as becoming more important. In this regard it is important to note that no part of the global political economy is immune from the spread of modernist ideas about what generates wealth. The question in this regard is whether *undeveloped* countries like the Solomons are destined to become *underdeveloped* ones as happened in Latin America. Mercantilist discourses of development argue for economic nationalism, state market protection and active attempts to nurture infant industries. Liberalist discourses of development argue for free market access to all national resources with maximum opportunity for entrepreneurs to create and foster economic enterprise. Socialist discourses of development argue for state planning so as to prevent market distortions and to return to citizens as much as possible of the commonweal in the form of educational, medical, communications and transport infrastructure in particular. Neo-marxist discourses of development see the outcome of liberalist access as being the emergence of a "comprador" elite that has more interest in selling national resources for its own gain and that of its immediate clan members and kin than using national income to build educational, health, communications and transport facilities. Those marginalized by modernity, such as women or environmentalists, articulate discourses of development that promote gender parity or sustainability. Meanwhile, modern communications media make considerably more visible to a global audience the consequences of a failure to build a national infrastructure. This is manifest, for example, in global awareness of the ongoing spread in countries like the Solomons of diseases like malaria, tuberculosis and HIV/AIDS. In terms of the social dimension to the Euro-American/modernist tale that the Solomons has to tell, it has failed so far to create a national identity commensurate with the sovereign identity of the state. The British bequeathed a Westminster version of democracy, based on liberal individualism, that continues to function after a fashion, though its local relevance is a matter for debate. More radically, there has been a failure to create a national identity. The Solomons do not cohere ethnographically (there are 70 languages spoken statewide) and nor are they likely to, at least, not in the short term. This does not bode well for the capacity of any Solomons government to win national legitimacy. A first-past-the-post electoral system, replete with competing parties and a relatively free press, has survived a succession of domestic crises, but the political system is at odds with non-Westminster modes of governance. It has not yet completely collapsed, but this may be more to do with the extent to which the system has been counter-colonized than anything else.

On the other hand, the Solomons is seen as part of the non-Euro-American construction of world affairs, that is, the "rest". As such it is seen as a clan-based, non-modernist or pre-modernist country whose culture runs counter to attempts to introduce human rights and democracy, a centralized capitalist market, and a sovereign state. Non-modernity is seen, that is, as continuing to foster communalist, subsistence and village-centered political norms rather than individualist, commodified, state-specific ones. Human rights claims, liberal entrepreneurialism and strategic autonomy, which are all modernist and rationalist, continue to be compromised in practice by customary obligations which are pre-modernist and traditionalist. While Solomon Islanders may recognize the benefits of important aspects of modernist culture, such as its scientific technology and more particularly its capacity to heal and provide contemporary means of communication and transport, they question the implications of this culture for their own.

The Solomon Islands: Competing conceptions of a politico-cultural reality

The competing conceptions of reality sketched above are evidence, from a Euro-American perspective, of important differences in perspective and approach. They token different ways of describing and explaining the world and of prescribing policies there.

This is not the only perspective, however. Hence the following attempt to consider these conceptions more closely, beginning with the underlying issue of modernity as opposed to pre-modernity or non-modernity (Firth, 1998):

> Thank God, white man
> You have educated me,
> Filled me with your Knowledge
> Almost to the brim,
> But leave me some space,
> Space for my own purpose.
>
> God gave me a culture,
> A totality of my life.
> I was religious long before, I was ruler
> Long before,
> Laws have I to direct my life.
>
> I like your knowledge, white man,
> But I like it built on me.
> Build it on my existence,
> Politics on my politics,
> Religion on my religion.
> My feet would stand firm.

(Fugui, 1977)

The author of this poem is an Anglican priest and a Solomon Islander. He was also a one-time member of the Solomon Islands' Legislative Assembly.

He is trying to highlight in what he writes how Solomon Islanders have been on the receiving end of European imperialism. As he is well aware, Solomon Islanders know they cannot regain the political autarky they enjoyed in pre-contact times or maintain it today. Too much has happened, the outside world is too immediate, and as he points out in his poem, there is too much that Solomon

Islanders now want from the outside world for autarky to be an option. Being an Anglican priest, Fugui is also well aware of the role Christianity has played in crafting the contemporary sense of reality in the Pacific. The initiatives of the early Christian missionaries were resisted, often violently so. Once entrenched, however, they became part of the local communities. They reinforced their unity and they served their own neo-colonial role by making it more difficult for these communities to change. Younger people in more recent times have become less religious or have joined fundamentalist groups funded by churches in the United States. These are no less neo-colonial in their cultural impact, even though the "liberation theology" some of them espouse is said to have proven a "helpful anti-dote" to the growth of a wealth- and status-based class system in towns like Honiara, which is the country's capital (Crocombe, 1989, p. 76).

As an eminent Nuiginian pointed out at the same time Fugui wrote: "We have been a colony, a trust territory, a dependency, or whatever. Now … we want to be free. Freedom [however] is more than merely getting rid of external constraints. It is, above all, self-possession. We want to possess ourselves as individuals and especially as Melanesians, people who are of dignity in our own right … It means that sooner or later we have to come to answer, to our own satisfaction, not to the satisfaction of expatriates, missionaries, company managers, [a]dministrators, or what have you, certain searching questions, such as: What are we really worth ourselves? What do we want to be as a people? And this leads to the far more fundamental question of whether we can be ourselves at all. Perhaps this is not a particularly good time … to be striking out on one's own. Being a poor, underdeveloped, powerless country, maybe we are lost before we start. Talking to our educators sometimes, one gains the impression that man is a slave to systems created by man and is doomed forever to this type of life. Even those who preach the 'good news' which comes to liberate us, the poor pagans of this country, themselves give the impression that we are all without hope. The answer to this question, the question of 'what are we all up to?', to me is this: we don't know. We don't know if indeed we can be a nation — all we know is that we must try" (Momis, 1972, p. 448).

Another local author to reflect on this key issue at this time was Francis Bugotu, the first Solomon Islands postgraduate. Bugotu learned the ways of Euro-American modernism in high school in Honiara. He subsequently earned a Master's degree in linguistics from the University of Lancaster. Despite his tertiary education, Bugotu remained close nonetheless to the village context which continues to define reality for the great majority of Solomon Islanders. This provided him with a hybrid perspective that makes his comments particularly acute.

In 1968 he gave a paper at the 2nd Waigani Seminar at the University of Papua New Guinea on the impact of Euro-American culture on Melanesian society. In 1973 he chaired a committee that produced a comprehensive report on educational policy for the Solomon Islands. This committee was mostly composed of Solomon Islanders and its work required him to travel extensively throughout the whole of the country, talking to people about what they wanted their children to learn. At this time he authored a paper with Roger Keesing, an anthropologist from the University of California, on the different ways in which the Solomons might develop, a paper that Keesing presented at the 7th Waigani Seminar in Port Moresby. In 1973 Bugotu published an article on decolonization and recolonization that drew heavily on this paper. Though an academic work, and hence an objectifying one, it was written with an intimacy and a personal understanding of its subject matter that remains relevant to this day.

The key point Bugotu made throughout his work was that while the British empire had come to an end, imperialism had not. The ongoing effect of modernist culture, and hence of the politics, economics and social relations characteristic of that culture, meant that a country that was supposed to have become independent had become dependent instead. Because of the deeds of what neo-marxists would call its comprador elite, the Solomon Islands had become a neo-colony.

Bugotu said that the neo-colonial reality was "disguised and often silent". He said that the "'light' of the civilized world" as preached to the "man who lives 'in darkness'" became under these circumstances "a newly imposed darkness which paralyses the thought processes of the beholder ...". He said that the result was "[s]tandards of living, of education, of behaviour, etc." which were "continually ... judged from ... [the] point of view of the outsider" and were "unrelated to the needs and wishes of the people within the country ..." (Bugotu, 1973, p. 77).

To remove this disguise and counter this silence, that is, to expose the reality of the Solomon Islands for what it was, it was necessary, Bugotu said, to seek a "broader range of alternatives for development ...". It meant, most fundamentally, remaining faithful to island culture. It meant looking to "traditional" ways of living. This meant looking in turn to "communal land rights and collective responsibility ... [as] the basis for co-operative work ... [to] decision-making by consensus [as the basis] ... for modern parliamentary procedures ... [to] the philosophy of shared responsibility for the young, the sick and the elderly [as the basis for] ... modern social welfare programmes ... [and to] classless and non-elitist society forms [as the basis for] ... newly planned educational structures" (Bugotu, 1973, p. 78).

The problem with what was happening in the Solomons, Bugotu said, was that those being neo-colonized took the colonizing "Other" as their role model and their reality. They internalized this role model and reality, he said, and they followed its prescriptions to the point of eschewing true freedom for themselves (Bugotu, 1973, p. 78). He concluded: " ... I feel strongly that the dramatic and abrupt realization of prestige and power in high places ... has caused the creation of a native elite instilled with false confidence and a 'know it best' attitude, mysteriously caged behind alien ideas, values, goals and visions. It is we the White Melanesians of Honiara who are confused. Our visions use the urban setting as the norm and we greatly delude ourselves that the rest of the Solomons want to be like us when they do not. We misinterpret the wishes of the people who are in the main village dwellers, and we desire high praise for the misrepresentations" (Bugotu, 1973, p. 79).

Bugotu saw African parallels in this regard. In a number of African countries, members of the local elite, who had been educated in

Europe, had become alienated from village life. In the people's name they had become "landowners, businessmen, civil servants or politicians ...". Wittingly or unwittingly they had become exploiters, only to be exploited in turn by foreigners who did not have their country's interests at heart (Bugotu, 1973, p. 79).

Bugotu called on his fellow citizens to become aware of the issue of contending realities by changing "from the inside". He called on them to confront any image put there by others (Bugotu, 1973, p. 78). The problems may be global, he said, but they first had to be addressed locally, that is, "from within". The problem of oppression, he said, had to be solved by the oppressed accepting that fact and then transforming it (Bugotu, 1973, p. 79). For example, Bugotu called on Solomon Islanders to see underdevelopment as an artifact of colonialism since it had not occurred because of what locals had done. After compromising the best that communal/traditional life had to offer, the colonialists had proceeded to add insult to injury. Their development strategies had promised progress but in practice had remained a dream. At worst, they had become the purveyors of an exploitative nightmare (Bugotu, 1973, p. 80).

No wonder Bugotu told Solomon Islanders to "look to themselves and the past" to find the requisite sense of reality and for strengths that the colonizers themselves seemed to have lost, that is, "for wisdom and values men everywhere seem to be seeking ..." (Bugotu, 1973, p. 80). No wonder he saw the world system in predatory terms and the way forward for the Solomons as requiring the capacity to look backwards, not in a negative sense but in a positive sense, that is, in such a way as to build for the present using resources harvested from the past. For Bugotu, in short, the dominant sense of reality in the Solomon Islands was still a colonized one. Colonialism had come to an end in principle but was still extant in practice.

Bugotu's reading of reality is by now a very well-articulated one. Linda Tuhiwai Smith talks in the same terms of research as inextricably linked to the sense of what is real and as defined by Euro-American imperialists and neo-colonialists. What annoys her most is the way Euro-American researchers and intellectuals "... assume to know all that it is possible to know of us, on the basis of their brief encounters with some of us" (Smith, 1999, p. 1). This is why Smith sees research itself as a "significant site of struggle" between Euro-American reality and interests and local reality and interests (Smith, 1999, p. 2).

Smith recognizes that for local peoples in the Pacific, reality is a neo-colonized one. This is accompanied by widespread poverty that, like these people's status, is not of their choosing. It is the result of forms of oppression, she says, that the oppressors justify in terms of what local peoples are told is their indolence, their ignorance, and their lack of "'higher' order human qualities" (Smith, 1999, p. 4).

Smith is a New Zealander/Aotearoan/Maori. As such, she says that to resist colonization is to "... remake ourselves. The past, our stories local and global, the present, our communities, cultures, languages and social practices — all may be spaces of marginalization ..." (Smith, 1999, p. 4).

Speaking in more abstract terms, Smith also says that discussing "*research methodology* and *indigenous peoples* together ..." means understanding the "complex ways in which the pursuit of knowledge" is "deeply embedded in the multiple layers of imperial and colonial practices" (Smith, 1999, p. 2). For each local intellectual who "succeeds in the academy ...", that is, there is a raft of issues about how they relate within and without their communities, within and without academia, and between these two very diverse realms (Smith, 1999, p. 14).

In the light of the above, Smith calls post-colonialism a "convenient invention" by modernist/rationalist analysts who want to retain the power to define the global reality and to co-opt what local academics have to say whilst continuing to leave out local peoples themselves. This suggests a reluctance to be identified with the concept. However, she does subsequently go on to describe her work from the same radically detached perspective and one that ostensibly includes the concept of post-colonialism. Smith is an accomplished epistemologist, after all, who, like Bugotu, moves between two primary realities with consummate ease (Smith, 1999, pp. 24, 28).

Smith goes on to look at the cultural foundations of imperial research, at the dichotomy it creates between the individual and society, and at the ideas it fosters of time and space. She then looks at the Enlightenment project and the way it is used to establish the "positional superiority" of Euro-American knowledge; the way, for example, it is used to structure local ways of knowing through the development of academic disciplines and the education of colonial elites (Smith, 1999, p. 59). She follows this with an account of some of the more informal ways in which information is collected about local societies and how it is "formally constituted" within a colonial context (Smith, 1999, p. 79). As she sees it, the result is local societies living under post-colonial conditions, that is, societies that, though ostensibly globalized and post-imperial, remain examples of "tribal development" (Smith, 1999, p. 97). Despite much having changed, that is, there is still a "fundamental clash" between Euro-American and local peoples, though not as the former construe it, since the contemporary "language of imperialism" divides the global population into a North and a South. "Territories are called markets ... prospectors mine for genetic diversity ... [f]ood is packed up and sold as Mc-something ... [t]elevision beams in live from America [and] ... imperial armies assemble under the authority of the United Nations defending the principles of freedom, democracy and the rights of capital" (Smith, 1999, pp. 97, 98, 99). Imperialism still works, in other words, to expropriate local resources — material, mental, emotional, cultural, and spiritual. At the same time, it still works to impose foreign ones (Smith, 1999, pp. 100–103). And while local peoples contest these hegemonic conceptions of global reality, and while Smith's work and that of the other authors cited above are evidence in themselves of politico-cultural resistance, the global reality remains an imperial one.

Opposition by local peoples makes more clear the hegemonic role modernist rationalism plays in underpinning contemporary world affairs and the dominance modernism therefore enjoys apropos traditionalism. The strength of modernist rationalism as a way of accounting for contemporary reality lies in the way it allows its practitioners to look back at the world, and at local peoples in the world, in an objectifying manner. It helps them to see the pattern the forest makes, lifting them above the complexities of the forest floor. At the same time, as Solomon Islanders are only too aware, its weakness lies in the way it limits and distorts a comprehensive understanding of what is real. They know that to compensate for the detached perspective of the Euro-American post-colonialist, it is necessary for the latter to get close and listen. If the research is not being done by someone local, that entails the researcher either accepting a mentor from the society being studied or seeking a lifelong relationship with that society extending well beyond the realms of the particular project — one that asks what the society wants to know and that tries to provide the appropriate answers (Smith, 1999, p. 177).

Opposition by local peoples also makes more clear how reducing what is rationalist and traditionalist to a cultural dichotomy occludes the extent to which both change. For example, modernist practices have become traditionalist ones to such an extent that local concepts like compensation have to be seen in the light of the country's imperial experience as well as the influence of Christianity and what Solomon Islanders have learned working for foreign companies. This is not to ignore the "existence or significance of Melanesian custom …". Rather, it is to highlight its "socially constituted nature …". And as with any social construct, it is "contested" at the same time as it is "regularly invoked" to legitimize a wide range of "often-conflicting political ends" (Hameiri, 2007, p. 419).

To highlight the difference between the reality that writers like Bugotu and Smith document and the reality promoted in the Euro-American world, it is necessary to do no more than consider the account of the Solomon Islands provided by the *Lonely Planet* guide. Here, Euro-American travelers are deemed to be getting close to listen and take part in what for them is a non-modernist culture. However, their listening is typically dominated by an inner monologue about what such travel means. As a result, taking part is often done so ineptly that it results in them moving past the locals rather than in meeting them in a meaningful way.

For example, the Solomon Islands is depicted in this guidebook as one of the "last South Pacific frontiers" and, as such, as likely to appeal to those who want to get off the "beaten path", particularly since in this part of the world it says that "there is no beaten path …". Indeed, it says that this part of the world feels like the "world's end".

Outside the capital, on the largest island, Guadalcanal, the country is said to have the "genuine look of a lost world". Meanwhile, some of the inhabitants of adjacent Malaita are said to "still worship ancestral spirits" (McKinnon, Carillet and Starnes, 2008, pp. 246–247, 274).

For those who inhabit the Solomon Islands, their country is no frontier. They are at the center of the world. The global frontier is somewhere else. Reality in their terms is the "beaten path" that goes from one village to another, by land or by canoe. For most Solomon Islanders, the village is the hub of human life while the paths that Euro-Americans tread are completely peripheral.

A guidebook like this is Euro-American post-colonial paternalism at its most offensive. It is commodified prose designed for sale to Euro-Americans, many of whom will do no more than travel by arm-chair. Those who do visit the Solomon Islands will often experience no more than the picturesque, or what to them is colorful and bizarre.

For example, a description of the "traditional 'bush'" people of Malaita, namely, the Kwaio, highlights how unmarried girls and women wear no clothes, while married women wear miniscule "T-pieces". Is this any more in the way of an "alternative universe" than a Euro-American nudist colony? Is there much difference between sartorial expectations among the Kwaio and those to be found among Brazilians on Copacabana beach? And as for worshipping ancestral spirits, during the Bon-time festival in Japan, the whole population practices precisely the same relationship with dead relatives. However, few would see Japan as being off the beaten path, or as a tourist frontier, or as a radically alternative politico-cultural universe with a commensurate simplicity capable of reducing Euro-Americans to tears.

This said, the guidebook does provide a brief account of early contact between Solomon Islanders and Euro-Americans that highlights the exploitative intentions of the explorers and settlers. A chapter on Melanesian culture also highlights the significance of what is a subsistence-based, village-centered clan or *wantok* system, and the speed with which local societies have been obliged to change in the face of large mining, logging and fishing companies and copra and palm oil plantations. The guidebook's authors and editors are well aware of the costs of contact with the outside world and how the clan system is basically an "egalitarian way for the community to share ... in rapidly changing circumstances ...". They are also well aware that these ideas become "nepotism and, at worst, corruption. In the public service, the police, the army and especially in politics [and the economy], this is a scourge ...". As such, McKinnon, Carillet and Starnes see it as a "microcosm" of the "battle [currently] being waged between the modern and the traditional ...", by which they mean the battle currently being waged between modernity and non-modernity, given that what is modern is what is contemporaneous and what is contemporaneous is both modernist and non-modernist (McKinnon, Carillet and Starnes, 2008, p. 37).

Though these sections are less offensive than the Indiana Jones-style depiction of the Solomon Islands provided elsewhere, the idea of the country that the guide promotes is highly problematic. This is hardly surprising since the view of reality it articulates is one that is particular to a Melbournian, a Parisian and an Aucklander. None of the authors are Solomon Islanders. None of them were born and raised there. None of them are permanently resident there. Once a local perspective is provided of the same events and issues, this becomes immediately apparent.

The Solomon Islands: Competing conceptions of the politico-strategic reality

The Solomon Islands became independent in July 1978. In 1981 the country went on to adopt a system of government that fell short of federalism but acknowledged the existence of a number of provinces. This recognized the nation's diversity and made allowance to some extent for it in the way the government worked, though it fell far short of a functioning Euro-American-style state.

From a Euro-American perspective, the reality of independence was manifest in the way one more administrative unit of the British empire had gained sovereign status. By becoming formally independent the Solomons had become autonomous, had joined the global state-system, and was recognized by other sovereign states as having done so. Modernist rationalism is most commonly articulated in politico-strategic terms using the discourse of state-centric "realism". This discourse highlights what it sees as the self-evident fact that the state-system is ungoverned. "Realists" subsequently charge state-makers with the duty to adopt policies that promote self-help. They also charge state-makers with the duty to foster their legitimacy by promoting a state-centric sense of national identity. From a Euro-American perspective, "realism" and its cognate discourse "nationalism" were the main ways to see the new Solomons state.

From a local perspective, however, the reality of Solomons independence was marked most notably by the country's ethnic pluralism and the challenge this presented to state coherence. Ethnically diverse states face not only an anarchic world system but also domestic cultural and social diversity. The latter can preempt any attempt to keep the state together. In an assessment of this attempt ten years after independence, then prime minister Ezekiel Alebua noted how a "lot of people from the provinces" were sharing in the celebrations (Alebua, 1992, p. 26). He deliberately tried to strike an optimistic note even though he was well aware of the problems Solomon Islanders faced in keeping such a wide range of locally-oriented peoples committed to the concept of a Solomons nation-state. His optimism proved ill-founded. Even Euro-Americans said that their institutions provided an "ill-fitting overlay" to the traditional structures underneath. As such, they were well aware that the Solomons "state" was never a "properly functioning" one (Wainwright, 2003, p. 488).

The issue of domestic pluralism came to a head in the late 1990s with what was called a "low-intensity civil war" (Barlow, 2002, p. 442) between two different groups, whose ethnic identities were actually relatively recent ones being a consequence of "colonialism and post-colonial development and migration" (Fry, 2000, p. 300), but who were at odds anyway. In order to benefit from the opportunities and the resources that the capital had to offer, people from Malaita had been moving to Guadalcanal since Honiara had been designated as such after World War Two. This prompted resistance from the Guale people who traditionally owned the land where most people from Malaita settled. Several issues were involved including demands for compensation. Eventually, armed militia began attacking settlers. This prompted an armed response in return. The situation was exacerbated by the fact that the police, who were mainly from Malaita, had access to the state armory. Honiara subsequently fell under Malaitan control, though an estimated 20,000 Malaitans fled back to their island to escape the depredations of the local militia that ringed the capital. Meanwhile, many people from Guadalcanal moved to the countryside.

The resulting reality, defined in Euro-American terms, was that of a "failed state", though the term was first said to have been used in this context in the *Solomon Star* by an American-born Solomon Islander, John Roughan (Kabutaulaka, 2005, pp. 295–297; Wainwright, 2003, pp. 485–486; Warner, 2004; McDougall, 2004; Moore, 2007; Hameiri, 2007; Dinnen, 2008). The phenomenon had heretofore been seen as largely an African one. The collapse of law and order, of social services, and subsequently of the standard of living, was seen as mostly characteristic of states like Somalia, Liberia, the Democratic Republic of the Congo and the Sudan, though the dis-integration of Yugoslavia had made it a European one as well. The discourse of state failure was accompanied by a discourse to do with transnational crime of various kinds. Unsupervised borders were seen as an open invitation to those involved in a range of nefarious activities to conduct them without sovereign state supervision. This included terrorist activities. After the attack on New York in September 2001 and the bombings in Bali in October 2002, Euro-American perceptions of the security environment radically changed and regional concerns with regard to the integrity of the Solomons state have to be seen in this light (Wainwright, 2003, p. 486; Kabutaulaka, 2005, p. 291).

Though the Solomon Islands had not yet failed, it was deemed in Euro-American terms to be in the process of failing. In June 2000 the Solomon Islands police, together with the Malaitan militia, staged a coup that ousted the prime minister Bartholomew Ulufa'alu (himself a Malaitan). Subsequent talks in Townsville resulted in a peace agreement and the intervention of a monitoring team, but this team did not achieve disarmament and was not able to effect reconciliation. The subsequent political chaos caused the economy to decline. Major industries on Guadalcanal like the Gold Ridge gold mine and the Solomon Island Plantation Limited were closed. State services, such as schools and medical facilities, were brought to a standstill, not only in urban areas but in rural ones as well.

In June 2003 the Australian government, after having ignored repeated earlier pleas to intervene, finally responded to a local prime ministerial request to lead a mission to the Solomon Islands to disarm the various gangs that had brought the country "to its knees" (Warner, 2004, p. 1). Once the Australians had gained the support of the Pacific Islands Forum and once the relevant legislation had been passed by the Solomon Islands parliament, they met with the foreign ministers of the former to get their collective endorsement. They subsequently mounted an armed intervention together with forces from New Zealand, Fiji, Papua New Guinea, Tonga, Samoa, Vanuatu, Kiribati and the Cook Islands. This was the Regional Assistance Mission to Solomon Islands (RAMSI), or, as it was called in *Pijin* English, Operation *Helpem Fren* ("helping the government and the people to help themselves"). The Australians not only wanted to pre-empt the consequences of state failure; they also wanted to deny any other power, such as Indonesia, the opportunity to do so in their stead (Kabutaulaka, 2005, p. 291). By intervening, they were acutely aware of not wanting to present as a neo-colonial power, hence the care they took to assemble a collective response that had local, regional, US and United Nations endorsement. They also knew that once committed to intervention, it was going to be a long-term task reconstructing a Euro-American-style state that was tenuous at best. Regardless of their intentions, this commitment did become a neo-colonial one.

From the Euro-American view of the realities of intervention, the short-term objectives were rapidly met (Joint Standing Committee on Foreign Affairs, Defence and Trade, 2004). A personal protection program was put in place to prevent another coup. A nationwide amnesty resulted in the recovery of a large number of weapons. A key secessionist leader from Guadalcanal's southern coast, Harold Keke, was persuaded to surrender and face the courts, which subsequently gaoled him for life for murders committed by him and his men. Other militants who had conducted violent crimes were arrested and tried. The Solomon Islands police force was purged and a new, merit-based system of recruitment was put in place (Warner, 2004). Indeed, the whole intervention operation was seen as a political "circuit-breaker". It was seen as one that the majority of Solomon Islanders themselves had wanted and as the only chance the country had to turn its fortunes around (Wainwright, 2003, p. 493).

From the Euro-American view of the realities of the intervention, the long-term objectives were not so readily met. The feud that had brought Solomons' state- and nation-making to a halt involved governance and development issues that were not easily addressed since they involved meeting the educational, health and employment needs of a rapidly expanding population and rebuilding institutional capacities radically compromised by the difference between pre-modernist or "traditionalist" values and modernist or "rationalist" ones. This was generally acknowledged to be a significant challenge, particularly given the extent to which the state had become the instrument of pre-modernist practices like that of customary "compensation" (McDougall, 2004, p. 214; Hameiri, 2007, p. 411; Dinnen, 2002, p. 289) and the extent to which comparing state weakness in the Solomons — or, indeed, anywhere — with abstract ideas of what strength might entail was arguably not apt (Larmour, 1998, p. 92).

What of the local notion of reality, though? What was the Solomons reality in this regard?

Not surprisingly, one reviewer of a Euro-American account of events (Fraenkel, 2004) felt "highly dissatisfied with the 'foreign-ness' of it all — or, put differently, frustrated with the almost complete lack of indigenous voices. One longs", the reviewer said, "to hear through first-hand interviews what any leading player believed he was trying to do then, and what now, with the benefit of hindsight, he believes actually happened on the ground … Can an account [such as Fraenkel's] really be judged as history, or even as a historical record, without the local people themselves being center stage?" In short: "Whose history is it?" (Richards, 2006, p. 443).

Another analysis of the same period was deemed to be superior since its author, Clive Moore (Moore, 2004), though not a Solomon Islander, was said to have a "much deeper" understanding than Fraenkel's; however, he provided "few interviews" with locals, either (Richards, 2006, p. 443). Nor did he do more than make a passing reference to the "exhausted people of Honiara" who gave the intervention forces a "rapturous welcome". Thus, Moore's study remains that of an "outsider looking in", while the "indigenous history, or rather the indigenous histories, of the crisis ... have yet to be published" (Richards, 2006, p. 444).

At the time of the intervention, there was an ongoing exchange between expatriate Solomon Islanders on an e-mail site called "Iu-Mi-Nao" or "It's Up To Us To Do It! And Now!" about the unfolding events. As Richards observes: "[w]ith further in-depth interviewing of the real participants while they are still alive, the accumulated postings of that e-mail chat group [if they have been stored anywhere] could yet provide something more like a view from the inside" (Richards, 2006, p. 444).

The Solomon Islands view of the reality of the crisis can also be gleaned from subsequent accounts by local academics such as Tarcisius Kabutaulaka. Commentators like these vividly document the culture of violence that prevailed at the time and the way politicians, police and public servants extorted large sums from the government in the form of customary compensation (Kabutaulaka, 2005, p. 292).

They make the key point that a sustainable peace was possible, given the pluralism of a state like the Solomons, only if both state and non-state entities were taken into account and strengthened. They also highlight the need for RAMSI not to create relationships of inter-state dependency (Kabutaulaka, 2005, p. 284).

Kabutaulaka refers in the first instance to the network of "churches, nongovernmental organizations, traditional political organizations and leaders, and 'special interest' groups such as women's and youth organizations" that the Solomons state has always worked with (Kabutaulaka, 2005, p. 299). As he comments elsewhere: "... my spirit is always lifted by the general sense of optimism among Solomon Islanders, however cautious they might be. It is always great to see people gather, chew betel nut, reflect on what has happened, and map ways forward. At all levels of society, people are working to heal the wounds of the social unrest. This optimism and work in mending relationships and rebuilding communities must be identified and nurtured by those wanting to help ..." (Kabutaulaka, 2006, p. 429).

He refers in the second instance to the large number of Australians in the police and justice, finance and customs and excise departments, and the extent to which the Solomons was placed under direct control from Canberra (Kabutaulaka, 2005, p. 299; Morgan and McLeod, 2006, p. 424). The post-crisis period was also marked by an influx of aid money, he says. This came from the World Bank and the International Monetary Fund as well as from the Asian Development Bank, the European Union and countries like the United Kingdom, Australia, New Zealand, Taiwan and Japan. All of these donors set conditions that were in effect neo-imperial ones, thereby carrying on a tradition that extended back to independence. Meeting these conditions, as well as those of the transnational corporations that continued to seek access to the country's timber, fish and plantations, meant a "long-term discount on national autonomy. And this, as it happens, is what is meant by neo-colonialism" (Pettman, 1977, p. 276).

More radically, Kabutaulaka questions whether a Euro-American-style concept of the state was one that was potentially commensurate with a Solomons nation anyway. It might be able to provide law and order and basic goods and services, but could it, he asks, create a viable nation? Could it do more than make for "band-aid" difference? Was the Euro-American notion that the diversity of the Solomons was a liability a way of not acknowledging this very diversity as the "rich" and "sustaining" seedbed for new ways to look forward (Bennett, 1987, p. 347)?

Given the events of 2006, when serious riots occurred in Honiara because of dissatisfaction with the results of the election of the prime minister (Dinnen and Firth, 2008), the emphasis Kabutaulaka places on the need not only to reestablish law and order but to understand the nature of relationships in the Solomon Islands seems to have proved highly prescient. The main issues at that time were not ones to do with whether the courts could deal with the large numbers of cases it still had to process, or the cost of keeping those found guilty in jail, or the difficulties experienced in restoring public confidence and trust, or even the problems presented by the Taiwanese paying money to local politicians to keep the Solomons under their diplomatic wing (Kabutaulaka, 2006, p. 425). They were more to do with the way in which the wrongs were typically "not between two individuals, but between groups … Generally, Solomon Islanders do not see imprisoning one individual as a way of mending basic social relationships" (Kabutaulaka, 2005, p. 3001). They were also to do with how Solomon Island voters were largely not interested in "overarching policies". They sought "immediate returns for their support, in the form of money, materials and employment opportunities …". For Solomon Island parliamentarians, therefore, the challenge was that of meeting the "immediate demands of constituents …". This was more significant than meeting "long-term goals … It is for these reasons that Solomon Islands politics … are commonly more about patronage than participation …" (Morgan and McLeod, 2006, p. 417). Most fundamentally of all, the riots were to do with the way the Westminster system works by encouraging histrionics and antagonism rather than consensus and how it is built on a first-past-the-post electoral system that can result in a government being voted in by a minority while assuming — erroneously in the case of the Solomons — that those elected will represent all (Kabutaulaka, 2008; see also Timmer, 2008, p. 207).

The riots targeted local Chinese traders, who had long constituted an enclave community whose members benefited from a range of capitalist activities. More recent Chinese emigrants were the most resented and the ones whose businesses were attacked, though locals had long harbored suspicions that Asian businessmen purchased electoral influence and helped corrupt in the process the local fishing and logging industries (Moore, 2008). The riots were certainly compelling evidence of RAMSI's failure to read the local scene.

In conclusion, Kabutaulaka highlights the difference between Australia's "failed state" discourse and its ostensible desire to build a viable state as opposed to the local emphasis on the quality of its leadership (Kabutaulaka, 2005, p. 301). A number of key Solomon Island commentators, he says, agreed that the problem with the Solomons was its poor leaders and that this issue was not one outsiders were likely to be able to address. Key Solomon Island analysts felt that the crisis was mostly to do with not having high-caliber leaders capable of carrying out their official duties honestly and a culture of leadership that made this mandatory. They also felt that only Solomon Islanders could successfully deal with a problem of this kind.

The distinction in this regard between the Australian view of the Solomon Islands reality and the Solomon Islands view of the Solomon Islands reality is marked, though one of the best informed of the Euro-American commentators does not subscribe to this distinction. A decade ago Bennett said that "[a]t the root [of the crisis that led to intervention …]" was the "irresponsible performance" of post-imperial governments and the way leaders set a "poor example of the use of power and undermined the qualified confidence the people had in the state" (Bennett, 2000, p. 383). This is consistent with a comment made by one of Kabutaulaka's erstwhile critics, namely, that the Solomon Islands conflict was not a crisis of governance but was best explained by the "growing marginalization of key interests" resulting from a range of "systemic" challenges to the "complex and dense patronage networks that hitherto worked to mitigate the effects of highly uneven economic development" (Hameiri, 2007, p. 413). From this perspective, RAMSI reinforced conflict and created tensions. It did not mitigate conflict or alleviate tensions.

In the longer term, that is, RAMSI's intervention was radically at odds with a view of reality that understood the "real risk" in the Solomons as being one of "rebuilding the very same institutions whose shortcomings led to the crisis that provoked … intervention in the first place" (Dinnen, 2008, p. 354). In imposing a Euro-American view of what success meant, RAMSI found the Solomons wanting. However, it failed to look at the Solomons in terms of what the locals themselves considered rational and reasonable in terms of what success meant.

RAMSI came to see the country as "irrational or pathological" (Dinnen, 2008, p. 354), particularly with regard to how pervasive the system of patronage happened to be. This became a core question given how those Solomon Islanders who did not help their fellow clan or kin were not liable to receive help when they needed it and even faced "social exclusion" or "sorcery" (Morgan and McLeod, 2006, p. 423).

This is significant since, as Bennett points out, "[w]here claims are acknowledged by clan and village, no Solomon Islander [is] denied garden land and the means to subsistence. The village still represents life and livelihood" (Bennett, 1987, p. 341).

The Solomon Islands: Competing conceptions of the politico-economic reality

In the same speech Prime Minister Alebua made to mark the tenth year of Solomon Islands independence that was cited above, he noted that the country had been bequeathed an open-market economy. He also noted that the country had been insufficiently nationalistic in economic terms. He said that it had left itself much too open to market forces and as a consequence had reached the point where it had little say in its material future. It had therefore become victim of a "general [economic] malaise" (Alebua, 1992, p. 27). He recommended a mercantilist strategy designed to reduce food imports and to supply the people with home-grown agricultural produce. He also recommended the domestic production of other goods the country required such as clothing and housing materials. The Solomons had become too dependent on other countries' exports, he said (Alebua, 1992, p. 31).

This view of the reality of the Solomons situation was one reinforced a decade later by analysts like Shahar Hameiri who saw it in terms of the way politico-economic power was occluded by Euro-American-style images of "state" and "society". Thus: "… rather than attempting to explain diverging social and political outcomes with ahistorical and unchanging terms like modern and tradition", Hameiri said, "we must apply a political economy perspective to explain the changing contours of state power in [the] Solomon Islands and the sort of conflicts that are likely to emerge" (Hameiri, 2007, p. 420).

Political economy is a modernist discourse that sees the world in competitive (economic nationalist), calculative (economic liberalist) and cooperative (economic socialist) terms. Critically, the above is the sort of discourse that highlights the global spread of capitalism and the class structures that capitalism creates (marxism and neo-marxism).

The dominant discourse of the current day is an exaggerated form of economic liberalism. It promotes the prevention of unbalanced budgets and the avoidance of large fiscal deficits; the reduction of state expenditure rather than increases in state revenue; the reduction of public subsidies, education and health expenditure and of public infrastructure investment; the broadening of the tax base and the reduction of marginal tax rates; the determination of interest rates by markets, not bureaucrats (who are supposed at the same time to discourage capital flight and increase savings — not easy under crisis conditions); the determination of exchange rates by market forces; greater import liberalization; more liberal foreign financial flows as well as more privatized commerce and industry; more deregulation; and more secure property rights (Williamson, 1991).

Economic liberalism has its roots in colonial times; indeed, it goes back to Adam Smith and his germinal discussion of the *Wealth of Nations* (1993 [1776]). Consistent with this doctrine, the first British commissioner for the Solomon Islands, Charles Woodford, saw the land and its resources as there for anyone able to exploit them. Land not used was deemed vacant despite any ancestral claims the locals might have to them. The forests, meanwhile, were only deemed fit to be razed and replaced with coconut plantations (Barlow, 2002, p. 245).

Economic liberalism was reinforced by the events of the Second World War and those that followed it. Not only were forests destroyed by fighting, but they were also destroyed by the logging that was carried out by both the Americans and the Japanese. At the same time, World War Two caused many Solomon Islanders to become less deferential to the colonial British (Barlow, 2002, p. 246).

Independence heightened the conflict between the central government's sense that forest resources fell within its purview and the assumption by locals that the forests were theirs. This conflict became more acute when foreign logging companies began bypassing the government to negotiate directly with local owners. Central government reliance on the income from forests to pay for its activities was directly jeopardized by this move.

The story of the struggle for control of the Solomon Island forests is a protracted and complex one (Frazer, 1997; Bennett, 2000). Crocombe says that confidential files show how "secret payments … to three cabinet ministers and senior officials … in cash, liquor, overseas trips, vehicles, restaurant charge-accounts, fictitious payments as directors" won loggers lucrative access rights and tax exemptions. These payments were not unusual (Crocombe, 2008, pp. 481–482).

As Barlow argues, however, following Bennett: "… Solomon Islanders should not be villainized [for selling their birthright] … [R]ural people have few viable alternatives for making their way into the modern economy", while "[s]hrinking forests and populations pressure are now forcing [a] reevaluation of resource exploitation and conservation" (Barlow, 2002, p. 247).

Economic liberalism continues to inform official analyses of the Solomon Islands' economy. Consider, for example, the report by the Economic Analytical Unit of the Australian Department of Foreign Affairs and Trade following the RAMSI intervention. This concludes that priority should be afforded "new private sector investment" and the attempt to gain a "competitive advantage" in a "globalised world". It also recommends reducing the public sector wage bill, removing regulatory barriers to income-earning activities and employment, privatizing state-owned enterprises, and directly addressing the issue of resource depletion and land tenure reform. Only liberalist policies like these it deems to be economically "sound" (Economic Analytical Unit, 2004, pp. 133–136). Built into this discourse is the notion that it is the only way to promote economic growth and that the benefits of such growth will "trickle-down" to the population at large. The uncritical acceptance of the need to make foreign investment and governmental outlays as small as possible continues to be seen as more advantageous than either economic nationalism or socialist planning.

Economic liberalism says nothing about Solomon Islanders having "gone berserk" over logging because of what they perceive as "easy money", however, and a mania fuelled "largely by the lavish way in which Asian logging companies bribe, cajole and [seek] unduly influence". It also says nothing about logging-led corruption extending up into the "highest echelons of government", while extending at the same time down to the "common man in the street" (Aqorau, 2008, pp. 247, 251).

While the Euro-American reality in this regard is that of neo-marxist dependency or populist post-development or participatory reflexivity (Pieterse, 1998), the local reality is much more graphic. It is also much more immediate.

The local reality initially involves subsistence, since an estimated 85% of Solomon Islanders still live by gardening and fishing. This reality has its own indigenous epistemology, which has been documented by one of the few studies to examine what development means in this context. This study notes how village communities have highly pragmatic knowledge resources. It also describes what happens when local entrepreneurs co-opt these resources (Gegeo and Watson-Gegeo, 2002).

The local reality can also involve foreign entrepreneurs, however. This reality is likely to be very different. Consider, for example, part of a poem by Jules Makini, which he entitles the "Greased Dinner": "Last night I was treated like a king/at a business dinner/Never before had I been treated thus/Along with ten of my wantoks/we who had never entered any hotel/were wined and dined at the Gizo Hotel/I sat with a roomful of strangers,/the table-littered with plates,/glasses on thin legs, ashtrays,/two sticks to use instead of fingers,/and handkerchiefs to blow my nose/with …". As Makini concludes: "The Roviana Bamboo Band/made too much noise [but]/I heard 'royalty', … 'timber rights' …/'roads, … clinics, … schools …'/but through stuffy ears and blurry eyes./Anyway we'd already talked it over in/the village/Our politician and lawyer were present/so I didn't have to read the 'small print'/I signed./zzzzzzzzzzzzzzzzzzzzzzzz/" (Bennett, 2000, p. 296; see also McDonald, 2003, pp. 20–21).

The Solomon Islands: Competing conceptions of the politico-social reality

The Euro-American reality in this regard is one where the attempt to reproduce Euro-American institutions in the local context predominates, particularly in the form of nationalism, and where kin or clan obligations are seen as distorting these attempts. It is one where the Euro-American penchant for modernist state-making in general and democratic state-making in particular is projected onto the world as the doctrine that should be globally preferred. It is one that promotes the Euro-American penchant for economic liberalism as the doctrine new states should accept as the most compelling way to become wealthy and stable. It is also one that highlights how "modernized" comprador classes emerge as prominent local families create networks of influence and obligation throughout the structure of the new government and its administration. The Euro-American sense of what is happening in the Solomons does not deny the dangers of it being neo-colonized by aid donors that want to know what their money is being spent on and by foreign corporations that want access to resources like timber, palm oil, gold and fish. RAMSI with its neo-liberalist agenda exacerbates both, however, not least because of the way it dismantles local patronage relationships without building a robust capacity for national leadership in their stead.

The local reality in this regard is more complex. It is one where social change does not necessarily work against local ways of behaving. It is one where social change results in "new particularisms" that fragment further a polity that is already highly fragmented. This in turn can reinforce the elite character of local politics and reinforce their factional, personalized and patron-client form (Heeger, 1974, p. 70). "Our perceptual front-yard", in other words, "tends to get overrun by the obvious — by the political machinery and by the legal and administrative structures that ... are in the process of formation; by any incipient process of party-formation [for example]; [and] by the process, even more conspicuous on occasion, of union formation in towns. We lose sight of a critical feature of politics under such conditions, which is their very diffuse and amorphous character" (Pettman, 1977, p. 273). In the local capital, institutions are in practice little more than shifting coalitions. In the rural hinterland, institutions are similar, though access to the state system and the potential it provides for elites to disperse patronage is usually more limited. The key point is that in local terms, "personalism" is so pervasive that it results in a political system not just "uninstitutionalized" but one that is actively "hostile to institutionalization" (Heeger, 1974, p. 70). It is one where patronage is not a matter of traditionalism versus modernism, but a matter of "coalition making in a context of limited … economic development, which is reliant [in turn] on foreign-owned, resource-intensive, and migrant labor-dependent export industries, in a geographically and ethnically fragmented country" (Hameiri, 2007, p. 422).

Conclusion

The concept of reality, like the concept of truth, is a Grail that modernists reach for in the terms that their modernism allows. This means that they reach for an understanding of what is real using the epistemological and ontological assumptions that underpin modernist rationalism.

This makes for a relatively detached and impartial account of what is real. It does not make for an absolutely detached and impartial account of what is real, however, since that would only be available to someone endowed with divine luminous wisdom. Very few have that. It does allow for a relatively objectified account of the world, though, as well as one that is centered on a version of the self that is relatively socially individuated and relatively culturally alienated.

Modernism is articulated in a range of ways that depend on the dimension to world affairs being discussed, the assumption about human nature being made, or the assumption about the essential nature of human nurturing practices being made. This provides a range of analytical languages that can be used to describe and explain (and prescribe policy for) a country like the Solomon Islands.

This concept of reality is at odds with that shared by most of those who live in a non-modernist environment like the Solomon Islands one, however. The latter is highly complex. It does not preclude modernist/rationalist understandings, but it does articulate ways of knowing and being in the world that modernism/rationalism mostly eschews.

The issue here is that those deeply embedded in their particular sense of reality, whether modernist or non-modernist, tend to see those who are not so embedded as psychopathological. A committed economic neo-liberalist, for example, will tend to see a committed neo-marxist as not just ideologically misguided or as simply articulating a different assumption about human nature or nurturing practices, but as actually insane. More radically, a modernist/rationalist will tend to see a committed non-modernist, for example, a committed sacralist such as a Buddhist or a Muslim, as psychopathologically challenged as well, not just as someone articulating a different epistemology, ontology and axiology.

There are, to be sure, individuals and whole societies that do lose touch with reality, for a short time or a long one. These individuals and societies are deemed to be neurotic or psychotic. Though there is no objective and agreed measure of what constitutes psychosis in such cases, it is generally agreed that it is possible to characterize individuals and societies in this way. This is psychopathology of a medical kind and it is the somewhat un-envious role of psychiatrists in particular to diagnose and treat individuals and societies who manifest such symptoms.

There are also individuals and societies that are in touch with a particular kind of psychological reality that has them constructing the world in a discourse-specific way that can seem psychopathological but is more to do with the choice they have made about what human nature is, or what the nature of human nurturing practices might be. They practice politics accordingly with the result that their view of the world is distorted to fit their discourse. This is not psychosis, though it can look like it. This said, persuading someone otherwise who thinks that neo-liberalism really is the politico-economic ideology the world should prefer can be as difficult, if not more difficult, than persuading someone who thinks they really are Santa Claus that they are not.

In the analysis above, ideas in the Solomon Islands were compared with those elsewhere to explore how psychological realities can differ from each other in this way. In the process, the modernist culture that underpins contemporary world affairs was compared with the non-modernist culture that still underpins much of the Solomons. Some of the analytical languages used to articulate modernism were also explored to see how they applied inside the Solomon Islands as compared to how they applied outside it.

It was the crisis in the late 1990s and the so-called "cooperative intervention" that heightened the awareness of analysts and practitioners of the different realities involved here (Nanau, 2008). The discourse used to justify the intervention, for example, was exclusively a modernist one. Modernism in turn was articulated in mostly realist and liberalist ways. The realists talked of "failed states" and of the need for law and order. The liberalists talked of the re-invigoration of investor confidence, the re-establishment of governmental finances, and the reconstruction of rational-legal institutions (Nanau, 2008, pp. 150–151).

Those critical, not necessarily of the intervention but of how it was conducted, did so in both modernist and non-modernist terms. They highlighted the shortcomings of the realist approach that intervention represented, how the whole episode was dominated by Australia, and how it threatened Solomon Islands' sovereignty by failing to build up local institutions. They highlighted how foreign donors disbursed funds in distorted ways, how Australia protected expatriates and a host of foreign advisors, how it collaborated with local leaders and sanctioned illegal activities, indeed, how it worked within a whole system that was not only corrupt but did not have the military reach it claimed to have and failed to bring to justice enough of the major players (Nanau, 2008, pp. 151–158).

Those articulating the dominant discourse saw any other perspective as not only misinformed but potentially insane. It took some time for local analysts to begin to articulate other insights capable of putting the dominant one in context and providing alternatives that could not be readily dismissed as psychopathological.

Conclusion

The most obvious way to talk about psychopathology and world politics is to review all of the mental maladies listed in a comprehensive account of them, like the DSM-IV, and to explore their relevance to global affairs (DSM-IV, 1994). It is to look at all the ways in which the brain/mind is said to malfunction and the effects such malfunctioning can have on how international relations works.

The DSM-IV lists a wide range of psychological disorders. These include the various forms of insanity characterized by symptoms such as poor acculturation, poor communication, maladjustment and bereavement.

It also lists a wide range of organic disorders. These include the various forms of insanity characterized by symptoms such as substance abuse, autism, dementia and schizophrenia.

The difference between psychological and organic disorders is entirely artificial in that all psychopathology is brain-based and therefore organic. All psychopathological conditions are manifest in terms of how the brain functions as a neuro-physiological and neuro-chemical whole. They are all also potentially treatable in these terms. For example, oestrogen is used to try and reduce the delusions that can accompany schizophrenia and electro-convulsive shock therapy is used to treat depression.

Nonetheless, like the nature/nurture dichotomy, the difference between brain-states and mind-states remains meaningful. This is so much so that the emergent properties of the brain that are the mind can not only be seen as different from the brain, but they can also be seen as working back upon the brain, changing and even determining how the brain works. Likewise, a traumatized brain can be seen as compromising the mind, rendering its properties a pale shadow of what they might otherwise be. This has implications not only for psychopathological diagnoses but also for treatment regimes.

As noted above, a comprehensive account of psychopathology and world politics is one that would consider in the first instance each and every psychological and organic disorder listed in a work like the DSM-IV and what it has to say about each and every leader and people that constitutes world affairs. This would be a vast task and one well beyond the scope of a single volume.

Because of the prohibitive scale of such an account, a more modest one is attempted here, though more modest does not mean less informative. While the work above explores only some of the fundamental issues to do with psychopathology and world politics, the ones it does explore seem to be sufficiently suggestive to show why an awareness of the psychopathological underside to rationalistic thinking is necessary to compensate for the limits and distortions of modernist/rationalist thinking in general and modernist/rationalist accounts of world affairs in particular.

The work above begins by looking at how psychopathology might be defined. It then looks, in very general terms, at what the relationship between psychopathology and world politics might be.

What follows is a case study on denial. A complementary account is provided on what in such a context telling the truth might mean.

What follows this is a case study on delusion. A complementary account is provided on what in such a context talking about reality might mean.

A case study on anxiety would have been just as apt, though in this instance a complementary account of how to resolve anxiety would have been called for (Horney, 1939, p. 205). Anxiety is an "emotional response to danger …". Unlike fear, however, it is diffuse, uncertain, and betrays something of a sense of helplessness. It denotes a "horror of the unknown" (Horney, 1939, p. 194). What causes anxiety also depends on the individual or society involved since different individuals and societies feel menaced in different ways. Some threats, like those to survival or status, seem to engender anxiety wherever they exist. Others seem to be more specific to a particular personality or society and to the external and internal issues that people and peoples confront (Horney, 1939, p. 194).

Anxiety is ubiquitous. It might even be necessary in terms of the requirements of natural selection and human survival.

Where anxiety is experienced despite there being no danger or very little danger present, then such a feeling is inappropriate. Where despite there being no or little danger present, such a feeling is extreme and is evidence of neurosis or even psychosis (Horney, 1939, p. 195).

In an anarchic environment like that of the world, a certain level of anxiety would seem to be entirely appropriate. It would seem to be part of the price people pay for living in an ungoverned international system.

Some states, however, seem to be unduly anxious. Consider Australia (Dibb, 2007). Originally a set of British colonies, "Australia" was established by imperial means. The land and its resources were taken from its original inhabitants in a particularly harsh fashion. The settlers/invaders then set about protecting themselves from regional, that is, Southeast and Northeast Asian, "others". A sense of national vulnerability was exacerbated by the Japanese imperial advance in World War Two — an advance that reached Darwin, Sydney and the continent's southern coast. This feeling remains relatively acute for many Australians because of the growth of China's blue-water navy and its submarine fleet. How meaningful is it, however? Is the level of threat that Australia currently faces so low in reality that the anxiety that is palpable in the country represents a neurotic or even a psychotic response? Australia's strategic situation would certainly not seem to warrant the mendicant way it has followed America into wars in Korea, Vietnam, Iraq and Afghanistan. Fearfulness has resulted in an attempt to take out global insurance with the global superpower and the payment of premiums in the form of military and diplomatic support for its various wars. In this regard, Australia's foreign policy would seem to be neurotic at least. Given that the "Asian" threat is still within living memory, it is arguably not psychotic, but given how much the world has changed since World War Two, this is credible too.

A case study on trauma would have been apt as well. In this regard, a complementary account of strategic remembrance, or one to do with reconstituting communities and local healing rituals, would have been called for.

Trauma in psychopathological parlance is used to describe the disorders that result when minds have to cope with organic insult or with what is psychologically simply too much for them. It can characterize individuals, collectives or whole communities.

Except for the most extreme examples of trauma, like those that result from total war, how the psychological form presents itself is culture-specific. This is why it is said that "[b]efore intervening, it is of crucial importance to first assess the ... explanatory models [of those involved], their interpretations of ... past and current events ... and their expectations ...". This can involve little more than asking those affected what they think caused their trauma, why it began when it did, what its symptoms are, how bad they are, what should be done to alleviate them, and what the best outcome might be (Drozdek, 2007, pp. 12, 21).

The above suggests that gaining access to accounts of individual or social trauma is relatively unproblematic. The reality is anything but. Trauma makes active remembering more fraught and selective forgetting more common. Both distort any account of what happened with "imaginary, fragmented or disjointed" elements and symbolic ones as well (Leydesdorff *et al.*, 1999, p. 1). In addition, there is the issue of how applicable the Euro-American idea of trauma might be in non-Euro-American contexts. Because of the modernist assumptions that underpin the Euro-American understanding of trauma, this can make the latter radically inappropriate in non-modernist environments, that is, in non-rationalistic ones (McNally, 2003, p. 283; Culbertson, 2007; deVries, 1996).

Trauma results from both the civil conflicts that abound in world affairs and the international ones that occur there. Given the high incidence of such conflicts, trauma is a common occurrence as well.

Understanding world affairs can be said to require understanding the traumatic consequences of armed conflict. While this is a psychopathological dimension to the discipline that ought to receive analytic attention, it does not receive the discussion it deserves. Any text on world affairs is evidence of this, given how every such text fails to consider trauma in a specific way.

Other case studies present themselves. Indeed, the more psychopathology and world politics is explored, the more examples proliferate of what might be discussed.

As a consequence, this work concludes by reiterating once again how only a beginning has been made here. Hopefully enough has been said, though, to demonstrate the way in which understanding psychopathology adds to an understanding of world politics. Hopefully, too, enough has been said to demonstrate that such an understanding is both abstract and applied.

References

Abrahamsen, David (1976) *Nixon vs. Nixon: An Emotional Tragedy* (Farrar, Straus and Giroux, New York).

Abse, D. Wilfred and Ulman, Richard (1977) "Charismatic political leadership and collective regression" in Robert Robins (ed.) *Psychopathology and Political Leadership* (Tulane University, New Orleans).

Adler, Alfred (1928) *Understanding Human Nature*, trans. Walter Wolfe (Allen and Unwin, London).

Alebua, Ezekiel (1992) "The State of the Nation at Tenth Year of Independence" in Ron Crocombe and Esau Tuza (eds.) *Independence, Dependence, Interdependence: The First 10 Years of Solomon Islands Independence* (Institute of Pacific Studies and the Solomon Islands College of Higher Education, Honiara).

Andrews, Allan *et al.* (1996) *Keys to the Japanese Heart and Soul* (Kodansha International Ltd., Tokyo).

Aqorau, Transform (2008) "Crisis in Solomon Islands: foraging for new directions" in Sinclair Dinnen and Stewart Firth (eds.) *Politics and State Building in Solomon Islands* (Asia Pacific Press, Canberra).

Armstrong, Karen (1993) *A History of God: From Abraham to the Present — the 4000-Year Quest for God* (Heinemann, London).

Barlow, Kathleen (2002) review of Judith Bennett (2000) *Pacific Forest: A History of Resource Control and Contest in Solomon Islands, c. 1800–1997* and Edvard Hviding and Tim Bayliss-Smith (2000) *Islands of Rainforest: Agroforestry, Logging and Eco-Tourism in Solomon Islands* in *The Contemporary Pacific*, v. 14 no. 1 (Spring), pp. 244–249.

Befu, Harumi (1990) "Four Models of Japanese Society and their Relevance to Conflict" in Shmuel Eisenstadt and Eyal Ben-ari (eds.) *Japanese Models of Conflict Resolution* (Kegan and Paul International, London and New York).

Bell, Vaughan, Halligan, Peter and Ellis, Hadyn (2003) "Beliefs about delusions" *The Psychologist*, v. 16 no. 8 (August), pp. 418–423.

Bennett, Judith (1987) *Wealth of the Solomons: A History of a Pacific Archipelago, 1800–1978* (University of Hawai'i Press, Honolulu).

———— (2000) *Pacific Forest: A History of Resource Control and Contest in Solomon Islands, c. 1800–1997* (Brill, Leiden).

Berrios, G. E. (1991) "Delusions as 'Wrong Beliefs': a conceptual history" *British Journal of Psychiatry*, v. 159 (supplement 14), pp. 6–13.

Bierce, Ambrose (1958) *The Devil's Dictionary* (Dover, New York).

Blackwood, Nigel *et al.* (2001) "Cognitive neuropsychiatric models of persecutory delusions" *American Journal of Psychiatry*, v. 158 no. 4 (April), pp. 527–539.

Bloch, Sidney (ed.) (2006) *An Introduction to the Psychotherapies*, 4th ed. (Oxford University Press, Oxford).

———— and Harari, Edwin (2006) "An historical context" in Sidney Bloch (ed.) *An Introduction to the Psychotherapies*, 4th ed. (Oxford University Press, Oxford).

Bohm, David (1980) *Wholeness and the Implicate Order* (Routledge and Kegan Paul, London).

Booth, Ken (1987) "Nuclear Deterrence and 'World War III': how will history judge?" in Roman Kolkowicz (ed.) *The Logic of Nuclear Terror* (Allen and Unwin, Boston).

Bortolotti, Lisa (2010) *Delusions and Other Irrational Beliefs* (Oxford University Press, Oxford).

Bracken, Patrick (2002) *Trauma: Culture, Meaning and Philosophy* (Whurr Publishers, London).

Bromberg, Norbert and Small, Vera (1983) *Hitler's Psychopathology* (International Universities Press, New York).

Brothers, Doris (1995) *Falling Backwards: An Exploration of Trust and Self-Experience* (W.W. Norton and Company, New York).

Brunner, Jose (1995) *Freud and the Politics of Psychoanalysis* (Blackwell, Oxford).

Bucke, Richard (1948 [1901]) *Cosmic Consciousness: A Study in the Evolution of the Human Mind*, 14th ed. (Dutton, New York).

Bugotu, Francis (1973) "Decolonising and Recolonising: the case of the Solomons" *Pacific Perspective*, v. 2 no. 2, pp. 77–80.

Buhle, Mari Jo (1998) *Feminism and Its Discontents: A Century of Struggle with Psychoanalysis* (Harvard University Press, Cambridge, Mass.).

Calder, Nigel (1970) *The Mind of Man* (British Broadcasting Commission, London).

Caldicott, Helen (1978) *Nuclear Madness* (Jacaranda, Brisbane).

Carpenter, Ted (1997) *Delusions of Grandeur: The United Nations and Global Intervention* (Cato Institute, Washington, D.C.).

Chadwick, Peter (1992) *Borderline: A Psychological Study of Paranoia and Delusional Thinking* (Routledge, London and New York).

Chafe, William (2005) *Private Lives/Public Consequences: Personality and Politics in Modern America* (Harvard University Press, Cambridge, Mass.).

Chang, Jung and Halliday, Jon (2005) *Mao: The Unknown Story* (Jonathan Cape, London).

Childs, W. (1984) "Nuclear Madness and Nuclear Sanity" in Graham Mann and Gregory Berry (eds.) *Preparing for Nuclear War: The Psychological Effects*, proceedings of the Second Annual Symposium of the Medical Association for Prevention of War (Australian Branch).

Chilton, Paul (ed.) (1985) *Language and the Nuclear Arms Debate: Nukespeak Today* (Frances Pinter, London).

Cohen, Stanley (2001) *States of Denial: Knowing About Atrocities and Suffering* (Polity, Cambridge).

Cohn, Carol (1987) "Sex and death in the rational world of defense intellectuals" *Signs: Journal of Women in Culture and Society*, v. 12 no. 4 (Summer), pp. 687–718.

Cooper, David (2001 [1961]) "Introduction" to Michel Foucault, *Madness and Civilization: A History of Insanity in the Age of Reason*, trans. Richard Howard (Routledge, London).

——— (1970) *Psychiatry and Anti-psychiatry* (Paladin, St. Albans).

Crocombe, Ron (2008) *The South Pacific*, 7th ed. (University of the South Pacific, Suva).

Crocombe, Ron (1989) *The South Pacific: An Introduction* (Institute of Pacific Studies of the University of the South Pacific, Christchurch).

Culbertson, Philip and Agee, Margaret (eds.) with Makasiale, Cabrini 'Ofa (2007) *Penina Uliuli: Contemporary Challenges in Mental Health for Pacific Peoples* (University of Hawai'i Press, Honolulu).

Datan, Merav *et al.* (2007) *Securing Our Survival: The Case for a Nuclear Weapons Convention* (International Association of Lawyers against Nuclear Arms; International Network of Engineers and Scientists against Proliferation; International Physicians for the Prevention of Nuclear War, Cambridge, Mass.).

David, Anthony (1999) "On the impossibility of defining delusions" *Philosophy, Psychiatry, and Psychology*, v. 6 no. 1 (March), pp. 17–20.

Davidson, Jonathon, Connor, Kathryn and Swartz, Marvin (2006) "Mental Illness in U.S. Presidents between 1776 and 1974: a review of biographical sources" *The Journal of Nervous and Mental Disease*, v. 194 no. 1 (January), pp. 47–51.

Davidson, Shamai (1989) "Avoidance and Denial in the Life Cycle of Holocaust Survivors" in E. L. Edelstein, Donald Nathanson and Andrew Stone (eds.) *Denial: A Clarification of Concepts and Research* (Plenum Press, New York and London).

Davies, Martin and Coltheart, Max (2000) "Introduction: pathologies of belief" in Max Coltheart and Martin Davies (eds.) *Pathologies of Belief* (Blackwell Publishers, Oxford).

Davis, Derek (1984) *An Introduction to Psychopathology*, 4th ed. (Oxford University Press, Oxford).

Dawkins, Richard (1986) *The Blind Watchmaker* (Penguin, London).

———— (2006) *The God Delusion* (Bantam Press, London).

Deary, Ian (1986) "The Wisdom of Deterrence — a Reply to Jim Dyer" *Bulletin of the Royal College of Psychiatrists*, v. 10 no. 7 (July), pp. 165–168.

Descartes, Rene (2006 [1637]) *A Discourse on the Method of Correctly Conducting One's Reason and Seeking Truth in the Sciences*, trans. Ian Maclean (Oxford University Press, Oxford).

Devos, George (1976) "The Interrelationship of social and psychological structures in transcultural psychiatry" in William Lebra (ed.) *Culture-bound Syndromes, Ethnopsychiatry, and Alternative Therapies* (The University Press of Hawaii, Honolulu).

deVries, Marten (1996) "Trauma in cultural perspective" in Bessel van der Kolk, Alexander McFarlane and Lars Weisaeth (eds.) *Traumatic Stress: The Effects of Overwhelming Experience on Mind, Body, and Society* (The Guildford Press, New York).

Dibb, Paul (2007) "Australia's Strategic Outlook 2017–2027", speech given at the Australian Defence Magazine Conference, 22 February, http://rspas.anu.edu.au/papers/sdsc/analysis/Dibb_Australia_Strategic_Outlook_220207.pdf (accessed 13 May 2011).

Dinnen, Sinclair (2008) "The Solomon Islands intervention and the instabilities of the post-colonial state" *Global Change, Peace and Security*, v. 20 no. 3 (October), pp. 339–355.

———— and Firth, Stewart (eds.) (2008) *Politics and State Building in Solomon Islands* (Asia Pacific Press/The Australian National University, Canberra).

———— (2002) "Winners and Losers: politics and disorder in the Solomon Islands 2000–2002" *The Journal of Pacific History*, v. 37 no. 3 (December), pp. 285–298.

Dore, Ronald (1969) "The Japanese Personality" in Guy Wint (ed.) *Asia Handbook* (Penguin, Harmondsworth).

Dower, John (2002) "'An Aptitude for Being Unloved': war and memory in Japan" in Omer Bartov, Atina Grossmann and Mary Nolan (eds.) *Crimes of War: Guilt and Denial in the Twentieth Century* (The New Press, New York).

Draguns, Juris and Tanaka-Matsumi, Junko (2003) "Assessment of psychopathology across and within cultures: issues and findings" *Behaviour Research and Therapy*, v. 41 no. 7 (July), pp. 755–776.

Drozdek, Boris (2007) "The Rebirth of Contextual Thinking is Psychotraumatology" in Boris Drozdek and John Wilson (eds.) *Voices of Trauma: Treating Psychological Trauma Across Cultures* (Springer, New York).

DSM-I (1952) *Diagnostic and Statistical Manual of Mental Disorders*, http://www.PsychiatryOnline.com (accessed 9 April 2009).

DSM-IV (1994) *Diagnostic and Statistical Manual of Mental Disorders*, 4th ed. (American Psychiatric Association, Washington).

Dufresne, Todd (2003) *Killing Freud: Twentieth-Century Culture and the Death of Psychoanalysis* (Continuum, London).

Duran, Bonnie, Duran, Eduardo and Brave Heart, Maria Yellow Horse (1998) "Native Americans and the Trauma of History" in Russell Thornton (ed.) *Studying Native America: Problems and Prospects* (The University of Wisconsin Press, Madison).

Dyer, Jim (1986) "The psychopathology of nuclear war" *Bulletin of the Royal College of Psychiatrists*, v. 10 no. 1 (January), pp. 2–5.

Economic Analytical Unit (2004) *Solomon Islands: Rebuilding an Island Economy* (Department of Foreign Affairs and Trade, Barton).

Edelstein, E. L., Nathanson, Donald and Stone, Andrew (eds.) (1989) *Denial: A Clarification of Concepts and Research* (Plenum Press, New York and London).

Edkins, Jenny (2003) *Trauma and the Memory of Politics* (Cambridge University Press, Cambridge).

Einstein, Albert and Freud, Sigmund (1933) *Why War?* (International Institute of Intellectual Cooperation, League of Nations, Dijon).

Eisenstadt, Shmuel (2000) "Multiple Modernities" *Daedalus*, v. 129 no. 1 (Winter), pp. 1–29.

———— (1990) "Patterns of Conflict and Conflict Resolution in Japan: some comparative indications" in Shmuel Eisenstadt and Eyal Ben-ari (eds.) *Japanese Models of Conflict Resolution* (Kegan Paul International, London and New York).

Enloe, Cynthia (1989) *Bananas, Beaches and Bases: Making Feminist Sense of International Politics* (University of California Press, Berkeley).

Evans, Gareth and Kawaguchi, Yoriko (2009) "A plan to eliminate the world's nuclear weapons" *Financial Times*, 18 December, http://www.icnnd.org/articles/181209_oped.html (accessed 13 May 2011).

Everly, George and Lating, Jeffrey (eds.) (1995) *Psychotraumatology: Key Papers and Core Concepts in Post-Traumatic Stress* (Plenum Press, New York).

Falk, Avner (2004) *Fratricide in the Holy Land: A Psychoanalytical View of the Arab-Israeli Conflict* (The University of Wisconsin Press, Madison).

Firth, Raymond (1998) "Reflections on Knowledge in an Oceanic Setting" in Verena Keck (ed.) *Common Worlds and Single Lives: Constituting Knowledge in Pacific Societies* (Berg, Oxford).

Foucault, Michel (2001 [1961]) *Madness and Civilization: A History of Insanity in the Age of Reason*, trans. Richard Howard (Routledge, London).

Foulkes, S. and Anthony, E. (1957) *Group Psychotherapy: The Psychoanalytic Approach* (Penguin Books, Harmondsworth).

———— (1990) "Some basic concepts in group psychotherapy" in Elizabeth Foulkes (ed.) *Selected Papers of S. H. Foulkes: Psychoanalysis and Group Analysis* (Karnac Books, London).

Fraenkel, Jon (2004) *The Manipulation of Custom: From Uprising to Intervention in the Solomon Islands* (Victoria University Press, Wellington).

Frank, Jerome (2006) "What is psychotherapy?" in Sidney Bloch (ed.) *An Introduction to the Psychotherapies* (Oxford University Press, Oxford).

———— (1982) "Pre-nuclear age leaders and the nuclear arms race" *American Journal of Orthopsychiatry*, v. 52 no. 4 (October), pp. 630–637.

———— (1967) *Sanity and Survival: Psychological Aspects of War and Peace* (Random House, New York).

Frankl, Viktor (1984) *Man's Search for Meaning: An Introduction to Logotherapy*, 3rd ed. (Simon and Schuster, New York).

Frazer, Ian (1997) "The Struggle for Control of Solomon Island Forests" *The Contemporary Pacific*, v. 9 no. 1 (Spring), pp. 39–72.

Freeman, Daniel and Garety, Philippa (2004) *Paranoia: The Psychology of Persecutory Delusions* (Psychology Press, Hove and New York).

Freud, Anna (1968 [1946]) *The Ego and Mechanisms of Defence*, rev. ed. (Hogarth Press, London).

Freud, Sigmund (1922) *Group Psychology and the Analysis of the Ego*, 3rd ed., trans. James Strachey (The Hogarth Press, London).

——— (1935) *A General Introduction to Psycho-analysis: A Course of Twenty-eight Lectures Delivered at the University of Vienna*, trans. Joan Riviere (Liveright Publishing Corporation, New York).

——— (1936) *The Problem of Anxiety* (W.W. Norton and Company, New York).

——— (1949) *An Outline of Psycho-analysis*, trans. James Strachey (W.W. Norton and Company, New York).

——— (1949 [1922]) *Group Psychology and the Analysis of the Ego* (The Hogarth Press, London).

——— (1957 [1914]) "On Narcissism: an introduction" in *The Standard Edition of the Complete Psychological Works of Sigmund Freud*, Vol. XIV (The Hogarth Press, London).

——— (1957 [1915]) "The Unconscious" in *The Standard Edition of the Complete Psychological Works of Sigmund Freud*, Vol. XIV (The Hogarth Press, London).

——— (1960 [1901]) "The Psychopathology of Everyday Life" in *The Standard Edition of the Complete Psychological Works of Sigmund Freud*, Vol. VI (The Hogarth Press, London).

——— (1961 [1925]) "Negation" in *The Standard Edition of the Complete Psychological Works of Sigmund Freud*, Vol. XIX (The Hogarth Press, London).

——— (1975 [1930]) *Civilization and Its Discontents* (The Hogarth Press, London).

——— and Bullitt, William (1999 [1966]) *Woodrow Wilson: A Psychological Study* (Transaction Publishers, New Brunswick).

Fridson, Martin (ed.) (1996) *Extraordinary Popular Delusions and the Madness of Crowds* [Charles Mackay, 1841] and *Confusion de Confusiones* [Joseph de la Vega, 1688] (John Wiley and Sons, New York).

Fromm, Erich (1970) *The Crisis of Psychoanalysis* (Holt, Rinehart and Winston, New York).

———— (1984) *The Fear of Freedom* (Ark, London).

Frosch, Stephen (1989) *Psychoanalysis and Psychology: Minding the Gap* (Macmillan, Houndmills).

———— (1997) *For and Against Psychoanalysis* (Routledge, London).

Fry, Greg (2000) "Political Legitimacy and the Post-colonial State in the Pacific: reflections on some common threads in the Fiji and Solomon Island coups" *Pacifica Review: Peace, Security and Social Change*, v. 12 no. 3 (October), pp. 295–304.

Fugui, Fr. Leslie (1977) "A Black Man Speaks" in D. Lulei, E. Nash and J. Saunana (eds.) *Twenty-Four Poems of the Solomon Islands* (University of the South Pacific, Solomon Islands Centre).

Gardner, Sebastian (1993) *Irrationality and the Philosophy of Psychoanalysis* (Cambridge University Press, Cambridge).

Garety, Philippa and Hemsley, David (1994) *Delusions: Investigations into the Psychology of Delusional Reasoning* (Oxford University Press, Oxford).

Gay, Peter (1988) *Freud: A Life for Our Time* (W.W. Norton and Company, New York).

———— (1990) *Reading Freud: Explorations and Entertainments* (Yale University Press, New Haven).

Gegeo, David and Watson-Gegeo, Karen (2002) "Whose knowledge? Epistemological collisions in Solomon Islands community development" *The Contemporary Pacific*, v. 14 no. 2 (Fall), pp. 377–409.

George, Alexander and George, Juliette (1964 [1956]) *Woodrow Wilson and Colonel House: A Personality Study* (Dover Publications, New York).

Glanzberg, Michael (2006) "Truth", Stanford Encyclopedia of Philosophy, http://plato.stanford.edu/entries/truth/ (accessed 16 March 2010).

Glass, James (1985) *Delusion: International Dimensions of Political Life* (The University of Chicago Press, Chicago).

Goffman, Erving (1962) *Asylums: Essays on the Social Situation of Mental Patients and Other Inmates* (Aldine Publishing Company, Chicago).

Goleman, Daniel (1985) *Vital Lies, Simple Truths: The Psychology of Self-Deception* (Simon and Schuster, New York).

Gomez, Lavinia (2005) *The Freud Wars: An Introduction to the Philosophy of Psychoanalysis* (Routledge, London).

Gruenberg, Ernest (1957) "Socially shared psychopathology" in Alexander Leighton, John Clausen and Robert Wilson (eds.) *Explorations in Social Psychiatry* (Tavistock Publications Ltd., London).

Grunbaum, Adolf (1993) *Validation in the Clinical Theory of Psychoanalysis: A Study in the Philosophy of Psychoanalysis* (International Universities Press, Madison).

Hameiri, Shahar (2007) "The Trouble with RAMSI: reexamining the roots of conflict in Solomon Islands" *The Contemporary Pacific*, v. 19 no. 2 (Fall), pp. 409–441.

Hardin, Russell (1986) "Risking Armageddon" in Avner Cohen and Steven Lee (eds.) *Nuclear Weapons and the Future of Humanity: Fundamental Questions* (Rowan and Allanheld, Totowa).

Harper, David (1992) "Defining delusion and the serving of professional interests: the case of 'paranoia'" *British Journal of Medical Psychology*, v. 65, pp. 357–369.

Heeger, Gerald (1974) *The Politics of Underdevelopment* (St. Martin's Press, New York).

Heise, David (1988) "Delusions and the construction of reality" in Thomas Oltmanns and Brendan Maher (eds.) *Delusional Beliefs* (John Wiley and Sons, New York).

Hitler, Adolf (1992 [1925–1926]) *Mein Kampf*, trans. Ralph Mannheim (Pimlico, London).

Holzman, Philip (1970) *Psychoanalysis and Psychopathology* (McGraw-Hill, New York).

——— (1993) "Introduction" in Adolf Grunbaum, *Validation in the Clinical Theory of Psychoanalysis: A Study in the Philosophy of Psychoanalysis* (International Universities Press, Madison).

Hook, Glenn *et al.* (2001) *Japan's International Relations: Politics, Economics and Security* (Routledge, London and New York).

Horney, Karen (1939) *New Ways in Psychoanalysis* (Kegan Paul, Trench, Trubner and Co., London).

———— (1967) *Feminine Psychology*, ed. by Harold Kelman (W.W. Norton and Company, New York).

Hsien-Li, Tan (2010) "Not just global rhetoric: Japan's substantive actualization of its human security foreign policy" *International Relations of the Asia-Pacific*, v. 10 no. 1 (January), pp. 159–187.

Huxley, Aldous (2004 [1945]) *The Perennial Philosophy* (Perennial Classics, New York).

International Commission on Nuclear Non-proliferation and Disarmament (2009) "Why this report, and why now", http://www.icnnd.org/reference/reports/ent/pdf/ICNND_Parts_Ipdf (accessed 23 February 2010).

James, William (1929 [1902]) *The Varieties of Religious Experience: A Study of Human Nature* (Modern Library, New York).

Jaspers, Karl (1972 [1913]) *General Psychopathology*, trans. J. Hoenig and Marian Hamilton (Manchester University Press, Manchester).

Jervis, Robert *et al.* (1989) *Psychology and Deterrence* (John Hopkins University Press, Baltimore).

Joint Standing Committee on Foreign Affairs, Defence and Trade (2004) *Report of the Parliamentary Delegation to the Solomon Islands, 17–18 December 2003* (The Parliament of the Commonwealth of Australia, Canberra).

Kabutaulaka, Tarcisius Tara (2008) "Westminster meets Solomons in the Honiara riots" in Sinclair Dinnen and Stewart Firth (eds.) *Politics and State Building in Solomon Islands* (Asia Pacific Press, Canberra).

———— (2006) "Political Reviews: Melanesia: Solomon Islands" *The Contemporary Pacific*, v. 18 no. 2 (Fall), pp. 423–430.

———— (2005) "Australian Foreign Policy and the RAMSI Intervention in Solomon Islands" *The Contemporary Pacific*, v. 17 no. 2 (Fall), pp. 283–308.

Kamino, Tomoya (2008) "The Twenty Years' Crisis, 1919–1939: an introduction to the study of international relations in Japan" in Kosuke Shimizu *et al.*, *Is There a Japanese IR? Seeking an Academic Bridge Through Japan's History of International Relations*, Afrasian Centre for Peace and Development Studies, Ryukoku University, Research Series 5, pp. 29–45.

Kernberg, Otto (1975) *Borderline Conditions and Pathological Narcissism* (J. Aronson, New York).

Kershaw, Ian (1998) *Hitler — 1889–1936: Hubris* (Allen Lane, London).

Kilminster, Richard (2007) *Norbert Elias: Post-Philosophical Sociology* (Routledge, London).

Klein, Hillel and Kogan, Ilany (1989) "Some Observations on Denial and Avoidance in Jewish Holocaust and Post-Holocaust Experiences" in E. L. Edelstein, Donald Nathanson and Andrew Stone (eds.) *Denial: A Clarification of Concepts and Research* (Plenum Press, New York and London).

Kolkowicz, Roman (1987) "Intellectuals and the Nuclear Deterrence System" in Roman Kolkowicz (ed.) *The Logic of Nuclear Terror* (Allen and Unwin, Boston).

Kosaka, Masataka (1989) *Japan's Choices: New Globalism and Cultural Orientations in an Industrial State* (Pinter Publishers, London and New York).

Kraepelin, Emil (1981 [1907]) *Clinical Psychiatry* (Delmar, New York).

Kubler-Ross, Elisabeth and Kessler, David (2005) *On Grief and Grieving: Finding the Meaning of Grief Through the Five Stages of Loss* (Simon and Schuster, London).

Kuhn, Thomas (1962) *The Structure of Scientific Revolutions* (University of Chicago Press, Chicago).

Kull, Steven (1985) "Nuclear nonsense" *Foreign Policy*, no. 58 (Spring), pp. 28–52.

Kurzweil, Edith (1995) *Freudians and Feminists* (Westview Press, Boulder).

Lacan, Jacques (2008) *My Teaching* (Verso, London).

Laing, Ronald (1967) *The Politics of Experience and the Bird of Paradise* (Penguin Books, Harmondsworth).

Langer, Walter (1973 [1943]) *The Mind of Adolf Hitler: The Secret Wartime Report* (Secker and Warburg, London).

Laqueur, Walter (1980) *The Terrible Secret: Suppression of the Truth About Hitler's 'Final Solution'* (Little, Brown and Company, Boston).

Larmour, Peter (1998) "Migdal in Melanesia" in Peter Dauvergne (ed.) *Weak and Strong States in Asia-Pacific Societies* (Allen and Unwin, St. Leonards).

Lasch, Christopher (1979) *The Culture of Narcissism: American Life in an Age of Diminishing Expectations* (W.W. Norton and Company, New York).

Lasswell, Harold (1960 [1930]) *Psychopathology and Politics* (The Viking Press, New York).

Lawrence, D. H. (1960 [1921]) *Psychoanalysis and the Unconscious and Fantasia of the Unconscious* (The Viking Press, New York).

Leeser, Jaimie and O'Donohue, William (1999) "What is a delusion? Epistemological dimensions" *Journal of Abnormal Psychology*, v. 108 no. 4 (November), pp. 687–694.

Leydesdorff, Selma *et al.* (1999) "Introduction: trauma and life stories" in Kim Rogers, Selma Leydesdorff and Graham Dawson (eds.) *Trauma and Life Stories: International Perspectives* (Routledge, London and New York).

Lifton, Robert (1982) "Beyond psychic numbing: a call to awareness" *American Journal of Orthopsychiatry*, v. 52 no. 4 (October), pp. 619–629.

Lipton, J. (1984) "Overcoming the Psychological Barriers to Disarmament" in Graham Mann and Gregory Berry (eds.) *Preparing for Nuclear War: The Psychological Effects*, proceedings of the Second Annual Symposium of the Medical Association for Prevention of War (Australian Branch).

Littlewood, Ian (1996) *The Idea of Japan: Western Images, Western Myths* (Secker and Warburg, London).

Maher, Brendan and Spitzer, Manfred (1993) "Delusions" in Patricia Sutker and Henry Adams (eds.) *Comprehensive Handbook of Psychopathology*, 2nd ed. (Plenum Press, New York and London).

Makari, George (2008) *Revolution in Mind: The Creation of Psychoanalysis* (Harper Collins Publishers, New York).

Markowitz, Gerald and Rosner, David (2002) *Deceit and Denial: The Deadly Politics of Industrial Pollution* (University of California Press, Berkeley).

Mathews, Freya (2008) "Metaphysics: a once and future discourse" *Dialogue: The Journal of the Academy of the Social Sciences in Australia*, v. 27 no. 2, pp. 51–56.

McDonald, Ross (2003) *Money Makes You Crazy: Custom and Change in the Solomon Islands* (University of Otago Press, Dunedin).

McDougall, Derek (2004) "Intervention in Solomon Islands" *Round Table*, v. 93 no. 374 (April), pp. 231–223.

McKinnon, Rowan, Carillet, Jean-Bernard and Starnes, Dean (2008) *Papua New Guinea and Solomon Islands* (Lonely Planet Publications, Footscray).

McNally, Richard (2003) *Remembering Trauma* (Harvard University Press, Cambridge, Mass.).

Meerlo, A. M. (1968 [1949]) *Delusion and Mass-Delusion* (Johnson Reprint Corporation, New York and London).

Melley, Timothy (2000) *Empire of Conspiracy: The Culture of Paranoia in Postwar America* (Cornell University Press, Ithaca).

Menninger, Karl, Mayman, Martin and Pruyser, Paul (1977 [1963]) *The Vital Balance: The Life Process in Mental Health and Illness* (Penguin Books, Harmondsworth).

Mezzich, Juan and Berganza, Carlos (eds.) (1984) *Culture and Psychopathology* (Columbia University Press, New York).

Milburn, Michael and Conrad, Sheree (1996) *The Politics of Denial* (The MIT Press, Cambridge, Mass.).

Millon, Theodore (2004) *Masters of the Mind: Exploring the Story of Mental Illness from Ancient Times to the New Millennium* (John Wiley and Sons, Hoboken).

Momis, John (1972) in R. May (ed.) *Priorities in Melanesian Development* (6th Waigani Seminar, Port Moresby).

Moor, James and Tucker, Gary (1979) "Delusions: analysis and criteria" *Comprehensive Psychiatry*, v. 20 no. 4 (July/August), pp. 388–393.

Moore, Burness and Fine, Bernard (eds.) (1995) *Psychoanalysis: The Major Concepts* (The Yale University Press, New Haven).

Moore, Clive (2008) "No more walkabout long Chinatown: Asian involvement in the economic and political process" in Sinclair

Dinnen and Stewart Firth (eds.) *Politics and State Building in Solomon Islands* (Asia Pacific Press, Canberra).

——— (2007) "*Helpem Fren*: the Solomon Islands, 2003–2007" *The Journal of Pacific History*, v. 42 no. 2 (September), pp. 141–124.

——— (2004) *Happy Isles in Crisis: The Historical Causes for a Failing State in Solomon Islands, 1988–2004* (Asia Pacific Press, Canberra).

Morgan, Michael and McLeod, Abby (2006) "Have we failed our neighbour?" *Australian Journal of International Affairs*, v. 60 no. 3 (September), pp. 412–428.

Morgenthau, Hans (1973 [1948]) *Politics Among Nations; The Struggle for Power and Peace*, 5th ed. (Alfred A. Knopf, New York).

Morris, Paul and Hill, Michael (2000) "The Millennium Show", *Radio New Zealand*, 1 January.

Morrison, James, http://www.psychnet-uk.com/dsm_iv/misc/complete_tables.htm (accessed 9 April 2009).

Moses, Jeremy and Iwami, Tadashi (2009) "From pacificism to militarisation: liberal-democratic discourse and Japan's global role" *Global Change, Peace and Security*, v. 21 no. 1 (February), pp. 69–84.

Moses, Rafael (1989) "Denial in Political Process" in E. L. Edelstein, Donald Nathanson and Andrew Stone (eds.) *Denial: A Clarification of Concepts and Research* (Plenum Press, New York and London).

Muhaiyaddeen, M. R. Bawa (1980) *The Wisdom of Man: Selected Discourses* (The Fellowship Press, Philadelphia).

——— (1994) *A Book of God's Love* (The Fellowship Press, Philadelphia).

——— (2003a) *Enough for a Million Years* (The Fellowship Press, Philadelphia).

——— (2003b) *The Tree That Fell to the West: Autobiography of a Sufi* (The Fellowship Press, Philadelphia).

Munro, Alistair (1999) *Delusional Disorder: Paranoia and Related Illnesses* (Cambridge University Press, Cambridge).

Nanau, Gordon Leua (2008) "Intervention and nation-building in Solomon Islands: local responses" in Greg Fry and Tarcisius

Kabutaulaka (eds.) *Intervention and State-Building in the Pacific: The Legitimacy of 'Cooperative Intervention'* (Manchester University Press, Manchester).

Nasion, Juan-David (1998) *Five Lessons on the Psychoanalytic Theory of Jacques Lacan*, trans. David Pettigrew and Francois Faffoul (State University of New York Press, New York).

Newberg, Andrew, D'Aquili, Eugene and Rause, Vince (2002) *Why God Won't Go Away: Brain Science and the Biology of Belief* (Ballantine Books, New York).

Nixon, Richard (1978) *The Memoirs of Richard Nixon* (Arrow Books, London).

Nobus, Dany and Quinn, Malcolm (2005) *Knowing Nothing, Staying Stupid: Elements for a Psychoanalytic Epistemology* (Routledge, London).

Oberg, James (1988) "Deterrence: punishment, anthropocentrism, absurd theatre", a paper presented to the *International Peace Research Association*, 14–19 August.

Oltmanns, Thomas (1988) "Approaches to the definition and study of delusions" in Thomas Oltmanns and Brendan Maher (eds.) *Delusional Beliefs* (John Wiley and Sons, New York).

Osgood, Charles (1962) "Toward International Behaviour Appropriate to a Nuclear Age" in *Psychology and International Affairs: Can We Contribute?*, proceedings of the International Congress of Applied Psychology, v. 1 (Munksgaard, Copenhagen).

Owen, David (2008a) "Hubris syndrome" *Clinical Medicine: Journal of the Royal College of Physicians of London*, v. 8 no. 4 (August), pp. 428–432.

——— (2008b) *In Sickness and in Power: Illness in Heads of Government During the Last 100 Years* (Methuen, London).

Oyebode, Femi (2008) *Sims' Symptoms of the Mind: An Introduction to Descriptive Psychopathology*, 4th ed. (Saunders Elsevier, Edinburgh).

Page, James (1975) *Psychopathology: The Science of Understanding Deviance* (Aldine Publishing Company, Chicago).

Papps, Daniel (1991) *Contemporary International Relations: Frameworks for Understanding*, 3rd ed. (Macmillan Publishing Co., New York).

Park, Bert (1986) *The Impact of Illness on World Leaders* (University of Pennsylvania Press, Philadelphia).

Pettman, Ralph (1977) "The Solomon Islands: a developing neo-colony?" *Australian Outlook*, v. 31 no. 2 (August), pp. 268–278.

———— (1989) "The Psychopathology of Nuclear Deterrence" in G. Rodley (ed.) *Beyond Deterrence* (Centre for Peace and Conflict Studies, University of Sydney).

———— (2004) *Reason. Culture. Religion. The Metaphysics of World Politics* (Palgrave, New York).

———— (2008) *Intending the World: The Phenomenology of World Affairs* (Melbourne University Press, Melbourne).

———— (2010) *Going for a Walk in the World*, http://theaikiacademy. com (accessed 14 January 2010).

Pieterse, Jan (1998) "My paradigm or yours? Alternative development, post-development, reflexive development" *Development and Change*, v. 29, pp. 343–373.

Poland, Jeffrey, Von Eckardt, Barbara and Spaulding, Will (1994) "Problems with the *DSM* approach to classifying psychopathology" in George Graham and G. Lynn Stephens (eds.) *Philosophical Psychopathology* (The MIT Press, Cambridge, Mass.).

Post, Jerrold (2004) *Leaders and Their Followers in a Dangerous World: The Psychology of Political Behavior* (Cornell University Press, Ithaca).

Raphael, B. (1984) "Thinking the Unthinkable" in Graham Mann and Gregory Berry (eds.) *Preparing for Nuclear War: The Psychological Effects*, proceedings of the Second Annual Symposium of the Medical Association for Prevention of War (Australian Branch).

Redlich, Fritz (1999) *Hitler: Diagnosis of a Destructive Prophet* (Oxford University Press, New York).

Rees, Martin (2000) *Just Six Numbers: The Deep Forces That Shape the Universe* (Basic Books, New York).

Richards, Rhys (2006) Book review of Jon Fraenkel (2004) *The Manipulation of Custom: From Uprising to Intervention in the Solomon Islands* and Clive Moore (2004) *Happy Isles in Crisis: The Historical Causes for a Failing State in Solomon Islands, 1988–2004* in *The Contemporary Pacific*, v. 18 no. 2, pp. 442–444.

Ricoeur, Paul (1970) *Freud and Philosophy: An Essay on Interpretation* (Yale University Press, New York).

Robins, Robert (1977) "Introduction to the topic of psychopathology and political leadership" in Robert Robins (ed.) *Psychopathology and Political Leadership* (Tulane University, New Orleans).

——— and Post, Jerrold (1997) *Political Paranoia: The Psychopolitics of Hatred* (Yale University Press, New Haven).

Rokeach, Milton (1981 [1964]) *The Three Christs of Ypsilanti: A Psychological Study* (Columbia University Press, New York).

Rosenhan, D. L. (1973) "On being sane in insane places" *Science*, v. 179 no. 4070 (January), pp. 250–258.

Saver, Jeffrey and Rabin, John (1997) "The Neural Substrates of Religious Experience" *The Journal of Neuropsychiatry and Clinical Neurosciences*, v. 9 no. 3 (August), pp. 498–510.

Schumaker, John and Ward, Tony (2001) *Cultural Cognition and Psychopathology* (Praeger, Westport).

Shultz, George, Kissinger, Henry, Perry, William and Nunn, Sam (2007) "A world free of nuclear weapons" *Wall Street Journal* (4 January), p. A15.

Sinha, Radha (2003) *Sino-American Politics: Mutual Paranoia* (Palgrave Macmillan, Basingstoke).

Smith, Adam (1993 [1776]) *An Inquiry into the Nature and Causes of the Wealth of Nations* (Oxford University Press, Oxford).

Smith, Linda Tuhiwai (1999) *Decolonizing Methodologies: Research and Indigenous Peoples* (Zed Books, London).

Spitzer, Robert (1975) "On pseudoscience in science, logic in remission, and psychiatric diagnosis: a critique of Rosenhan's 'On being sane in insane places'" *Journal of Abnormal Psychology*, v. 84 no. 5, pp. 442–452.

Starr, Steven (2009) "Catastrophic Climatic Consequences of Nuclear Conflict", research paper commissioned by the International Commission on Nuclear Non-proliferation and Disarmament, http://www.icnnd.org/articles (accessed 23 February 2010).

Stern, Kenneth (1993) *Holocaust Denial* (The American Jewish Committee, New York).

Stone, Tony and Young, Andrew (1997) "Delusions and Brain Injury; the philosophy and psychology of belief" *Mind and Language*, v. 12 no. 3/4 (September/December), pp. 327–364.

Storr, Anthony (1989) *Freud* (Oxford University Press, Oxford).

Szasz, Thomas (1974) *The Myth of Mental Illness: Foundations of a Theory of Personal Conduct*, rev. ed. (Harper and Row, New York).

Tamamoto, M. (1999) "The Uncertainty of the Self: Japan at century's end" *World Policy Journal*, v. 16, pp. 119–128.

Taylor, F. Kraupl (1966) *Psychopathology: Its Causes and Symptoms* (Butterworths, London).

Taylor, Jill (2008) *My Stroke of Insight: A Brain Scientist's Personal Journey* (Viking, New York).

Taylor, Tony (2008) *Denial: History Betrayed* (Melbourne University Press, Carlton).

Thomas, Lewis (1983) *Late Night Thoughts on Listening to Mahler's Ninth Symphony* (Bantam, New York).

Thompson, James (1985) *Psychological Aspects of Nuclear War* (John Wiley and Sons, Chichester).

Timmer, Jaap (2008) "*Kastom* and theocracy: a reflection on governance from the uttermost part of the world" in Sinclair Dinnen and Stewart Firth (eds.) *Politics and State Building in Solomon Islands* (Asia Pacific Press, Canberra).

Tucker, Robert (1965) "The Dictator and Totalitarianism" *World Politics*, v. 17 no. 4 (July), pp. 555–583.

Ueshiba, Morihei (2002) *The Art of Peace*, trans. and ed. John Stevens (Shambhala Publications, Boston).

Underhill, Evelyn (1949 [1912]) *Mysticism: A Study in the Nature and Development of Man's Spiritual Consciousness*, 17th ed. (Methuen, London).

UNESCO (2010), http://www.unesco.org/culture/ich/index.php?pg=00011 (accessed 18 January 2010).

van der Kolk, Bessel, McFarlane, Alexander and Weisaeth, Lars (eds.) (1996) *Traumatic Stress: The Effects of Overwhelming Experience on Mind, Body and Society* (The Guildford Press, New York).

Volkan, Vamik (1979) *Cyprus — War and Adaptation: A Psychoanalytic History of Two Ethnic Groups in Conflict* (University Press of Virginia, Charlottesville).

———— (1988) *The Need to Have Enemies and Allies: From Clinical Practice to International Relationships* (Jason Aronson Inc., Northvale, New Jersey).

————, Montville, Joseph and Julius, Demetrios (1990) *The Psychodynamics of International Relationships: v. 1 Concepts and Theories* (Lexington Books, D.C. Heath and Company, Lexington).

———— (1991) *The Psychodynamics of International Relationships: v. 2 Unofficial Diplomacy at Work* (Lexington Books, D.C. Heath and Company, Lexington).

———— (1997) *Bloodlines: From Ethnic Pride to Ethnic Terrorism* (Farrar, Straus and Giroux, New York).

———— (2005) "Politics and International Relations" in Ethel Person, Arnold Cooper and Glen Gattard (eds.) *Textbook of Psychoanalysis* (American Psychiatric Publishing, Inc., Washington, DC).

Wainwright, Elsina (2003) "Responding to state failure — the case of Australia and Solomon Islands" *Australian Journal of International Affairs*, v. 57 no. 3 (November), pp. 485–498.

Waite, Robert (1977) *The Psychopathic God: Adolf Hitler* (Basic Books Inc., New York).

Walker, Chris (1991) "Delusion: what did Jaspers really say?" *British Journal of Psychiatry*, v. 159 (supplement 14), pp. 94–103.

Wangh, Martin (1989) "The Evolution of Psychoanalytic Thought on Negation and Denial" in E. L. Edelstein, Donald Nathanson and Andrew Stone (eds.) *Denial: A Clarification of Concepts and Research* (Plenum Press, New York and London).

Warner, Nick (2004) "Operation Helpem Fren: rebuilding the nation of Solomon Islands", speech to National Security Conference by RAMSI Special Coordinator, Department of Foreign Affairs and Trade, 23 March.

Webb, Gisela (1994) "Tradition and Innovation in Contemporary American Islamic Spirituality: the Bawa Muhaiyaddeen Fellowship" in Yvonne Haddad and Jan Smith (eds.) *Muslim Communities in North America* (State University of New York Press, Albany).

———— (2006) "Third-wave Sufism in America and the Bawa Muhaiyaddeen Fellowship" in Jamal Malik and John Hinnells (eds.) *Sufism in the West* (Routledge, London).

Webster, Richard (1995) *Why Freud was Wrong: Sin, Science and Psychoanalysis* (Basic Books, New York).

Weiner, Bernard (1975) "'On being sane in insane places': a process [attributional] analysis and critique" *Journal of Abnormal Psychology*, v. 84 no. 5, pp. 433–441.

Westermeyer, Joseph and Wintrob, Ronald (1979) "'Folk' criteria for the diagnosis of mental illness in rural Laos: on being insane in sane places" *The American Journal of Psychiatry*, v. 136 no. 6 (June), pp. 755–761.

Whyte, Lancelot (1978) *The Unconscious before Freud* (Julian Friedmann Publishers, London).

Williams, Mary and Sommer, John (eds.) (1994) *Handbook of Post-Traumatic Therapy* (Greenwood Press, Westport).

Williamson, John (ed.) (1991) *Latin American Adjustment: How Much Has Happened?* (Institute for International Economics, Washington).

Wilner, Ann (1984) *The Spellbinders: Charismatic Political Leadership* (Yale University Press, New Haven).

Woodward, Bob (2006) *State of Denial* (Simon and Schuster, New York).

World Health Organization (WHO) (2007) *International Statistical Classification of Diseases and Related Health Problems*, 10th revision, http://www.who.int/classifications/apps/icd10online/ (accessed 9 April 2009).

World Heritage Center (2010), http://whc.unesco.org (accessed 14 January 2010).

Wurmser, Leon (1989) "Cultural Paradigms for Denial" in E. L. Edelstein, Donald Nathanson and Andrew Stone (eds.) *Denial: A Clarification of Concepts and Research* (Plenum Press, New York and London).

Young, Andrew (2000) "Wondrous Strange: the neuropsychology of abnormal beliefs" in Max Coltheart and Martin Davies (eds.) *Pathologies of Belief* (Blackwell Publishers, Oxford).

Index